ULTIMATE
COVER
LETTERS

ULTIMATE
COVER
LETTERS

THIRD EDITION

A guide to job search letters, online
applications and follow-up strategies

MARTIN JOHN YATE

KoganPage

LONDON PHILADELPHIA NEW DELHI

First published in the United States in 1992 as *Cover Letters that Knock 'em Dead* by Adams Media Corporation

First published in Great Britain in 2003 as *The Ultimate Job Search Letters Book* by Kogan Page Limited
Reprinted in 2007
Second edition published in 2008 as *Ultimate Cover Letters*
Third edition 2012
Reprinted 2012 (twice)

Published by arrangement with Adams Media Corporation, 57 Littlefield Street, Avon, MA 02322, USA

120 Pentonville Road	1518 Walnut Street, Suite 1100	4737/23 Ansari Road
London N1 9JN	Philadelphia PA 19102	Daryaganj
United Kingdom	USA	New Delhi 110002
www.koganpage.com		India

© Martin John Yate, 1992, 1995, 1998, 2001, 2002, 2003, 2008, 2012

The right of Martin John Yate to be identified as the author of this work has been asserted by him in accordance with the Copyright, Designs and Patents Act 1988.

ISBN   978 0 7494 6405 9
E-ISBN   978 0 7494 6458 5

British Library Cataloguing-in-Publication Data

A CIP record for this book is available from the British Library.

Typeset by Graphicraft Limited, Hong Kong
Printed and bound in India by Replika Press Pvt Ltd

CONTENTS

READ THIS FIRST

Selling yourself with the written word is always a challenge. And with everything you have to stay on top of in your professional life, packaging yourself in job search letters is probably one thing you haven't made a priority.

But the writing skills displayed in your letters and CVs can have a *major* impact on your job search. Ignore developing these critical skills and you can stay longer in that going-nowhere job, or be longer unemployed.

This book has helped millions of people around the world craft hard-hitting letters that helped them win interviews and job offers. It can do the same for you. Use these techniques and your letters will position you as someone worth taking seriously.

You'll find job search letters of every conceivable type here: from cover letters to follow-up after telephone and face-to-face meetings, networking, resurrection, acceptance, rejection, and those oh-so-happy letters of resignation.

These letters work, giving you an edge in a highly competitive job market. They are *real* letters that have already worked in someone's job search. Some of these letters I've helped people write, others have been sent to me by career coaches, professional CV writers, headhunters, HR managers and grateful readers. They will work for you too when you customize them to your own unique circumstances and your voice. What do I mean by 'your voice'? I mean that as you learn to customize and create your own letters, they will work best when the tone of the letter sounds natural, and that means staying away from words you wouldn't normally use in a professional context.

Throughout this book the words 'mail', 'letter', and 'e-mail' are intended to be interchangeable, unless otherwise noted. Written communications can be delivered by either e-mail or traditional mail, with the majority known going by e-mail. However, I don't want you to ignore traditional mail, because when you do something other job hunters aren't doing, you stand out.

How recruitment works

A good cover letter and subsequent follow-up letters can speed your application through the four stages all employers go through in the recruitment screening and selection cycle. They won't win you the job in and of themselves but they can make a big difference in the way you are perceived as a professional and as a person, thus differentiating you from the competition.

The four stages are:

1 *Long-list development.* Multiple recruitment strategies to develop the largest manageable field of qualified candidates, usually 10 to 12.

2 *Short-list development.* The long list of candidates is screened for best-fit-to-the-job, reducing the long list to four or six candidates. Those who make the cut become the 'short list' and are invited in for an interview, after first passing the additional screening of a telephone interview. A dossier is created for each candidate, including both print and electronic documents.

3 *Short-list prioritization.* Through a series of interviews, usually one, two, or three, the short-list candidates are ranked for ability and fit.

4 *Short-list review and decision.* Each candidate's dossier is reviewed for one last time before the final decision. The dossier will include your CV, the employer's notes, and any cover and follow-up letters you have been smart enough to send during the interview process. These letters make additional points, clear up mistakes and omissions, and brand you as a competent professional and real human being who would be a pleasure to work with.

> Your letters cut to the point, they don't waste time, they are friendly and respectful; they are not pompous, distant and death-in-the-family formal.

In each of these steps, letters have a role to play in separating you from other candidates (part of a process called professional branding, which we'll discuss later) and easing your passage through each step of the selection cycle. Letters support your application and remind employers of your relevant skills, professionalism, continued existence, and interest and suitability for the job, all the way through to the offer.

Job search professionals know that when there is no major difference between two top candidates, the offer will always go to the most enthusiastic; your follow-up letters after meetings help make that enthusiasm clear to your prospective employer.

Passing through each step of the interview cycle, you are presented with significant opportunities to advance your application. You can add additional information after a meeting, clear up a misunderstanding or a poor answer ('I'm good at my job, but not so good at interviews, just haven't had that many. When we were talking about _____ perhaps I didn't make it clear that …').

By sampling a phrase from this letter and few words from that letter, you will create unique letters that reflect the real you. *Read this book with a highlighter in hand so you can flag phrases or sections for later reference.*

Because your comments are in a letter, it speaks for you when you aren't there to speak for yourself; a strong written dimension to your job search can double your effectiveness. The different types of letters you create during the interview cycle demonstrate your writing skills, attention to detail, professionalism, and that all-important enthusiasm. Each letter adds another meaningful plus to your application.

With this book on your desk, you won't waste time creating letters from scratch, and once settled in a new position, you can apply these same strategies and tactics to the written communications that are an integral part of every successful career.

1
Cover letters: the secret weapon of your job search

Letters can play a critical role in a successful job search. They are far too often overlooked or underused.

When you build a great CV but don't learn how to use it properly, your job search will take longer and the job you get may not be the best your skills deserve. You can use cover letters when you don't have a name, but if you develop a plan of attack that includes reaching out directly to employers, you'll find more interviews happening more quickly. Whenever someone in a position to hire you reviews your CV, the odds of getting that interview increase dramatically, because you have skipped right over getting pulled from the CV database, sidestepped the recruiter's evaluation process, and you are speaking directly to the hiring authority.

The primary goal of every job search is to get into conversations, as quickly and frequently as possible, with people in a position to hire you; without conversations, job offers can't be made. Rarely reaching employers with your message is one of the major reasons why many job searches stall. This happens because most job searchers involve themselves, almost exclusively, with posting CVs to CV banks and responding to job postings by uploading CVs into other CV databases.

However, when you can get your CV, personalized with a cover letter, in front of employers, you differentiate yourself. And by differentiating your message and your brand you substantially increase your chances of landing an interview. In addition, the unusual way you got the interview helps differentiate you.

If all you are planning to do is load your CV into CV databases, a cover letter can still help. Its main strength is in personalizing your message to a specific company and ideally a particular person. When you develop a plan of attack for your job search that includes reaching out directly to decision makers, the personalizing touch of a letter really increases your impact.

The job titles to target during your job search are:

- Those job titles most likely to be in a position to hire you. Usually this will be managers one to three levels above your target job.

- Those job titles most likely to be involved in the selection process. Usually this will be managers working in related departments, recruitment and HR. Whenever you have a name in one of these disciplines, use a letter to stand out.

When an e-mail or envelope is opened, your cover letter should be the first thing seen. A cover letter personalizes your application for a specific job in ways that are impossible for your CV to do, given its impersonal structure. The cover letter sets the stage for the reader to accept your CV, and therefore you, as something and someone special. It can create common ground between you and the reader and demonstrate that you are well qualified and suitable for *this* job with *this* company.

Your ideal target for direct communication is always someone who can hire you, although any management title offers opportunity for referral. Even Human Resources contacts are valuable. HR contacts can't make the hiring decision (although s/he can have a strong influence), but the pivotal nature of HR jobs means the professionals in this area are aware of all areas within a company that could use your skills.

Any name and title you capture in a job search is valuable. With the internet at your fingertips there are countless ways to identify the names of people who hold the titles you need to reach, and if a name and title is of no use to you, it might be just the contact another job hunter needs, so it can be a valuable commodity to develop in your networking activities. There is a whole chapter on how to find the names of hiring authorities later in the book.

Five tactics that help your cover letter work

Address your target by name

Your first step is to grab the reader's attention and arouse interest, so whenever possible address the letter to someone by name.

Approaching employers directly is one of the very best tactics for getting job offers, because as I noted, it cuts many of the recruitment screening steps: the CV, databases, the external recruiter (headhunter) review and the internal recruiter review (HR recruiter). Right now, just get it fixed in your mind that names are a powerful secret weapon in your job search. Whenever you can find the names of any one of these titles involved in the recruitment and selection cycle, approach them directly and address them by name.

Make your letter readable

Your customer, the reader, is always going to be distracted, so your letters need to be easily readable, focused, clear and brief. You can also grab the reader's attention with the appearance of your letter, which should echo the fonts and font sizes of your CV, giving you a more professional look.

The font and font size are important because they must be legible for managers. Anyone who has been staring at computer screens for 10 or more years and has 10 other priorities pressing for attention is likely to have problems with tiny font sizes and elaborate but unreadable type faces. I recommend a minimum of 11- or 12-point font size (more on this later).

Remember to apply these rules of matching font and font size to *e-mail and print* letters. It is easy to do and yet so often overlooked.

Emphasize your personal brand

Branding is the process by which you consistently draw attention to the ways you are special, the sum of these special attributes that makes you unique. The cover letter is part of the packaging that captures the professional you. If it looks good, carries a succinct, relevant, readily accessible message, and shows you to be a professional with a clear sense of self, you're well on the road to establishing a viable professional brand. When your actions differentiate you from others, your standing as a candidate is empowered.

- Getting your CV directly under the nose of a manager, who just wants to make a good decision and get back to work, makes you special.

- Getting your CV to the manager in a creative way and showing that you know what you are doing makes you special. Your letter might say in part, 'I sent my CV by e-mail but thought you might appreciate a screen break, so you'll find it attached to this letter…' In that case, your e-mail should say, 'As well as attaching my CV to this e-mail, in case you need a screen break I've also sent it by traditional mail.'

- Writing a strong cover letter that presents your CV and establishes connectivity between you and the manager makes you special.

- Keeping your message clear and succinct makes you special.

- Following up your meetings with thoughtful letters that continue the messaging of a consummate professional makes you special and confirms your professional status.

- Making sure in all your letters and CVs that your paper is good quality and that the fonts are legible and coordinated makes you special.

Good brands are those that live up to their promise or value proposition. Integrate this brand-building behaviour with the other strategies discussed and your application is going to gain more attention. To emphasize the consistency of your personal brand:

1 Use the same font choices and paper for your letters as you use for your CV.

2 Make the font you employ for contact information and headlines in both your CV and your letterhead the same.

3 Use the same font you chose for your CV's body copy for the message in your letter.

4 Use the same font choices for all your e-mail communications. Smart idea: set the chosen font as your default e-mail font.

5 Get matching paper for CV, cover letters and envelopes. Every office superstore has them. You need printed CVs to take to interviews. Also, sending your cover letter and CV by traditional mail when the opportunity arises is a way to get your CV read because most job hunters don't think to do this. This means that managers get far fewer CVs by mail. A busy manager likes a break from the computer screen and because s/he enjoys this screen break, the manager will spend more time reviewing your CV.

Be succinct and on-message

A good cover letter gets your CV read with serious consideration. Time is precious. Recruiters and managers won't waste it on a letter that rambles. Your letter should always reflect a professional whose CV will have something to say.

When you can, make a specific reference to a job's key requirements. You want the reader to move from your letter to the CV already thinking that here's a candidate who can do this job, and referencing a job's most important requirements does just that.

If an advertisement, a job posting, or a telephone conversation with a potential employer reveals an aspect of a particular job opening that is not addressed in your CV (and for some reason you haven't had time to update it), use the Executive Briefing cover letter to fill in the gaps; you'll see samples shortly.

Remember: brevity is important. Leave your reader wanting more. The letter doesn't sell you – that's the CV's job. Rather, the letter positions you for serious consideration: whet the reader's appetite, no more.

End with a call to action

Your letters should always include a call to action. Explain when, where and how you can be contacted. You can also be proactive, telling the reader that you intend to follow up at a certain point in time if they have not contacted you. Just as you worked to create a strong opening, make sure your closing carries the same conviction. It is the reader's last personal impression of you, so make it strong, make it tight, and make it obvious that you are serious about entering into meaningful conversation.

Every step of the job search and selection cycle offers opportunities to use letters to promote your application. A good, strong letter will get your foot in the door, differentiate you from other contenders, and ultimately help you define a distinctive professional brand. Although the majority of your communications will be e-mails, stand out by sending letters on really important topics as both e-mails and traditional letters. If nothing more, your important communication gets read twice which increases the odds of your point being understood.

2
The six types of job search letters

Wholesale adoption of the internet as the primary recruitment vehicle has completely changed the way you need to approach the job search.

Every year the number of CVs loaded into commercial CV databases grows exponentially. Currently the larger databases each house more than 36 million CVs. Many individual CV banks have over 1 million CVs stored, and social networking sites like LinkedIn have over 70 million CVs and professional profiles registered. This has made life easier for recruiters, since they can usually find enough qualified candidates in the top 20 CVs from any database, and given the large number of potential candidates, they rarely dig deeper.

In the CV databases that allow attachments to your CV, a cover letter helps you stand out by making additional and supportive comments about your capabilities. When you also send your CV directly to a potential employer by using their name and title, your CV and cover letter have even greater impact because you can differentiate yourself by addressing the manager or recruiter by name and by customizing your message.

Here are six types of cover letters that you will get high mileage from in your job search. Each is a composite letter I built from scouring the examples that appear later in the book, taking a word from one example and a phrase from another. It's a useful technique you can use to build your own unique letters. In each example, I have underlined the borrowed phrases to give you an idea of how easy it is to create your own original documents with a little cut and paste. The six letters are:

1 The cover letter for when you do not know of a specific job but have the name of someone to send the letter to or are uploading to a CV bank where you can attach it to your CV.

2 The executive briefing. A very effective cover letter for when you have knowledge of the job's requirements.

3 A cover letter in response to an online job posting.

4 A cover letter aimed at headhunters.

5 A networking letter for getting the word out to the professional community about your search.

6 A broadcast letter, in which you introduce yourself without a CV.

A cover letter when you do not know of a specific job opening

This letter is designed to be uploaded to a database as an attachment or sent to a potential employer whose name you've garnered from your research. Of course, if you are sending this to an individual it should be personalized with a salutation at the very least, and will ideally include references to the company or the establishment of some common ground between you and the recipient.

When you do not know of a specific job opening

James Sharpe
1 Any Street • Anytown, AA1 1AA
12345 678901

2 October 20–

Jackson Bethell, V.P. Operations
DataLink Products
111 Any Avenue
Anytown, AA1 1AA

Dear Jackson Bethell:

Recently I have been researching the leading local companies in data communications. My search has been for companies that are respected in the field and that provide ongoing training programmes. The name of DataLink Products keeps coming up as a top company.

I am an experienced voice and data communications specialist with a substantial background in IBM environments. If you have an opening for someone in this area, you will see that my CV demonstrates a person of unusual dedication, efficiency and drive. My experience and achievements include:

- the complete redesign of a data communications network, projected to increase efficiency company-wide some 12 per cent;

- the installation and troubleshooting of a Defender IV call-back security system for a dial-up network.

I enclose a copy of my CV, and look forward to exploring any of the ways you feel my background and skills would benefit DataLink Products. While I prefer not to use my employer's time taking personal calls at work, with discretion I can be reached at 10987 654321 to initiate contact. However, I would rather you call me at _____ in the evening. Let's talk!

Yours sincerely,

James Sharpe

James Sharpe

When you do not know of a specific job opening

JANE SWIFT
1 Any Street, Anytown, AA1 1AA
12345 678901

David Doors, Director of Marketing   14 January 20–
Martin Financial Group
111 Any Avenue
Anytown, AA1 1AA

Dear David Doors:

I have always followed the performance of your company in *Mutual Funds Newsletter.*

Recently your notice regarding a Market Analyst in *Investor's Business Daily* caught my eye – and your company name caught my attention. Your record over the last three years shows exceptional portfolio management. Because of my experience with one of your competitors, I know I could make significant contributions.

I would like to talk to you about your personnel needs and how I am able to contribute to your department's goals.

An experienced market analyst, I have an economics background (MA London) and a strong quantitative analysis approach to market fluctuations. This combination has enabled me to consistently pick the new technology flotations that are the backbone of the growth-orientated mutual fund. For example:

I first recommended XYZ Fund six years ago. More recently my clients have been strongly invested in ABC Growth (in the high-risk category), and DEF Growth and Income (for the cautious investor). Those following my advice over the last six years have consistently outperformed the market.

I know that CVs help you sort out the probables from the possibles, but they are no way to judge the personal calibre of an individual. I would like to meet you and demonstrate that along with the credentials, I have the professional commitment that makes for a successful team player.

Yours sincerely,

Jane Swift

Jane Swift

The executive briefing

The executive briefing is a different and effective form of cover letter to use *whenever you have information about a job opening* from an online job posting, a lead, or a prior conversation with one of your network contacts. The executive briefing gets right to the point and makes life easy for the reader. It introduces your CV, as well as customizing and supplementing it. Why is an executive briefing so effective?

1 It quickly matches job requirements against the skills you bring to the table, making analysis much easier for the reader and a successful outcome more likely for you.

2 While an initial screener, someone who quickly sorts through cover letters and CVs to separate the wheat from the chaff, may not have an in-depth understanding of the job's requirements, the executive briefing matches the job's requirements, point-by-point to your abilities.

3 The executive briefing allows you to emphasize your skills in a particular area or fill any gaps in your CV with job-specific information.

4 If an opportunity comes along that is right for you but your CV isn't up to date or doesn't have the right focus, the executive briefing allows you to bring that work history right up to date. It's a godsend when you have spoken to someone and they ask to see your CV, you say it isn't up to date, but they ask to see it anyway. The executive briefing is a very professional quick fix.

The executive briefing ensures that each CV you send out addresses the job's specific needs. It provides a comprehensive picture of a thorough professional, plus a personalized, fast, and easy-to-read synopsis that details exactly how your background matches the job description.

A cover letter in response to an online job posting

If you are writing as a result of an online job posting, you should mention both the website and any reference codes associated with the job:

'I read your job posting on your company's website on 5th January and felt I had to respond...'

'Your online job posting regarding a _____ on _____.com caught my eye, and your company name caught my attention.'

'This e-mail, and my attached CV, is in response to your job posting on _____.'

An executive briefing e-mail

From:	top10acct@anyserver.co.uk
To:	rlstein@McCoy.com
Cc:	
Subject:	**Re: Accounting Manager**

Dear Ms Stein:

I have nine years' accounting experience and am responding to your recent posting for an Accounting Manager on Careerbuilder. Please allow me to highlight my skills as they relate to your stated requirements.

Your Requirements	My Experience
Accounting degree, four years' experience	Obtained a degree in 2000 and have over four years' experience as an Accounting Manager
Excellent people skills and leadership	Effectively managed a staff of 24; ability to motivate staff, including supervisors
Strong administrative skills	Assisted in the development of a base reference skills-library with Microsoft Excel for 400 clients
Good communication skills	Trained new supervisors and staff via daily coaching sessions, communication meetings and technical skill sessions

My CV, pasted below and attached in MSWord, will flesh out my general background. I hope this executive briefing helps you use your time effectively today. I am ready to make a move. I hope we can talk soon.

Yours sincerely,

Joe Black

Joe Black

E-mail response to online job posting (legal administrator)

From: Helen Darvik [darviklegalpro@earthlink.net]
To: ggoodfellow@budownoble.com
Cc:
Subject: Administrator/mgmnt/mktg/cmptr/acctg/planning/personnel

Dear Ms _____:

I am responding to your job posting on Hotjobs.com for a legal administrator of a law firm. I wrote to you on (date) about law administrator positions in the _____ area. I have attached another CV of my educational background and employment history. I am very interested in this position.

I have been a legal administrator for two law firms during the past six years. In addition, I have been a law firm consultant for over a year. Besides my law firm experience, I have been a medical administrator for over 10 years. I believe that all of this experience will enable me to manage the law firm for this position very successfully. I possess the management, marketing, computer, accounting/budgeting, financial planning, personnel, and people-orientated skills that will have a very positive impact on this law firm.

I will be in the _____ area later in the month, and hope we can meet at that time to discuss this position. I look forward to hearing from you, Ms _____, concerning this position. Thank you for your time and consideration.

Yours sincerely,

Helen Darvik
12345 678901
darviklegalpro@earthlink.net

Recruitment agencies and executive recruiter

Headhunters deserve your appropriate respect. They are, after all, the most sophisticated salespeople in the world – they alone sell products that talk back! A headhunter will be only faintly amused by your exhortations 'to accept the challenge' or 'test your skills by finding me a job' in the brief moment before s/he throws your letter in the waste bin.

When approaching and working with headhunters – whether they are working for the local employment agency or a retained search firm – bear in mind these two rules and you won't go far wrong:

1 Tell the truth. Answer questions truthfully and you will likely receive help. Get caught in a lie and you will have established a career-long distrust with someone who probably possesses a very diverse and influential list of contacts.

2 Cut immediately to the chase in your letters and conversations. For example:

> *'I am forwarding my CV because I understand you specialize in representing employers in the _____ field.'*

> *'Please find the enclosed CV. As a specialist in the _____ field, I felt you might be interested in the skills of a _____.'*

> *'Among your many clients there may be one or two who are seeking a thorough professional for a position as a _____.'*

Remember that in a cover letter sent to executive search firms and employment agencies, you should mention your salary and, if appropriate, your geographic considerations.

An example of a cover letter you might send to a recruitment agency is on page 13.

Letter to a recruitment agency

James Sharpe
1 Any Street • Anytown, AA1 1AA
12345 678901

2 December 20–

Dear Mr O'Flynn:

I am forwarding my CV, as I understand that you specialize in the accounting profession. As you may be aware, the management structure at _____ will be reorganized in the near future. While I am enthusiastic about the future of the agency under its new leadership, I have elected to make this an opportunity for change and professional growth.

My many years of experience lend themselves to a finance management position in any medium-sized service firm, but I am open to other opportunities. Although I would prefer to remain in London, I would entertain other areas of the country, if the opportunity warrants it. I am currently earning £65,000 a year.

I have enclosed my CV for your review. Should you be conducting a search for someone with my background at the present time or in the near future, I would greatly appreciate your consideration. I would be happy to discuss my background more fully with you on the phone or at a personal interview.

Yours sincerely,

James Sharpe

James Sharpe

JS
CV attached

Networking letters

Nothing works like a personal recommendation from a fellow professional. It is no accident that successful people in all fields know each other; they helped each other become successful because they stayed in touch. You get the most out of networking by being connected to your profession and the professionals within it.

There are important considerations to bear in mind with networking letters:

1 Establish connectivity. Recall the last memorable contact you had, someone in common that you have both spoken to recently. Use past employers, membership of professional associations, common interests or a topical event as a bridge builder.

If you are writing (and calling) as the result of a referral, say so and quote the person's name if appropriate:

> *'I am writing because our mutual colleague, John Stanovich, felt my skills and abilities would be valuable to your company…'*

> *'The manager of your Bristol branch, Pamela Bronson, suggested I contact you regarding the opening for a _____.'*

> *'I received your name from Henry Charles, the branch manager of the XYZ Bank last week, and he suggested I contact you. In case the CV he forwarded is delayed in the mail, I enclose another.'*

> *'Arthur Gold, your office manager and my neighbour, thought I should contact you about the upcoming opening in your accounting department.'*

2 Tell them why you are writing:

> *'It's time for me to make a move; my job just got sent to Mumbai, India, and I'm hoping you can help me with a new sense of direction.'*

3 Do not talk about your ideal job. This only narrows the opportunities people will tell you about. Instead, just let contacts know your qualifications/experience and the job title you are most likely to work under. Don't let ego cost you a valuable job lead.

4 Ask for advice and guidance:

> *'Who do you think are the developing companies in the area today?'*

> *'Could you take a look at my CV for me? I really need an objective opinion and I've always respected your viewpoint.'*

5 Never ask directly, 'Do you have a job?' 'Can you hire me?' or 'Can your company hire me?' Instead, ask to talk on the telephone for a few minutes. Then by all means ask for leads within specific target companies.

6 When you do get help, say thank you. If you get the help in conversation, follow it up in writing; the impression is indelible and it just might get you another lead.

The broadcast letter

The broadcast letter acts as a brief introduction of the skills you bring to the table and is designed to be sent without a CV. You can use it when:

- you don't have a relevant CV;

- your CV is inappropriate for the position;

- your CV isn't getting the results you want, and you want to try something different while you are renovating it.

To be effective, the information you use in a broadcast letter must be relevant to the specific needs of a job posting or be focused on the needs of this job as you have determined them from your CV's target job deconstruction exercises (more on this shortly). This is because the intent of the broadcast letter is to *replace* the CV as a means of introduction and to initiate conversation. Keep in mind that although a broadcast letter can get you into a telephone conversation with a potential employer, that employer is still likely to ask for a CV.

While I am not a big fan of broadcast letters, people have used them effectively, so you need to be aware of them. As they pretty much require you have a name to send them to, my feeling is that, as a CV is going to be requested anyway, you should take the time to customize your CV properly. I don't advise using this kind of letter as the spearhead or sole thrust of your campaign, but you can use it as a stop-gap measure when you are renovating an ineffective CV or otherwise regrouping.

Networking letter (computer and information systems manager)

This letter was sent to follow up a meeting with a medical school dean.

DAVID KENT

1 Any Street • Anytown AA1 1AA
12345 678901 • dkent@alohanet.com

14 January 20–

John Jones, MD
Dean, School of Medicine
University of Hawaii
111 Any Avenue
Honolulu, Hawaii 96822

Dear Dr Jones:

Perhaps you remember our chance meeting at the Bio Asia-Pacific Conference at the Sheraton Waikiki on 18 and 19 August 20–. In our brief conversation, I shared with you the idea of using Web Development as an administrative tool. You expressed interest in the possibility of implementing such a system within the School of Medicine.

May I suggest a formal meeting to explore the idea?

I have some exciting and creative ideas, which may encourage you to take the next step towards realizing the positive impact a content management system would have in the School of Medicine. This would also be a great opportunity for us to discuss your goals and how an administrative intranet would help you reach them in a more timely and cost-effective manner.

In addition, there has recently been spirited discussion within the IT community on the topic of organizational continuity and its potential vulnerability due to advances in technology. I think you'll find the specific strategies I have to share with you worthy of consideration.

If you recall, my background is in Web Planning and Development, with specific skills in developing administrative intranets and public websites, and designing web-based software to address the internal and external reporting needs of organizations.

Enclosed is my CV attesting to my experience and specialities. I will contact you within the next few days to discuss the possibility of meeting with you.

Yours sincerely,

David Kent

David Kent
Computer and Information Systems Manager

Enclosure: CV

Broadcast letter

JANE SWIFT
1 Any Street, Anytown, AA1 1AA
12345 678901

2 October 20–

Dear _____ :

For the past seven years I have pursued an increasingly successful career in the sales profession. Among my accomplishments I include:

SALES
As a regional representative, I contributed £1,500,000, or 16 per cent, of my company's annual sales. I am driven by achievement.

MARKETING
My marketing skills (based on a BA in marketing) enabled me to increase sales by 25 per cent in my economically stressed territory, at a time when colleagues were striving to maintain flat sales. Repeat business reached an all-time high. I am persistent and pay attention to detail.

PROJECT MANAGEMENT
Following the above successes, my regional model was adopted by the company. I trained and provided project supervision to the entire sales force. The following year, company sales showed a sales increase 12 per cent above projections. I am a committed team player, motivated by the group's overall success.

The above was based on my firmly held zero price-discounting philosophy. I don't cut margins to make a sale. It is difficult to summarize my work in a letter. The only way I can imagine providing you the opportunity to examine my credentials is for us to talk to each other. I look forward to hearing from you. Please call me at _____.

Yours sincerely,

Jane Swift

Jane Swift

3

Know the job, know your customer

When you listen to what your customers are saying, you will find that they will usually tell you what they want to hear.

If your job is in sales, marketing, marketing communications, or in any way close to bringing in revenue for your employer, you will understand the importance of 'getting inside your customer's head' to find out what is important to them, because this allows you to sell the product or service based on the customer's needs. If you are not connected to revenue generation you might not know this. Either way, understanding what is important to your customer (the employer) is very helpful for anyone engaged in a job search because it helps you understand what it is that customer wants to buy. Knowing what a customer wants to buy makes it much easier to customize your message to meet their needs.

Now applying this to the job search we have bad news and good news.

Bad news: Normally you have to get into conversations with your customers to find out what it is they want to buy.

Good news: Fortunately the insights you need are all available to you in *job advertisements.* Let me just repeat that, because it's very important: All the insights you need about your target job are already available to you in job ads. *All you need to do is learn how to translate it into useable information*, which is what we are going to do now.

On the next couple of pages is a simple exercise called Target Job Deconstructions. *Do not skip this exercise – it can make an enormous difference to this job search and to your entire future career development.* It will tell you precisely how to prioritize the information you offer employers, and will give you illustrations for your letters, a new way of looking at your work and what it is you actually get paid for. The exercise will also tell you the areas of greatest inquiry at interviews and prepare you with illustrations for your answers to interview questions.

The Target Job Deconstruction process was designed to help you create the most powerful CV possible. The exercise is geared toward determining the precise requirements of the job you want, matching your skills to those requirements, and identifying the story you need to tell in your cover letter and CV to make these documents effective. The most difficult part of any letter is knowing what to say and how to say it, but this approach ensures that the topics your letter addresses are going to be of the highest relevance to your customers and the words you should use will have greatest likelihood of resonating with the reader.

> **Step 1.** Collect six job ads or online postings for jobs you can do and jobs you would enjoy. If you are interested in more than one job you must prioritize them.
>
> **Step 2.** Create a new document and title it 'TJD for _____ (your chosen target job title)'.
>
> **Step 3.** Start with a first subhead reading 'Target job titles'. Then copy and paste in all the variations from your samples. Looking at the result, you will be able to say, 'When employers are hiring people like this, they tend to describe the job title with these words.' From this you can come up with a generic Target Job Title to use in your cover letters (and as a target job title for your CV) that is likely to have the widest response.
>
> **Step 4.** Add a second subhead to the TJD: 'Skills/Responsibilities/ Requirements/Competencies, etc.'
>
> **Step 5.** Look through the job postings (it might be easier to print them out and spread them across your desk). You are looking for a requirement that is common to all of your job postings. When you find both the requirement and the most complete description of it, copy and paste it into your document beneath the second subhead (with a 6 beside it, signifying it is common to all six of your samples).
>
>   Underneath, add any additional words and phrases used in the other job postings to describe this same area. Repeat this exercise for any other requirements common to all six of your job postings.
>
> **Step 6.** Repeat the exercise but now consider requirements common to five of the jobs, then four, and so on, all the way down to those requirements mentioned in only one job ad.

You now have something unique: a template for how employers prioritize and express their needs when they hire someone like you.

Step 7. At their most elemental level, all jobs are the same – they all focus on problem identification, avoidance and solution. No matter what your job title is, you are being paid to prevent problems occurring whenever possible within your areas of responsibility and to solve them whenever they do crop up.

Imagine yourself, for a moment, as a manager looking at a cover letter and accompanying CV. Is this exactly the person you are looking for – someone who recognizes and knows how to handle the challenges of the job? Of course it is. When you as a job seeker register the underlying problem-solving nature of your target job, you gain a valuable insight into the mind of every recruiter, interviewer and manager you are ever going to meet.

Step 8. Now go back to your TJD and start with that first requirement, the one common to all six job postings. Note the problems you will typically need to identify, solve and/or prevent in the course of a normal workday as you deliver on this requirement of the job. Then list specific examples, big and small, of successful identification, prevention and/or solution to such problems that you've performed in the past.

Step 9. Repeat this with each of the TJD's other requirements, identifying the problems that come up in each aspect of the job and examples of how you deal with them. You'll want to include some of these examples in your cover letters. Others you'll use in your CV. Additional ones will provide you with the ammunition to answer all those interview questions that begin, 'Tell me about a time when...' and still others may appear in the follow-up letters after the interview.

Step 10. Look at each of the competencies/requirements you identified in steps 5 and 6, and for each one think of the *best* person you have ever seen doing this job and what made him or her stand out. Describe his or her performance, professional behaviour, interaction with others, and appearance.

This step has importance for today, tomorrow, and for your long-term success. This is the behavioural profile interviewers want to see in your cover letters, your CV, and at job interviews, and this is the person they would love to see showing up to work every day. In fact, this is the exact behavioural profile of the person who gets welcomed into the inner circle and gets the plum assignments, raises and promotions.

Repeat this behavioural identification exercise for each and every requirement listed in your TJD.

Step 11. Think of the *worst* person you have ever seen doing this job and answer for yourself what made that person stand out in such a negative way. Describe his or her performance, professional behaviours, interaction with others, and appearance. You are describing the person that no one wants to hire or work with; this valuable step gives you a behavioural profile for professional suicide.

Once you complete and review your TJD, you will have a clear idea of exactly the way all employers think about, prioritize and express their needs when they hire someone for the job you want. This tells you exactly the points to put in your cover letter that are most likely to get a positive response and prepares you in other ways for job interviews and for success in the job you ultimately choose as your next step.

4
Develop your professional identity

Competition is always fierce in a job search, so how you stand out from that competition is a big part of your success.

In this chapter, we'll talk about the issues and challenges of establishing a professional identity, and how to communicate that through your letters.

Written communication is a central component of your professional identity. It is easy for an interviewer to forget what someone is like, how they talk and what they say, but the written word has the capacity to bring you and your application back to life again in the interviewer's mind.

Your cover letter enables you to mark yourself out from the moment of introduction, and throughout the interview process when it presents a clear image of a unique, consummate professional. So, it helps to create a desirable professional identity that gives you focus and motivation and offers others an easy way to differentiate you from the crowd.

Identifying the components

A professional identity requires that you identify those skills and behaviours – your best professional qualities – that make you different and desirable. It's the capture and conscious positioning of those qualities in your letters, e-mails and on your CV that will make you stand out.

There are particular skills, values and behaviours that are admired by employers the world over. They are at the heart of all professional success because they can be applied in any job, at any level, in all professions.

I have broken this list of critical attributes into three sections:

1 Transferable skills

2 Professional values

3 Business values

Knowing its value to employers, when you identify one of these transferable skills, professional behaviours or core values as something you possess, make it part of your professional identity. When you identify a skill, behaviour or core value as something you need to develop, make it part of your ongoing personal development programme, because developing these attributes underlies your long-term survival and success.

Transferable skills

The National Association of Colleges and Employers (NACE), has defined seven transferable skills that every professional entering the workplace should develop:

Technical skills

Having technical skills means you know which tools are needed for a particular task and possess the know-how to use them productively and efficiently. These skills vary from profession to profession. Staying current with these skills is an integral part of your ongoing professional growth. Mentioning the course you just completed to upgrade your computer skills could be the perfect finish to a cover or follow-up letter.

Communication skills

Every professional job today requires communication skills; promotions and professional success are impossible without them.

The primary communication skills are:

- *Verbal skills:* What you say and how you say it.

- *Listening skills:* Listening to understand, rather than just waiting your turn to talk.

- *Writing skills:* Your ability to craft succinct, clear messages. Excellent written communication is essential for any professional career. It creates a lasting impression of who you are, and it's an important expression of your professional identity.

- *Technology communication skills:* Technology has changed the way we communicate and your ability to navigate the new communication media can and will have an impact on your professional success.

Teamworking skills

The professional world revolves around complex challenges and requires teams of people to provide solutions. This demands that you work efficiently with others who have different responsibilities, backgrounds, objectives and areas of expertise.

Critical thinking skills

Critical thinking, analytical, or problem-solving skills allow the successful professional to think through and clearly define a challenge and its desired solutions, and then evaluate and implement the best solution for that challenge from all available options.

Time management and organization skills

The ability to manage time and organize activities increases productivity. The people who do this are thought of as high achievers because they get so much done. In fact, these are just people who learned how to organize themselves and consequently work with more purpose.

Creativity

There's a difference between creativity and just having ideas. Creativity is developing those ideas with the strategic and tactical know-how that brings them to life. In a professional context, it is the generation of new ideas as they relate to a specific situation, challenge or goal. It is a skill that can be learned and applied to anything you do.

Leadership skills

Your job as a leader is to make your team function, so your teamwork skills give you the ability to pull your team together as a cohesive unit.

Your technical expertise, critical thinking and creativity skills help you to define the challenges and their solutions.

Your communication skills enable your team to understand its tasks and goals.

Your time management and organization skills enable you to create a practical blueprint for success and for your team to take ownership of the task and deliver the expected results.

Professional values

Successful professionals display these values in everything that they do. They'll open the doors of opportunity for you, too:

- *Motivation:* Employers realize that a motivated professional will do better on every assignment. Motivation expresses itself in a commitment to the job and the profession, an eagerness to learn and grow professionally, and a willingness to take the rough with the smooth.

- *Energy:* Motivation is invariably expressed by the energy someone demonstrates in his or her work, and is demonstrated by always giving that extra effort to get the job done and to get it done well.

- *Commitment:* These qualities include dedication to your profession and understanding the role it plays in the larger issues of company success. Knowing how your role contributes to the greater good gives you a strong sense of commitment.

- *Reliability:* Your dedication will also express itself in your reliability: Showing up is half the battle; the other half is your performance: not relying on anyone else to ensure the job is done.

- *Determination:* Determination is the quality of a resilient professional who doesn't get worn down or back off when a situation gets tough. It marks out the man or woman who chooses to be part of the solution rather than standing idly by and being part of the problem.

- *Pride:* Taking pride in yourself as a professional means always making sure you do your job to the best of your ability. It means paying attention to the details and to the time and cost constraints.

- *Integrity:* Integrity means taking responsibility for your actions, both good and bad, and it also means treating others, within and outside of the company, with respect at all times and in all situations. As a professional with integrity, your actions will always be in the ethical best interests of the company, and your decisions will never be based on whim or personal preference.

Business values

Companies have very limited interests: making money, saving money, and saving time. Developing business values that demonstrate sensitivity to the profit impera-tive of a business is the mark of a true professional.

These are all qualities that should be reflected in your professional identity, which in turn should appear in your job search letters and CV:

- *Productivity:* You should always work towards enhanced productivity through efficiencies of time, resources, money and effort. Most problems have two solutions, and the expensive one isn't always the best. Ideas of efficiency and economy engage the creative mind in ways that others would not consider.

- *Procedures:* You recognize the need for procedures and that they are implemented only after careful thought. You understand and always follow the chain of command and don't implement your own 'improved' procedures or organize others to do so.

Develop and apply these values in your professional life and you will become more credible, more visible and more successful as the result of having a developed professional identity.

However, that you possess these skills is one thing. That I know you possess them is another. Their inclusion in all your written communications should be an obvious step that we'll look at a little later in this chapter.

The examples of your skills and the impact of these values on your work can be used in all your job search letters to make positive statements about your suitability.

Identifying your competitive difference

Now that you have looked at the skills and values that mark successful professionals the world over, let's move on to pinpointing your competitive difference. This is another theme that must run throughout all your job search letters.

The people who hire you must be able to separate you from the other candidates. Your letters will reflect the qualities we discussed above, and this will help in that process, but we need more ammunition to make sure that you stand out. The following questions will help you identify the combination of factors that make you unique:

- What are the transferable skills, professional behaviours and business values that capture the essence of the professional you?

- What have you achieved with these qualities?

- What excites you most about your professional responsibilities?

- What are your biggest achievements in these areas?

- What gives you greatest satisfaction in the work you do?

- What value does this combination of skills, behaviours and achievements mean you bring to your employer?

- Make three one-sentence statements that capture the professional you.

- Take these three statements and rework them into one sentence. This is the essence of your competitive difference.

Weaving your professional identity into letters

These questions should help you to define your competitive difference and objectively sum up the professional you. These become the basis of the statements you use in your job search letters, CV and other written communications when it is necessary to talk about yourself.

Sometimes these will be bold statements and at other times an inference or subtle reference to make a point, but they all say, in effect, 'These are the benefits my presence will bring to your team and to your company.'

Your professional identity is communicated throughout your cover letter and CV, but especially in these statements.

Here is a statement from a pharmaceutical sales management professional:

I have attached my CV, where you will see a history of achievement with major pharmaceutical companies. I am well equipped to continue this success and would be honoured to join your team, where I believe I can outperform all prior achievements.

Implicit in this statement is a promise that this professional will repeat a history of achievement. She feels confident in doing so because her track record is underpinned with a clear sense of the skills this success is based upon. A couple of sentences in her cover letter demonstrate her value and make for a powerful presentation.

In another statement, a compelling message – 'I understand what is at the core of success in my job and I care about it' – is clearly emphasized:

> With reference to your Customer Service posting on www.sales.com, are you looking for a customer service associate who treats every customer interaction as critical to the company's success?

Here are some more examples:

- I believe I can bring sound technical skills, strong business acumen, and real management skill to technical projects and personnel in a fast-paced environment.

- Five years' experience in a retail environment has taught me that customer service is the company's face to the world and I consequently treat every customer interaction as critical to financial success.

- Leadership by example and conscientious performance management underlies my department's consistent customer satisfaction ratings.

Job search letters are short documents with much to convey. Your cover letters and all your job search letters should support your professional identity by addressing the skills, behaviours and values that identify you as a professional.

5
Elements of a great cover letter

There is a fine line between pride in achievement and insufferable arrogance when writing about your experiences and who you are as a professional.

Now that you have a clearer idea of what makes you different, and you've captured that in a personal brand statement, you're ready to reflect this in your cover letters and all the other types of letters you can use to make yourself stand out during the job hunt.

Differences between electronic and print cover letters

Today's workplace tends to demand 50 or more hours weekly from busy, multi-tasking professionals. Executives often base their decisions on whether to return a call or respond to an e-mail on the first few words or moments of the message. If you can't cut to the chase, they think they shouldn't waste their time because of your communication inadequacies. *Your cover letter and CV, whether sent by e-mail or snail mail, competes for the attention of this audience.* The key is to construct a clear, well-ordered, compelling, *succinct* letter.

A cover letter is a collection of sequenced sentences organized around a single goal: to get your CV read with serious attention. It is likely that you will need to create more than one type of cover letter, so my advice is to concentrate on one general letter first. You can then use this letter as a template to cut, paste and otherwise adapt other letters going to specific contacts, headhunters and so on. Ultimately, any letter is only as good as the individual sentences that carry the message; the most grammatically correct sentence in the world won't necessarily get you interviews, because it can read as though every breath of life has been squeezed out of it. Your goal is to communicate an energizing message and entice the reader to action.

The amount of e-mail traffic is growing exponentially, so hit your main points quickly and with clarity or lose your reader's attention. A good subject line grabs attention, but if the first two sentences don't succinctly state your purpose and maintain that initial attention, the reader has little reason for wasting any more precious time on the rest of your message.

Your cover letter will typically consist of three to five carefully constructed paragraphs. Because a second page simply won't get read, whether it is going by e-mail or traditional mail it is not going to exceed one standard MS Word page.

Your cover letters will only ever exceed this one-page rule if you have already spoken to the recipient and he has asked you to send a CV. Even in this instance, make every effort to contain your message to three to five short paragraphs. Just as you would limit a paper cover letter to one page, you should try to keep an e-mail cover letter to one screen that's as compact as possible. Edit yourself sternly and decisively. If you cannot get your entire letter in one screen view, at least make an effort to be certain that the meat of your pitch is on that first full screen.

Your letters should always be laid out with short paragraphs and lots of white space so that reading is easy on the eye; your letters have the same reader accessibility concerns as your CV.

Written communication is a critical skill in the workplace. Typos are *verboten*! Don't trust yourself to do the final proofread of your letter. Instead, ask a friend (or, preferably, several friends) to read it through, looking for typos, errors in formatting, and wording that isn't as clear as you'd like.

Cover letter ingredients

Your letters will be most effective when you do each of the following seven things:

1 Address someone by name… and, whenever possible, someone involved in the recruitment and selection cycle, ideally a hiring authority, as we noted – typically one to three management levels above your title.

2 Explain why you are writing.

3 Tailor the letter to the reader/company as far as is practical.

4 Include information relevant to the job you are seeking. As with the TJD you undertook earlier, this is possible even when you do not have a job posting.

5 Show concern, interest and pride in your profession; the branding exercises from the last chapter will help you with this.

6 Maintain a balance between professionalism and friendliness.

7 Ask for the next step in the process clearly and without apology or arrogance.

Before discussing formatting, let's take a minute to talk in more detail about some of these issues.

What makes a cover letter work?

Your first step is to grab the reader's attention and arouse interest. Use the first paragraph to introduce yourself with conviction and establish your reason for writing, perhaps integrating a phrase that foreshadows the opening brand statement from your CV. Whenever possible, your letter should start with a personalized greeting/salutation. E-mail has increased our ease of communication with the written word and has relaxed a number of letter writing rules, but you must use a greeting to open your letter if you expect to be regarded as a professional in your field. If you do not start your letter with a greeting you are immediately seen as someone who does not have a basic grasp of business communication. Remember my comments about that first five-second scan? Because written communication is so important in today's workplace, no salutation can mean your letter is rejected immediately.

Whenever possible, open the letter by using a person's name, spelled correctly and using one of the following forms:

- Dear Mr Yate (standard);

- Hello, Mr Yate (more casual but still okay; not as acceptable in the professions of law, medicine and education);

- Dear Martin Yate or Hello, Martin Yate (acceptable if you are an experienced professional, but not so much if you are at the entry level or in your first two or three years in the professional workplace).

Do not use first names (Hello, Martin or Dear Carole) unless the reader of the letter can clearly see by your signature that you are someone of equal stature. First names are okay once you have spoken and are clearly on a first-name basis.

Starting the letter

Everything you need to say must be short and to the point so that your copy never exceeds one page. At the same time, you quickly want to find common ground with your reader, present yourself in the best way, and cut to the chase.

Here are a few examples:

When you have a referral or prior frame of reference

First things first, Carole Mraz over at C-Soft asked me to say hello. You and I haven't spoken before but Carole thinks we might have an interesting conversation, especially if you anticipate the need for an industrious young marketing acolyte who comes equipped with a great education, two ears and one mouth, and a great desire to start at the bottom learning from an acknowledged master in the field.

Our mutual colleague, John Stanovich, felt my skills and abilities would be valuable to your company...

The manager of your Brighton office, Pamela Bronson, has suggested I contact you regarding the opening for a _____.

I received your name from Henry Charles, the branch manager of the ABC Bank, last week and he suggested I contact you. In case the CV he forwarded is delayed in the mail, I enclose another.

Arthur Gold, your office manager and my neighbour, thought I should contact you about the upcoming opening in your accounting department.

A colleague of mine, Diane Johnson, recommended your recruitment company to me as you recently assisted her in a strategic career move. I understand that your company specializes in the consumer products industry.

I met you briefly at the import/export symposium last _____ and really resonated with your comments about productivity being pulled down by sloppy communications, and as I am looking to harness my _____ years of logistics expertise to an organization with a major role in global distribution...

When you have no referral and no job posting

I have been researching the leading local companies in _____ , and the name of _____ Products keeps coming up as a top company. This confirmed an opinion I've developed over my three years as a committed distance-learning educator.

Right after my mentor mentioned _____ as one of the top companies in our industry, I saw you speak at the association meeting last year. I really resonated with your comments about productivity, and as I am looking to harness my _____ years of logistics expertise to a major player, I felt this was the right time to introduce myself.

I understand you are a manager who likes to gets things done, and who needs competent, focused, goal-orientated employees…

I'm focused on finding the right boss to bring out the best in a consistently top-producing _____ . I am a highly motivated producer who wants to make a contribution as part of the hard-driving team of the industry leader.

I thought the best way to demonstrate my drive and creativity was to deliver my CV in this priority mail envelope. I also sent it to you by e-mail and into your company CV bank, but sales is all about stacking the odds, and I knew you'd also appreciate a break from the computer screen.

I've been meaning to contact you ever since I attended/read/heard about _____ . It encouraged me to do a little research, which has convinced me that you are the kind of company I want to be associated with, and that I have the kind of analytical focus coupled with creative drive that can be successfully applied to your current projects.

I have been following the performance of your company in Mutual Funds Newsletter. With my experience working for one of your direct competitors in office support in the critical area of customer service I know I could make significant contributions… I am a detail-orientated problem solver and am used to working with different, often frustrated people.

Recently, I have been researching the local _____ industry. My search has been focused on looking for companies that are respected in the field and that prize a commitment to professional development. I am such an individual and you are clearly such a company. I bring sound technical skills, strong business acumen, and real management skills for complex technical projects in a fast-paced environment.

Although I am currently employed by one of your major competitors, I must admit that I was captivated by your company's mission statement when I visited your website.

Within the next few weeks, I will be moving from Glasgow to _____ . Having researched the companies in _____ , I know that you are the company I want to talk to because…

The state of the art in _____ changes so rapidly that it is tough for most professionals to keep up. The attached CV will demonstrate that I am an exception and eager to bring my experience as a _____ to bear for your company.

When you are responding to a job posting

Your job posting no. 23567 cited the need for drive and creativity. I thought a good way to demonstrate my drive and creativity was to deliver my CV in this priority mail envelope. Of course, I sent it to you by e-mail, but marketing communications is all about psychology and results… so I knew you'd get the message, appreciate the contrarian thinking, and enjoy a break from the computer screen.

I read your job posting on your company's website on 5th January and felt I had to respond…

Your online job posting regarding a _____ on _____.com caught my eye, and your company name caught my attention.

This e-mail, and my attached CV, is in response to your job posting on _____ .

I read your advertisement in the Daily Press *on 6th October for a _____ and, after researching your company website, felt I had to write…*

Reference job no. C/AA 5670. As you compare your requirements for a _____ with my attached CV, you will see that my entire background matches your requirements exactly.

This letter and attached CV are in response to your posting in _____ .

I was excited to see your opening for the accounting vacancy (job no. S9854) on careerbuilder.co.uk. As my attached CV demonstrates, the open position is a perfect match for my 15 years' payroll, general ledger, and accounts receivable experience.

While browsing the jobs database on monster.co.uk, I was intrigued by your Regional Sales Manager job posting.

Presenting yourself

If you haven't managed to build in the reason for writing into your opening as we see in some of the above examples, introduce it now and go on to identify something desirable about the professional you.

I am writing because…

My reason for contacting you…

… you may be interested to know…

If you are seeking a _____ , you will be interested to know…

I would like to talk to you about your staffing needs for _____ and how I might be able to contribute to your department's goals.

If you have an opening for someone in this area, you will see that my CV demonstrates a person of unusual dedication, efficiency and drive.

You then go on to define the kind of work you do with a brief statement and/or two to three statements that highlight your capabilities. With a short paragraph or a couple of bullets you might highlight one or two special contributions or achievements. These can include any qualifications, contributions and attributes that brand you as someone with talent and energy to offer.

You can also use this part of the letter if an aspect of a particular job opening is not addressed in your CV, and for some reason you don't have time to update it.

Or you can use the cover letter to emphasize a priority requirement(s) from the posting.

In my CV you will find proof points for my PR acumen including:

- *demonstrated track record of strategic communications and influential public relations;*

- *accomplished media relations and story placement, from* BBC World News *to ZDNet;*

- *team, account, budget, client and C-level executive management;*

- *client loyalty and satisfaction;*

- *knowledge of high-tech industry and players;*

- *new business success;*

- *self-motivated team player.*

Although I am currently employed by one of your competitors, I have kept my eye open for an opportunity to join your organization. Over the past year I have:

- *built a sales force of seven reps, reduced turnover, and increased individual productivity an average of 14 per cent;*

- *implemented a customer service plan that successfully reduced client turnover 18 per cent;*

- *initiated warranty tracking, increasing upsells by 7 per cent;*

- *increased revenue by £4.3 million.*

As a Marketing Director with 12 years' experience in consumer products, I have:

- *doubled revenues in just 18 months;*

- *introduced a new product that captured a 38 per cent market share;*

- *successfully managed a £5 million ad budget.*

I have an economics background from Cambridge and employ cutting-edge quantitative analysis strategies to approach cyclical fluctuations. This has enabled me to consistently anticipate all major peaks and valleys in the last 12 years.

If an advertisement or a telephone conversation with a potential employer reveals an aspect of a particular job opening that is not addressed in your CV (and for some reason you don't have time to update it), you can use the cover letter to fill in the gaps. Or you can use the cover letter to emphasize a priority requirement, for example:

I noticed from your posting that training experience in a distance-learning environment would be a plus. You will see in my enclosed CV that I have five years' experience writing and producing sales and management training materials in new media.

You are looking for a database administrator with experience in intranet implementation and management. As my attached CV demonstrates, I have done that type of work for six years with a regional organization on a platform of 15,000 users.

Desk technology upgrades:

- *responsible for hardware and peripheral selection;*

- *coordinated installation of workstations;*

- *trained users.*

Full upgrade achieved under budget and within deadline. Savings to company: £25,000.

You want the reader to move from your letter to the CV already primed with the feeling that you can do this job; the above reference to a job's key requirement does just that. Since you want the reader to move quickly to your CV, brevity is important. Leave your reader wanting more; the letter doesn't sell you – that's the CV's job – but it should position you for serious consideration. Whet the reader's appetite, no more.

Make it clear to the reader that you want to talk

Explain when, where and how you can be contacted. You can also be proactive, by telling the reader that you intend to follow up at a certain point in time if contact has not been established by then. Just as you worked to create a strong opening, make sure your closing carries the same conviction. It is the reader's last personal impression of you, so make it strong, make it tight, and make it obvious that you are serious about entering into meaningful conversation.

Useful phrases include:

It would be a pleasure to give you more information about my qualifications and experience…

I welcome the opportunity to discuss your specific projects and explore the possibility of joining your team.

I look forward to discussing our mutual interests further…

While I prefer not to use my employer's time taking personal calls at work, with discretion I can be reached at _____ .

I will be in your area around the 20th, and will call you prior to that date. I would like to arrange…

I have attached my CV for your review and will call you in the next couple of days to discuss any openings for which your firm is currently conducting searches.

I hope to speak with you further, and will call the week of _____ to follow up.

The chance to meet you would be a privilege and a pleasure, so to this end I shall call you on _____ .

I look forward to speaking to you further, and will call in the next few days to see when our schedules will permit a face-to-face meeting.

May I suggest a personal meeting where you can have the opportunity to examine the person behind the CV?

My credentials and achievements are a matter of record that I hope you will examine in depth when we meet. You can reach me at _____ .

I look forward to discussing any of the ways you feel my background and skills would benefit [name of organization]. I look forward to hearing from you.

CVs help you sort out the probables from the possibles, but they are no way to judge the calibre of an individual. I would like to meet you and demonstrate that I have the professional personality that makes for a successful _____ .

I expect to be in your area on Tuesday and Wednesday of next week, and wonder which day would be best for you. I will call to determine. In the meantime, I would appreciate you treating my application as confidential, since I am currently employed.

With my training and hands-on experience, I know I can contribute to _____ , and want to talk to you about it in person. When may we meet?

After reading my CV, you will know something about my background. Yet you will still need to determine whether I am the one to help you with current problems and challenges. I would like an interview to discuss my ability to make meaningful contributions to your department's goals.

You can reach me at [home/alternate no.] to arrange an interview. I know that the investment of your time in meeting with me will be repaid amply.

Thank you for your time and consideration; I hope to hear from you shortly.

May I call you for an interview in the next few days?

A brief phone call will establish whether or not we have mutual interest. Recognizing the demands of your schedule, I will make that call before lunch on Tuesday.

Some people feel it is powerful in the closing to state a date – 'I'll call you on Friday if we don't speak before' – or a date and time – 'I'll call you on Friday morning at 10 am if we don't speak before' when they will follow up with a phone call. The logic is that you demonstrate that your intent is serious, that you are organized, and that you plan your time effectively, all of which are desirable behavioural traits and support the brand of a goal-oriented and consummate professional.

A complete idiot in my profession once said that an employer would be offended by being 'forced' to sit and await this call. In over 30 years of involvement in the hiring process, as a headhunter, as a hiring manager, as an HR executive and as a writer on these issues who speaks to executives all over the world, I have never met anyone who felt constrained to wait by the phone for such a call. What sometimes does get noticed, though, is the person who doesn't follow through on commitments as promised. Therefore, if you use this approach, keep your promise: it's part of the value proposition in your professional brand.

Now that you have a frame of reference for the factors that impact cover letters and any other job search letters, let's move on to the nuts and bolts of making them work.

Later in the book you'll find five types of cover letters, plus follow-up letters; networking letters; thank you letters; resurrection letters; and acceptance, rejection, and resignation letters.

A question of money

Recruitment advertisements sometimes request salary information, either current salary, salary requirements or salary history. Over the years this issue has taken far more of people's attention than it deserves.

Recruiters and employers ask about your salary for two principal reasons:

1 *Because all jobs have approved salary ranges* and no matter what your skills, it is hard to win an exception to an approved salary range.

2 *Because it tells about your salary trajectory*, the offer you are likely to accept and the raises you are used to.

There are other considerations as well: interviews take precious time, and managers are reluctant to waste it on candidates who could never be hired because of their salary needs.

The usual exception, when there is one, is if you are in a hot job within an in-demand professional area or you have a unique skill set that gives you a competitive edge.

In a down economy when money is tighter and they have more options, it is known as a buyer's market and employers have far less incentive to negotiate out-side the approved salary.

Writing that your salary is 'negotiable', annoys HR people: they already know salary is negotiable, and the reply doesn't answer the question they need answered.

With an in-demand job in a good economy, 'negotiable' is rarely grounds for refusing to talk to a candidate, but in a buyer's market 'negotiable' might not always have the desired result.

Given this understanding, if you have the skills and you are in the approved range you'll get an interview. If you aren't... well, then your energies are probably better invested in finding other opportunities, but make the pitch anyway. You have nothing to lose.

When your salary requirements are requested, don't restrict yourself to one figure; instead, give yourself a range. All job openings have an approved salary range so this dramatically improves your chances of 'clicking onto' the salary range that is authorized for every position.

If you are asked about your current salary and choose to answer, be honest. This isn't something you can ever fudge on. It can and does get verified, and any discrepancies can result in you being dismissed; such an event will dog your career for years. Here is one way to address the topic of money in your cover letter. You will find other examples later in the book.

Depending on the job and the professional development environment, my salary requirements are in the £_____ to £_____ range.

Address this issue in the cover letter or in a document attached to the cover letter but never in the CV itself. This is because your CV may be kept in a database for years and your salary range may typecast you as, say, an entry-level professional in the eyes of that company's computer.

Here is an example of a salary history attachment.

Calvin Tompkins
1 Any Street, Anytown AA1 1AA
Home 12345 678901 • Mobile 1098765 4321 • sharplogistics@gmail.com

Salary History
XYZ Avionics, Kings Weston – 2008 to 2010
Chief Operations Officer / Aviation Training School Officer in Charge
Salary – £55,207
ABC Aviation, Leicester – 2006 to 2008
Aircraft Maintenance Chief – General Operations Manager / Plant Manager
Starting Salary – £44,484 / Ending Salary – £50,500
XYZ Systems, Birmingham – 2002 to 2006
Plant Manager / Senior Operations Manager
Starting Salary – £40,507 / Ending Salary – £44,200
ABC Engineering – 1998 to 2002
Recruitment Manager
Starting Salary – £35,545 / Ending Salary – £42,500

Contact information

This should include address, telephone number and e-mail address. Once you have determined a primary contact number for your job hunt, you must ensure that it will be answered *at all times*. There is no point in mounting a job search campaign if prospective employers can never reach you. Your telephone company offers you voice mail; use it and keep the message businesslike and, once recorded, replay it and listen carefully to the message for clarity, tone of voice, and recording quality. Does it present you as a clear-spoken, confident professional, and does it reflect the professional brand you are trying to create?

In your cover letter, you should always list your e-mail address immediately beneath your telephone number, as initial contact is often by e-mail. Never use your company telephone or e-mail for any job search activities, ever.

If you're sending out your cover letters by e-mail with CV attachments, be sure to hyperlink your e-mail address in your CV. That way, recruiters can send an e-mail back to you with one click of the mouse directly from your CV. Remember, it's all about making it *easy* for hiring managers to contact you. The less work you make them do, the better your chances of success.

6
Assembling your job search letter

Having pulled together the elements of your letter, it's time to start organizing them into a coherent, effective whole. There are six steps to this process.

Step one: identify your target job

Your job search – and the CV and letters that go with it – will be incalculably more productive if you begin by clearly defining a target job that you can land and in which you can be successful. Start by identifying this target job title.

Step two: research the target job

Any evaluation of your background must begin with an understanding of what potential employers will be looking for when they come to your cover letter and CV. Collect 6 to 10 job postings that carry this target job title. Once you have a selection, deconstruct them as described in the Target Job Deconstruction process.

Step three: go through your recent work history

Once you know what your readers are looking for and therefore will respond to, it is time to start working through your work history. Knowing what your customers want to buy (as revealed in the Target Job Deconstruction) and how to illustrate your abilities to deliver on their needs is part of this story. So consider, for example, the following elements:

A Current or last employer

Identify your current or last employer by name and location, and follow it with a brief description (five or six words) of the company's business/products/services.

Write down the following information:

Starting date: _____

Starting title: _____

Starting salary: _____

Leaving date: _____

Leaving title: _____

Reason for leaving: _____

Potential references for this job: _____

Leaving salary: _____

B Make a prioritized list of the duties/responsibilities/deliverables in this position.

C What special skills or knowledge did you need to perform each of these tasks well? Which transferable skills, behaviours, values helped you execute each of these tasks successfully?

- What educational background and/or credentials helped prepare you for these responsibilities?

- You are being paid to solve problems within the area of your professional expertise. For each area of responsibility consider the daily problems that arise and also major crises. Recall the analytical processes, subsequent actions, the transferable skills and successful solutions you implemented to achieve a successful outcome. There is a four-step technique you will find useful here called PSRV:

P. Identify the *project* and the problem it represented, both from a company perspective and from the point of view of your execution of duties.

S. Identify your *solution* to the challenge and the process you implemented to deliver the solution.

R. What was the *result* of your approach and actions?

V. Finally, what was the *value* to you, the department, and the company? If you can, define this in terms of meaningful contribution: time saved, money saved, or money earned. This is not always possible, but it is very powerful whenever you can employ it.

Step four: consider transferable skills, behaviours, and values used

Which transferable skills helped you succeed with this particular task? Come up with examples of how you used each behaviour in the execution of each of your major duties at this job. The examples you generate can be used in your CV, in your cover letters and as illustrative answers to questions at interviews.

Step five: add your previous work history

Now repeat Steps 3 (the problem solving aspect of your job) and 4 (how you used the seven transferable skills, learned behaviours, and values in your work). Do not skimp on this process. Everything you write may not go into the final version of your first cover letter, but you'll be able to use the information in another letter, in your CV, or in response to an interview question. What you are doing here is identifying the building blocks of what it takes to be successful in your profession, and the information you need at your fingertips to explain what you do objectively. The ultimate pay-off is more and better job offers and a more successful career.

Step six: compile compliments

Looking at each of your major areas of responsibility throughout your work history, write down any positive verbal or written commentary others have made on your performance. As you will see in some of the sample letters in Chapter 9, words about you that come from someone else often have a much greater impact than any description you could come up with yourself.

Now, these compliments don't always happen that often, and then all too often you sometimes push the accolades away. That's okay – lots of people do – but from now on you will make a point of capturing them for use in the future.

How did you work productively with co-workers, subordinates, and management? What different levels of people do you have to interact with to achieve your job's goals? What have you learned about productivity and communication from these experiences, and what does this say about you?

Compile a networking map

Now, while you are thinking so closely about work projects, also think about the job titles of people with whom you work on an ongoing basis. This can be very useful in your job search because these are the people:

- Who are most likely to hear about job openings of interest to you.

- Who you are most likely to stumble across job openings for, when looking for jobs for yourself. Such leads help the give and take of networking.

The different levels of people you have to interact with in your day-to-day work are all people and titles you will want to reach out to in your networking and other job search activities. *Don't confine yourself just to the people you already know with these job titles*, but constantly seek out new contacts with these titles. You can help each other.

Create punchy sentences

Your goal is to communicate an energizing message and entice the reader to action. Concise, punchy sentences grab attention.

Verbs always help energize a sentence and give it that short, cut-to-the-chase feel. For example, one professional – with a number of years at the same law firm in a clerical position – had written:

> *I learned to manage a computerized database.*

Sounds pretty ordinary, right? Well, after looking at her job as an ongoing problem-solving exercise, certain exciting facts emerged. By using verbs and an awareness of employer interests as they relate to her target job, this sentence was charged up and given more punch. Not only that, but for the first time the writer fully understood the value of her contributions, which greatly enhanced her self-confidence for interviews:

> *I analysed and determined need for comprehensive upgrade of database, archival and retrieval systems. I was responsible for selection and installation of 'in the clouds' archival systems. Company-wide archival system upgrade completed in one year.*

Notice how the verbs show that things happened when she was around the office and put flesh on the bones of that initial bare statement. Such action verbs and phrases add an air of direction, efficiency and accomplishment to every cover letter. Succinctly, they tell the reader *what* you did and *how well* you did it.

As you recall information that will contribute to your cover letter, rewrite the chosen phrases to see if you can give them more depth with the use of action verbs. While a cover letter is typically one page, or one screen, don't worry about the length right now. The process you go through helps you think out exactly what it is you have to offer and also creates the language and ideas you will use to explain yourself during an interview.

Varying sentence structure

As noted in the previous section, your letters will be most effective when they are constructed with short, punchy sentences. As a rule, try keeping your sentences under about 25 words; a good average is around 15. If your sentence is longer than the 25-word mark, change it. Either shorten it through restructuring, use semicolons to save space by obviating the need for the words necessary to orient a whole new sentence, or make two sentences out of one. At the same time, you will want to avoid choppiness, so vary the length of sentences when you can.

You can also start with a short phrase ending in a colon:

- followed by bullets of information;

- each one supporting the original phrase.

These techniques are designed to enliven the reading process for readers, who always have too much to read and too little time. Here's how we can edit and rewrite the last example.

Analysed and determined need for comprehensive upgrade of database, archival and retrieval systems:

- *Responsible for hardware and software selection and system-wide compatibility.*

- *Responsible for selection and installation of 'in the clouds' archival systems.*

- *Responsible for compatible hardware and software upgrades.*

- *Trained users from manager down to administrators.*

- *Achieved full upgrade, integration and compliance in six months.*

- *Manager stated, 'You brought us out of the dark ages, and neither you nor the firm missed a beat!'*

K.I.S.S. (keep it simple, stupid)

Persuading your readers to take action is challenging because many people in different companies and with different agendas see your letters and make judgements based on those agendas. This means you must keep industry jargon to a reasonable level (especially in the initial contact letters – covers, broadcast and the like); the rule of thumb is to use only the jargon and acronyms necessary to communicate your abilities. There will be those who understand the intricacies and technicalities of your profession, but many more who do not.

Within your short paragraphs and short sentences, beware of name dropping and acronyms, such as 'I worked for Dr A Witherspoon in Sys. Gen. SNA 2.31.' Statements like these can be too restricted to have meaning outside the small circle of specialists to whom they speak. Unless you work in a highly technical field, and are sending the letter and CV to someone by name and title that you know will understand the importance of your technical language, you should use technical phrases with discretion.

You want your letters to have the widest possible appeal, yet they need to remain personal in tone, so obviously you don't want them to sound like they're from Publishers Clearing House. You are not writing a novel but rather trying to capture the essence of the professional you in just a few brief paragraphs. Short words in short sentences help make short, gripping paragraphs – good for short attention spans!

Voice and tense

The voice you use for different letters depends on a few important factors:

- fetting a lot said in a small space;
- packaging your skills and credentials for the target job;
- being factual;
- capturing the essence and personality of the professional you.

There is considerable disagreement among the 'experts' about the best voice, and each option has both champions and detractors. The most important point is that whichever voice you use in your letters, you must be consistent throughout that letter.

Sentences can be truncated (up to a point), by omitting pronouns such as *I, you, he, she, they*:

Analysed and determined need for comprehensive upgrade of database...

In fact, many authorities recommend dropping pronouns as a technique that both saves space and allows you to brag about yourself without seeming boastful. It gives the impression of another party writing about you. Some feel that to use the personal pronoun – *'I analysed and determined need for comprehensive upgrade of database…'* – is naive, unprofessional, and smacks of boasting.

At the same time, still others recommend that you write in the first person because it makes you sound more human.

In short, there are no hard-and-fast rules – they can all work, given the many unique circumstances you will face in any given job search. Use whatever style works best for you and for the particular letter you are writing. If you do use the personal pronoun, try not to use it in every sentence; it gets a little monotonous, and it can make you sound like an egomaniac. The mental focus should be not on 'I' but on 'you', the person with whom you are communicating.

A nice variation is to use a first-person voice throughout the letter and then a final few words in the third person. Make sure these final words appear in the form of an attributed quote, as an insight to your value:

> *Manager stated, 'You brought us out of the dark ages, and neither you nor the firm missed a beat!'*

Don't confuse professionalism in your job search letters with stiff-necked formality. The most effective tone is one that mixes the conversational and the formal, just as we do in our offices and on our jobs. The only overriding rule is to make the letter readable so that the reader can see a human being and a professional shining through the page.

Length

As I indicated earlier, the standard length for a cover letter is usually one page, or the equivalent length for e-mails; typically this is as much as you can see on your screen without scrolling. Subsequent letters stemming from verbal communications – whether over the telephone or face-to-face – should also strive to adhere to the one-page rule, but can run to two pages if the complexity of content demands it.

With conscientious editing over a couple of days, that two-page letter can usually be reduced to one page without losing any of the content, and at the same time it will probably pack more punch. As my editor always says, 'If in doubt, cut it out.'

Having said this, I should acknowledge that all rules are made to be broken. Occasionally a two-page letter might be required, generally in one of the following instances:

1   You are at a level, or your job is of such technical complexity, such that you cannot edit down to one page without using a font size that is all but unreadable.

2   You have been contacted directly by an employer about a specific position and have been asked to present data for a specific opportunity.

3   An executive recruiter who is representing you determines that the exigencies of a particular situation warrant a dossier of such length. (Often such a letter and CV will be prepared exclusively – or with considerable input – by the recruiter.)

You'll find that thinking too much about length considerations will hamper the writing process. Think instead of the story you have to tell, and then layer fact upon fact until your tale is told. Use your words and the key phrases from this book to craft the message of your choice. When *that* is done you can go back and ruthlessly cut it to the bone.

Ask yourself these questions:

- Can I cut out any paragraphs?

- Can I cut out any sentences?

- How can I reduce the word count of the longer sentences?

- Where have I repeated myself?

Whenever you can, cut something out – leave nothing but facts and action verbs! (There's a list of action verbs in the next chapter.) If at the end you find too much has been cut, you'll have the additional pleasure of reinstating your deathless prose.

7

How to polish and edit your letters for maximum impact

A professional look is easy to recognize in business communications like cover letters but more difficult to define, because so much of that professional look comes from powerful messaging captured in elegant simplicity. Cover letters are defined as much by what they omit as by what they contain. This is what we are going to talk about now: the physical appeal and accessibility of your e-mails/letters and how to make sure every word counts.

Readability

Your CV and letter are typically going to arrive on a reader's desktop when he or she has a dozen other priorities. You can expect your letter to get *a maximum five-second scan to see if it is worth reading*; this will cover the subject line/opening sentence, spelling of the recipient's name and general readability. If it passes the scan test, you probably have *30 seconds* to make your point, and that's assuming your letter cuts to the chase and speaks to the reader's needs.

Mistakes to avoid

Letters that never get read have four things in common:

- They have too much information crammed into the space and are difficult to read – clearly the customer isn't coming first.

- The layout is unorganized, illogical and uneven; it looks shoddy and slapdash – and no one wants an employee like that.

- The recipient's name is misspelled – that's disrespectful.

- The letter contains typos – not acceptable in an age of spell-checkers.

Get your head into clear communication mode

Your CV and cover letters will always compete for the attention of a consistently distracted audience. The good news is that while your cover letters have a difficult job to do, if you apply just a few simple tactics, you can create cover letters that will improve the impact of your CV alone.

Advertising copywriters, with their ability to entertain and sell us stuff in a 30-second commercial, are arguably society's most effective communicators. They all share one common approach to their work: they get inside, and stay inside, the customer's head throughout the writing process. They focus on what features their product possesses and which benefits are most likely to appeal to the customer.

With a job posting or Target Job Deconstruction in hand, you know with considerable accuracy what your customer wants to hear about. From the Competitive Differentiation Questionnaire you know what features and benefits you have to offer. With this self-knowledge, you have everything you need to polish the draft you have just created.

How long should it be?

We've been here before, and the answer's still the same. Long enough to make your point and not a word longer. The standard length for a cover letter is usually one page (about 300 words); with an e-mail, the equivalent is typically as much as you can see on your screen without scrolling. They can also be much shorter. Here is a cover letter that gets to the point in 71 words:

> *Your colleague, Bill Jacobson, suggested that I send you my CV. He mentioned that your department is looking for a database administrator with experience in intranet*

implementation and management. As my attached CV demonstrates, I have done that type of work for six years with a regional organization on a platform of 15,000 users. I welcome the opportunity to discuss your specific projects and explore the possibility of joining your team.

With conscientious editing (spread over a couple of days to give you an objective distance), you can get any letter down to 300 words. The result will pack more punch.

Ask yourself these questions:

- Can I cut out a paragraph because it duplicates information?

- Is every sentence strictly necessary to get my point across?

- Can I use a strong element from a weaker sentence to beef up the better one?

- How can I reduce the word count of the longer sentences?

- Where have I repeated myself? (If you haven't found at least one repetition, you aren't really trying.)

Whenever you can, cut something out: 99 per cent of the time it will improve your message.

Avoid acronyms and professional slang

The rule of thumb is that if it is mentioned in the job postings you can use it. If not, find another way of saying it.

Every profession has its acronyms and professional slang/jargon, but there will be people in the recruitment and selection cycle who don't get it all. The acronyms and jargon have their place in your CV, but try to keep them under control in your letters.

Give action to your statements with verbs

The focus of your letter comes from your TJD and the results of your Differentiation questionnaire. It echoes the prioritization of keywords found in the job postings. These words are invariably nouns, and simply listing them doesn't make for an interesting story. Use verbs that show you in action.

- Responsible for all Accounts Payable

- Reduced Accounts Payable by…

- Streamlined Accounts Payable by…

- Managed all Accounts Payable…

Verbs always help energize a sentence and give it that short, cut-to-the-chase feel.

Because verbs show you in action, they give the reader a point of view, a way to see you. Verbs are very much part of creating your professional brand, bringing an air of direction, efficiency and accomplishment to your written communications. Succinctly, they tell the reader *what* you did and *how well* you did it and by implication anticipate you performing to the same standards when on the letter reader's payroll.

To help you in the process, here are more than 175 action verbs you can use. This list is just a beginning. Just about every word-processing program has a thesaurus; you can type any one of these words into one and get more choices for each entry.

accomplished	calculated	cut	executed	initiated
achieved	catalogued	decreased	expanded	innovated
acted	chaired	delegated	expedited	inspected
adapted	clarified	demonstrated	explained	installed
addressed	classified	designed	extracted	instigated
administered	coached	developed	fabricated	instilled
advanced	collected	devised	facilitated	instituted
advised	compiled	diagnosed	familiarized	instructed
allocated	completed	directed	fashioned	integrated
analysed	composed	dispatched	focused	interpreted
appraised	computed	distinguished	forecast	interviewed
approved	conceptualized	diversified	formulated	introduced
arranged	conducted	drafted	founded	invented
assembled	consolidated	edited	generated	launched
assigned	contained	educated	guided	lectured
assisted	contracted	eliminated	headed	led
attained	contributed	enabled	identified	maintained
audited	controlled	encouraged	illustrated	managed
authored	coordinated	engineered	implemented	marketed
automated	corresponded	enlisted	improved	mediated
balanced	counselled	established	increased	moderated
budgeted	created	evaluated	influenced	monitored
built	critiqued	examined	informed	motivated

negotiated	produced	referred	schooled	systematized
operated	programmed	regulated	screened	tabulated
organized	projected	rehabilitated	set	taught
originated	promoted	remodelled	shaped	trained
overhauled	provided	repaired	solidified	translated
oversaw	publicized	represented	solved	travelled
performed	published	researched	specified	trimmed
persuaded	purchased	restored	stimulated	upgraded
planned	recommended	restructured	streamlined	validated
prepared	reconciled	retrieved	strengthened	worked
presented	recorded	revitalized	summarized	wrote
prioritized	recruited	saved	supervised	
processed	reduced	scheduled	surveyed	

Vary sentence length

Your letters will be most effective when they are constructed with short, punchy sentences. As noted, try keeping your sentences under about 25 words; a good average is around 15 to 20. If your sentence is longer than the 25-word mark, either shorten it through restructuring, or make two sentences out of one. You can also start with a short phrase ending in a colon:

- Followed by bullets of information.
- Each bullet supporting the original phrase. Doing this enlivens the reading experience, keeping the reader engaged.
- When possible, substitute short words for long words, and one word where previously there were two.

Your letters have the same reader-accessibility concerns as your CV. Short sentences should be part of short paragraphs creating plenty of white space so that reading is easy on the eye. Everything you need to say is said succinctly so that your letter never exceeds one page.

Fonts

The font you choose has a big impact on the readability of your work. Stay away from script-like fonts, and use only those accepted as suitable for professional communication. A script may be more visually appealing, but the goal is accessibility for a reader who is ploughing through stacks of CVs when he or she gets your message.

The font(s) you choose must be used in a size legible for managers. Anyone who has been staring at computer screens for 10 or more years is likely to suffer from eyestrain and have problems with 10-point fonts; 11- or 12-point fonts are recommended.

Your branding message stays strong and consistent by using the same font choices (and paper) for your letters as you use for your CV.

The font you used for contact information and headlines in your CV is the same font you will use for your letterhead. The font you chose for your CV's body copy is the same as you will use for the message in your letters.

Good for Headlines/Your Contact Information/Signature

Arial
Times
Century Gothic
Verdana
Gill Sans
Lucida Sans

Good for Body Copy of Your Letters

Bodoni
Garamond
Georgia
Goudy Old Style

Note: copy written in all capital letters, in any font, is harder to read.

How to brighten the page

Once you decide on a font, *stick with it*. Apart from headlines and contact information, more than one font on a page can look confusing. You can do plenty to liven up the visual impact of the page within the variations of the font you have chosen.

Use the same fonts as you use in your CV, one for contact information and headlines, the other for body copy; the result will be cohesion and the desired professional look.

All the recommended fonts come in regular, bold, italic, underlined, and bold italic, so you can vary the impact of key words with *italics*, underlined phrases, and

boldface for additional emphasis. For example, when you are sending a cover letter and CV in response to an internet job posting or recruitment advertisement, you can bold or italicize those words used by the employer in the ad, emphasizing your match to their needs.

You should stay away from exclamation points and emoticons. In the samples section you will find little variation on the font choice beyond an occasionally italicized word or word in bold. In the end, it's your judgement call. Just don't overdo the typographic pyrotechnics.

Another no-no is the use of clip art to brighten the page. Those little quill pens and scrolls may look nifty to you, but they look amateurish to the rest of the world.

E-mail considerations

Do not include your address, because contact information for the medium and the date and time of your communication are entered automatically. If you are attaching a CV, your address will be seen there.

Subject line

Provide a revealing and concise subject line. It should allow the receiver to know immediately who you are and what you want.

The use of a powerful subject line can mean the difference between someone opening your e-mail or hitting the delete key. For example, with the headline for a magazine article, the intention is to grab the reader and draw him or her into the story. With an e-mail your subject line is your headline; it is what draws the reader into your e-mail. Your subject line needs to be intriguing and it also needs to be professional.

Do not use a subject line that states the obvious, like 'CV' or 'Jim Smith's CV'. If you are responding to a job posting, the job title and job posting number are necessary, but just a start. Combine this factual information with a little intriguing information, such as:

Financial Analyst no. MB450 – CPA/MBA/8 yrs exp

Posting 2314 – MBA is interested

Job no. 6745 – Top Sales Professional Here

Or if there is no job posting to refer to:

IT Manager – 7 yrs IT Consulting

Fundraiser – Non-profit Exp in Cheltenham

Referral from Tony Banks – Product Management Job

You can also try longer subject lines, for example:

Your next HR Manager – CIPD, FCIPD, & Dip PM

A message in your inbox will typically reveal a maximum of 60 characters, the above example is just 56 characters, and an opened message will show up to 150 characters. To be safe, try to get your headline in the first 30 characters,

Your next HR Manager – CIPD, FCIPD

but feel free to use all this extra headline space for a subhead; this example is just 144 characters:

Your next HR Manage – CIPD, FCIPD, Dip PM, HSA. 10 years exp all HR includes arbitration, executive recruitment, selection, compensation, T&D.

> All the social networking sites (Facebook, LinkedIn) have special interest groups that are used by recruiters. It is becoming increasingly common for job hunters to post pitches about themselves in the discussion groups. This helps them become visible to recruiters. This is done effectively with just the technique you see above. At 144 characters, this subject line does double duty as an online CV for group discussions.

The same thinking you underwent about extended subject lines applies to your discussion group posts. These aren't the place for 'out-of-the-box-thinking'. Rather, you need hard-hitting statements like this:

'HR Management – CIPD, FCIPD, Dip PM, HSA, T&D, arbitration, executive recruitment, selection, compensation, restructuring.'

Greeting

It is unprofessional to start an e-mail (or any business communication) without a salutation. There are basic professional courtesies that you must recognize. Don't address the recipient on a first-name basis unless you are already familiar with your contact.

Begin your messages:

Dear Tiffany Carstairs,

Or refer to a specific job, followed by salutation:

Ref Job no. 2376

Dear Ms Carstairs,

Or with any one of the other appropriate greetings we mentioned earlier.

Sign off

End your e-mails with your name followed by contact information:

Thomas Torquemada

12345 678901

Although there is a reply button built into every e-mail program, some people add a hyperlinked (live) e-mail address here on the basis that it encourages a response. If you decide to do so, place it before the telephone number:

Thomas Torquemada
mailto:ThomasTorquemada@hotmedia.com
12345 678901

You could also finish with a signature in a script-like font:

Thomas Torquemada
mailto:ThomasTorquemada@hotmedia.com
12345 678901

When you receive an e-mail that contains what appears to be a real signature, it makes an impression. However, *you should never use your real signature*; with the littlest bit of technical expertise anyone could copy it, and electronic signatures can have the same legal validity as a written signature. Don't risk your online security for the sake of style. Instead use one of the more legible script fonts. It's a nice touch that most people don't use and becomes part of the branding process that differentiates you. But only do this when everything else about your CV and letter package is complete and consummately professional.

Custom stationery

A number of e-mail programs now support the creation of customized stationery for your e-mails. This is a 'nice to have' look when you are sending directly to an individual and all other aspects of your CV and letter are perfect. There is little point in having fancy e-mail stationery if the wording of your letter is sloppy. It sends entirely the wrong message about who you are as a professional and works against your brand.

If you pursue the option of creating e-mails that look more like traditional business letters, you will follow the same rules for font choice, layout and page colour as you would sending traditional mail communications.

Paste and attach

It is normal when sending CVs without a prior conversation to attach an MSWord/ PDF version of your CV and to paste an ASCII version of your CV into the e-mail after your signature. You do this because some employers will not open attachments from people they do not know, for fear of viruses. With PDF documents the layout is fixed and will appear exactly as you send it. With MS Word docs the layout sometimes gets messed up. Both ways are acceptable, and there are even people who attach their CV in both formats to give the reader a choice.

Your cover letter will address this by saying, perhaps toward the end of your message,

I have attached my CV in MSWord (or PDF) and also pasted it below the signature in ASCII for your convenience.

Beware if you are crafting a cover letter for mass distribution using the mail merge feature of a word-processing program. All too often, the program will fill in the blanks: 'Dear _____' with *italics* (Dear *Fred Jones*) or ***bold italics*** (Dear ***Fred Jones***).

This detracts from all your efforts to be seen in a positive light. All you've achieved is to make it clear that this is a form e-mail, probably sent to thousands of people.

Spell-checking options

You can and should set your e-mails to check spelling before each and every message is sent, but never forget that *automatic spell-check is not completely reliable*.

Before you send any online, or print CV, cover letter or any other job search communication, remember to proofread and get additional outside help in proofreading. Ask family and friends to review your deathless literary prose to make sure that what you believe you are sending is received in the way you intended.

Traditional mail still works

Whenever you send your CV by more than one communication medium, it greatly improves your hit ratio. With e-mail the standard communication medium, most managers get far less traditional mail than they used to, so when you send an e-mail cover letter and also one by traditional mail, you at least *double* your chances of getting your CV read by someone in a position to interview and hire you. We all like to open the mail; it helps us get started at the beginning of the day and fills in those gaps before lunch and as we are winding things down at the end of the work day.

Coordinate your stationery

Letter stationery should always match the colour and weight of your envelopes and CV. Sending a white cover letter – even if it is your personal stationery – with a cream CV detracts from the statement you are trying to make. As for colours, white, cream and grey are all acceptable. Do not use pastel shades unless your target job involves interaction with the very young, aged or infirm where your colour sensitivity may then speak to the personal sensitivity that is relevant with such professions.

Paper quality

The quality of the paper you use matters because it affects the way others perceive you. It tells the recipient something about your values and the importance you attach to the message. This is something that deserves proper attention as an integral part of establishing your professional brand.

All the office supply superstores carry good quality matching CV paper and envelopes. When you print out CVs, print some letterheads at the same time.

Consistency

Contact information on your letters should be the same as the contact information on your CV and will use the same font. Likewise, the body copy of your letters will use the same font as the body copy on your CV; matching paper and coordinated and complementary fonts speak of a person who proceeds with intent in his or her professional life. It is another subtle way in which you establish a professional brand.

All subsequent letters (follow-up letters after interviews, for example) should be on the same matching paper and envelopes, using the same matching fonts in the same or similar font sizes.

Your written communication is likely to be filed in a candidate dossier. Prior to the hiring decision, a manager will review all the written materials on all the short-list candidates. A thoughtfully packaged written communication aspect of your job search campaign will paint the picture of a thoroughgoing professional, and the sum of your letters will become a powerful and expressive component of the total professional you.

Envelopes send messages, too

What goes on the envelope affects the impact of the message inside. Over the years, I've spoken with countless line managers and human resources professionals about the appearance of the envelopes they receive. Did it affect the likelihood of the letter being read and, if so, with what kind of anticipation? Here's what I heard:

'I never open letters with printed pressure-sensitive labels; I regard them as junk mail, and I simply don't have the time in my life for ill-targeted marketing attempts.'

'I never open anything addressed to me by title but not by name.'

'I will open envelopes and read letters or e-mails addressed to me by misspelled name, but I am looking with a jaundiced eye, keen for other examples of sloppiness.'

'I always open correctly typed envelopes that say "personal" and/or "confidential", but if they're not, I feel conned. I don't hire con artists.'

'I always open neatly handwritten envelopes. What's more, I open them first, unless there's another letter that is obviously a cheque.'

This last comment is especially interesting in an age when just about all correspondence is printed. In an entirely unscientific test, over a two-week period, every letter I had to send I sent with a hand-addressed envelope, and about 50 per cent of the recipients actually commented on not having seen a handwritten envelope in ages.

I once received an intriguing CV and cover letter. Both had attached to the top right-hand corner a circular red sticker. It worked as a major exclamation point. I was impressed. I was even more impressed when I realized that once this left my hands, no other reader would know exactly who had attached the sticker, but they *would* pay special attention to the contents because of it.

If your letter is going by traditional mail and is more than one page, it should be paginated with contact information on every page.

Checklist

Remember that the first glance and feel of your letter can make a powerful impression. The letter's appearance should go hand in hand with its professional-sounding, clear content. Before you seal the envelope, go through this checklist:

Appearance and formatting

❏ Is the paper A4, and is it of good quality with a nice weight to the paper?

❏ Have you used white, off-white, cream or pale grey paper?

❏ Did you use only one side of the page?

❏ Is contact information on every page?

❏ If there is more than one page, have you paginated your letter?

❏ CVs should *not* be stapled to the cover letter.

❏ Did you spell-check and grammar-check and then proofread carefully just to make sure everything's correct?

Content

❑ Does your letter state why you are writing?

❑ Is the letter tied to the target company? Does it refer to a specific job or job posting code when this is relevant?

❑ Is it focused on a target job whenever possible?

❑ Does it include a reference to relevant skills/behaviours/values?

❑ Does it use verbs to show you in action, making a difference with your presence?

❑ Are your most relevant and qualifying experiences prioritized to lend strength to your letter?

❑ Have you avoided wasting more space than needed with employer names and addresses?

❑ Have you omitted any reference to reasons for leaving a particular job? Reasons for making a change might be important at the interview, but they are not relevant at this point. Use this precious space to sell, not to justify.

❑ Unless they have been specifically requested, have you removed all references to past, current or desired salaries?

❑ Have you removed any references to your date of availability?

❑ Do you mention your highest educational attainment only if it is especially relevant and adds credence to the message?

❑ Have you avoided listing irrelevant responsibilities or experience?

❑ Have you given examples of your contributions/achievements, when relevant and possible?

❑ Have you avoided poor focus by eliminating all extraneous information?

❑ Is the letter long enough to whet the reader's appetite for more details, yet short enough not to satisfy that hunger?

❑ Have you let the obvious slip in, like heading your letter 'Letter of Application' in big bold letters? If so, cut it out.

❑ Do you have complete contact information – name, address, postcode, telephone number and e-mail address?

Proofing and printing

It simply isn't possible for even the most accomplished professional writer to go from draft to print, so don't try it. Your pride of authorship will blind you to blemishes you can't afford to miss.

You need some distance from your creative efforts to give yourself detachment and objectivity. There is no hard and fast rule about how long it should take to come up with the finished product; if you think you have finished, leave it alone, at least overnight. Then come back to it fresh. You'll read it almost as if it were meeting your eyes for the first time.

Before you e-mail or print your letters make sure that your writing is as clear as possible. Three things guaranteed to annoy cover letter readers are incorrect spelling, poor grammar and improper syntax. Go back and check all these areas.

8
The plan of attack

A successful job search needs an integrated overall plan that includes all the most practical job search strategies.

Great cover, broadcast and follow-up letters won't get you a job if they sit on your desk like rare manuscripts. You have to do something with them.

On a call-in radio show during this recession I took a call from a woman who explained that she had sent out almost 300 letters and still wasn't employed. After I asked her a couple of questions, I learned that she had been job-hunting for almost two years and had responded to two or three job postings a week. I also learned that, as an accountant, there were some 2,000 companies for whom she could work.

This job search used only one largely passive approach to finding a job (responding to job postings) when there are at least five practical ways to find work. During her search she managed to approach just 15 per cent of her potential employers in two years. Two employer contacts per week will not get you back to work.

This chapter will focus on tactics that can double, triple and quadruple your chances of getting interviews from job postings by identifying and approaching the people most likely to be in a position to hire you.

Online job postings

When you see a job you can do, respond to the posting in the requested way, but also note all the contact information for the company, including the website and mailing address.

When you can find the names and job titles of managers likely to have a say in the ultimate hiring decision, you can approach them directly in three different ways, each approach increasing your chances of getting an interview:

1 E-mailing your CV directly to that manager with a personalized cover letter doubles your chances of a hit.

2 Sending a CV and personalized cover letter by traditional mail to that manager triples your chances of a hit.

3 Making a follow-up telephone call to that manager first thing in the morning, at lunchtime, or at 5 pm quadruples your chances of a hit.

Internet research tactics for finding names

With a little work you can find the names, titles and contact information for a lot of the people who have the ultimate authority to hire someone like you.

For a start, check out company websites. On the 'about us' pages you can often find names and sometimes contact information for management.

Also try keyword searches on Google, Bing and other search engines. They will all deliver names, and they'll all get different results. Do a standard Google search first, then a Google News search, which looks for mentions of your keywords in media coverage.

When you do a search for a company and find relevant information, you can use it as an opener for your cover letter. Refer to the article and its relevance in your letter. Then copy and paste a URL to the reference if you're sending an e-mail, or enclose a copy of it with a traditional letter.

Try other keyword phrases. You will come up with job openings and job sites. And if you go beyond those first couple of pages of results for your search, which you should always do, drilling down until the well is dry, you will come up with job titles and names to go with those titles.

Why find names?

The more frequently you get into conversation with managers who have the authority to hire you, the faster you will land that new position. In embarking on these conversations, you've skipped over being pulled from the CV database, you have sidestepped the recruiter's evaluation process, and you have the attention of the actual decision maker. You can make a direct and personal pitch.

Your target for a direct approach is always someone who can hire you, although any management position offers an opportunity for referral. For example, while HR people may not have the authority to hire you, the pivotal nature of their work makes them aware of all the areas within a company that could use your skills.

Getting a CV to the 'right someone' by name and making a personalized pitch gives you a distinct advantage; this is never more important than when the economy is weak or in recovery. At such times competition is fierce, and employers always regard initiative and motivation as desirable features.

Who to target in your job search

These are the job titles to target during your job search. As you read, make a list of the specific titles that apply in your professional world, because a list of titles will make it easier to find the names that go with them:

1 Those job titles most likely to be in a position to hire you. Usually one, two and three management positions above you.

2 Other titles likely to have knowledge of an opening:

   - management positions one to three levels above you in departments that have an ongoing interaction with your department;

   - peers holding similar positions (a little less desirable).

3 Titles most likely to know people involved in the selection process and be able to refer you:

   - management positions one to three levels above you in any department;

   - internal recruiters and HR professionals.

Any name is better than no name, and with the internet at your fingertips there are endless opportunities to identify the names of people who are in a position to help you.

Networking

One of the best ways to find names and get introductions to employers is to talk to people. And because getting into conversation with the people who can actually offer you a job is the only way you are going to get hired, the more ways you have to get into these conversations, the more successful you are going to be.

When they are integrated into every aspect of your job search, properly executed networking strategies deliver incredible results. We are going to look at some effective ways of building relevant professional networks almost instantly.

Professional associations

One of the best things you can do for your job search and your long-term career success is to become an active member of one or two professional associations. You'll get job leads and a useful network immediately, and such organizations provide great vehicles for increasing your credibility and visibility in the profession. In fact, if you have heard disgruntled job hunters mutter, 'It's not what you know, it's who you know', it probably means they don't understand networking and are probably not members of a professional association.

Associations have monthly meetings in most major areas, plus national get-togethers every year. The local meetings are of immediate interest, and unless you work on a national level, membership in the local branch of a national association will be quite adequate for your needs.

When you join an association and attend the meetings, you get to know and be known by the most committed and best-connected people in your profession. Your membership will help you to stay attuned to what is going on in your profession as associations often offer ongoing training that makes you a more knowledgeable and therefore a more desirable employee.

The professional association is an 'old boy/old girl' network for the modern world. Your membership becomes a link to colleagues, almost all of whom will gladly talk to you, based on your mutual connection through the association.

Most industries and professions have associations, many of which could be valuable, depending on your needs.

If you fit the profile of a special interest or minority group, you will also find professional associations that cater to another dimension of the professional you. These include – but are by no means restricted to – associations for different ethnicities, professionals with disabilities, and women. If you can find a niche association that fits, join that as well: it represents another, even more finely tuned network.

To find appropriate professional associations, try a Google search for relevant keywords. For example, 'legal association' will generate listings of associations for the legal profession; while 'Asian legal association' will generate a listing of local associations for Asian professionals working in the legal field.

When you join an association, you'll benefit greatly from attending the meetings, because this is where you will meet other professionals in your field. But don't just attend the meetings; get involved. Associations are largely volunteer organizations and always need someone to set out chairs or hand out nametags. The task itself doesn't matter, but your willingness to be an active participant most certainly does and will get you on first-name terms with people you would probably never otherwise meet. Others are more likely to help you when they see you making an effort toward the common good.

It is easier to get to know people than you might think, because all professional association members are there at least in part to advance their careers through networking. You don't have to go straight from introductions to asking for leads on jobs. In fact, it can be more productive to have initial conversations where you make a contribution to the group.

Use the association database or directory

If an association directory comes with your membership package, it will provide you with a superb networking resource for telephone and e-mail networking campaigns.

You can feel comfortable calling any other member on the phone and introducing yourself: 'Hi, Brenda Massie? My name is Martin Yate. We haven't spoken before, but we are both members of the Teachers Association. I need some advice; can you spare a minute?'

Your mutual membership will guarantee you a few moments of anyone's time, a courtesy you should always return.

You can also use the directory to generate introductions for jobs you have heard about elsewhere. For example, you might have found an interesting job posting on www.careerbuilder.co.uk, or perhaps on a company website, with the request that you upload your CV. Apply as requested, then turn to your membership directory to find people who work for that company.

A judicious call or two will frequently get you a personal referral and some inside information, and you have doubled your chances of landing that interview. Once you have an interview, these same contacts can help you prepare for it with insider knowledge about the company, the department and the manager.

Professional associations all have online newsletters and many have a jobs section on their website, where companies advertise because of the suitably qualified response. So you will often see job postings there that don't appear anywhere else. In difficult economic times, a savvy employer will use an association website to skim the cream of available talent while screening out the less committed. You will also notice that association members write the articles in the newsletters. As everyone likes to have their literary efforts appreciated, telling a member you have read an article that he or she has written gives you a great introduction to a networking call or letter.

Active association membership puts you on the radar of all the best-qualified and connected professionals in your area. You can also list it at the end of your CV under a Professional Affiliations heading. This is guaranteed to get a second glance, as it signifies professional awareness. Employers and headhunters will sometimes use words like association, club and society in their keyword searches, so association membership will also help to get your CV pulled up from the databases for investigation by human eyes.

How to make networking work

Professional associations are just one of a dozen approaches for networking, all of which can be tremendously beneficial to your job search and overall career success, if you nurture them.

Think of networking as professional connectedness, because becoming properly connected to your profession is the activity that will generate the widest range of relevant contacts for your job search.

An effective job search requires more than writing to and chatting with old cronies on the telephone. It's important to move beyond your personal network of friends and acquaintances because you may well discover that your network is not as comprehensive as you might have wished.

Besides, just because you worked with someone five years ago doesn't mean he or she still regards you as a friend, especially if you haven't spoken to that person since then. Surveys show that we all respond in these understandable ways:

- To those requests from people I didn't know, I asked for a CV (of course, if they had an introduction or were fellow members of an association, things would be different).

- If I received it in good time with a thoughtfully prepared accompanying letter, I would give that person help if I could.

- To requests from people with an introduction from someone I liked and respected, I gave time and consideration and, wherever possible, assistance.

- To requests from friends, people I had worked with at one time and who had kept in touch since we had worked together, I provided leads and even made calls on their behalf.

- To requests from people who regarded themselves as friends but who had not maintained contact, or who had only re-established contact when they wanted something: for some reason I was unable to help them. I wished them the best of luck, but, 'Sorry I couldn't help you. If something comes to mind, I'll be sure to call.'

Nothing works like a personal recommendation from a fellow professional – and you get that by being a fellow professional, by being connected to your profession, the professionals within it and by becoming a colleague – someone who shares. It is no accident that successful people in all fields know each other; they helped each other become successful because they stayed in touch, through good times and bad, and helped each other whenever they could.

If you are going to use business colleagues and personal friends in your job search, don't do it half-heartedly. We live in a mobile society, so in addition to family, friends and the colleagues you know naturally, it is a smart long-term career management strategy to establish yourself as a member of your professional community.

Social networking

Social networking has become an integral part of cutting-edge job search and career management strategies. It revolves around social and/or professionally oriented online networks that help you reach out to people you know, once knew, or would like to know. You can extend your professional reach by connecting with others in your field, along with people with whom you share common experiences or interests.

You will find social networking sites especially important when you are planning a career change. If you know you are moving out of one profession and into another, you can use social networking sites to build a network of people who do the target job in your chosen profession and, whenever possible, people who have made a similar transition.

Here's an example: a soldier who was leaving the army sought my help in her search for a new civilian career. First, to find other individuals with a similar background, I put in the word army at www.linkedin.com, the online networking site. I got more than 4,000 profiles of people who shared her military experience. We then tried a search using the phrase 'information technology' (her desired career change) and got 39,000 profiles. Both these potential networks would have relevance to her job search, but it got even better when we combined both the keywords: 'information technology and army'. This pulled up 908 profiles of people who shared her life experience and who had, in about half the hits, already made the transition to her desired profession. Such a degree of initial connectivity ensured she could hold helpful conversations with an enormous number of people, each of whom could be relevant to her job search.

Social networking sites are seen by recruiters and headhunters, and this should shape the information you make available about yourself.

For the professional in a job search this will start with simply cutting and pasting your CV into your official profile. You make yourself visible but because this is a social networking site and not a CV bank you do it without an 'I'm for sale' sign, which is useful when you are employed and looking for a new position.

Social networking can get you useful introductions to people throughout your profession, the country and the world – people who might know of jobs at their own companies or who can introduce you to people at companies that have openings. This new application of technology enables you to reach out into an almost limitless community of like-minded professionals.

It works simply: you join a social networking site and find people you have worked with in the past. Then expand your network by joining the discussion groups that exist on all social networking sites and then connect with other members of those groups.

For employers and recruiters, networking sites constitute a reliable pathway to recruit qualified candidates, while for a job hunter they constitute a reliable pathway to jobs through the people connected to them. You can search a site's database by location, job title, company or any keywords of your choice. The database will pull up the profiles of people who match your requirements and allow you to initiate contact directly, through your common membership in groups or through the chain of people who connect you.

There are just too many sites to list, and the more they proliferate, the more specialized they become. It is probably a good idea to have a presence on two of the biggest, linkedin.com and facebook.com, but you'll also find networking sites for special interests, languages, gender, race and more.

A very smart networking idea

Intelligent networking encourages you to form relationships with people in your profession and industry at many levels. Almost anyone in your industry or location can be useful regardless of position or experience, but the people of most interest will probably fall into these categories:

1 Those who are one to three levels above you, who might hire you, now or in the future. With this group you can initiate contact by sending an e-mail to introduce yourself and ask him/her to look at your profile. If this proceeds to a conversation and interviews, fine; if not, you can ask your contact to connect you to others.

2 Those at or below your level but with similar professional experience.

3 Those who work in related areas within the same profession or industry.

It's best to build a relationship by finding common ground. You can initiate relationships by asking for advice, and many people will give you a few minutes of their time. You will develop the best relationships, though, by reaching out to others with help and advice, because when you offer something, forging a relationship with you becomes important to the other person. It is easy to do this by taking an active part in the special interest groups and also searching the social sites for people in your profession who are actively looking for jobs.

The challenge then becomes how to encourage a relationship that shares introductions and job leads. The answer is logical and painless: use the job leads you hear about that are inappropriate for your own use.

It's a not-so-funny thing about the job search: when you are just out of school no one is hiring entry-level workers; they all want you to call back in five years.

Five years later when you are once again looking for a job, they now only want someone just out of school or with 10 years' experience.

In your job search activities you are constantly coming across positions that aren't right for you but that could be just what someone else is aching to hear about. Offer these leads to others as part of your introduction. Here's how it can work: sometimes you have to send an e-mail stating why you want to make contact, and sometimes you can communicate immediately – it depends on a number of variables. In the first instance you send an e-mail simply stating you have a job lead that he or she might find interesting. This is a nice gesture and will get you lots of introductions.

In the second instance, where you are actually in direct e-mail communication, state your business: 'I am involved in a strategic career move right now, and I have come across a job that isn't right for me but which could be perfect for you. If you'd like to talk, let's exchange telephone numbers. I'll be happy to pass the lead on, and perhaps you have heard about something that would suit me… I am moving into the private sector and have been looking for jobs in IT in the South… .'

(When networking, never talk about what you want in that ideal next job. It reduces the odds of someone telling you about an opening. Instead, talk about what you can do.)

Your job search has you scouring the job sites for job leads, and now you have a use for all those positions that aren't quite right for you. Build your own database of the jobs that are not suitable for you and pass them on to all those people above and below you in your profession who will make symbiotic networking partners.

How social networks expand your options

When you find suitable jobs on the job sites, you are usually faced with uploading your CV into a company or headhunter's database, but now, along with your professional association memberships, your social networks give you additional approaches. Somewhere on one of your social networking sites there are people who work at that company, either now or in the past. Search for them, using the company name in your keyword search, then look for job titles one, two and three levels above your own, and then those at the same level or one or two beneath you.

The more you reach out, the better your reputation becomes and the more others will reach out to you.

Networking letters

When you write networking e-mails and letters, use these guidelines for your structure. You can also use them as frameworks for networking conversations:

1 Establish a connection, something or someone in common or information likely to be of interest.

2 You can use your common membership in professional associations as a bridge to other members.

3 Let contacts know what you can do. They will invariably want to help, but you have to give them a framework to target their effort. DO NOT tell them about your dream job, or the promotion you hope for; talking about dreams only reduces their options to help.

4 Try to be specifically vague: 'I'm looking for something in operations within the medical devices area' gives the listener the widest possible opportunity for coming up with leads.

5 Tell whoever you are writing or calling: 'It's time for me to make a move' or 'My job just got sent to Mumbai, and I'm hoping I could pick your brain.'

6 Don't ask specifically, 'Can you hire me?' or 'Can your company hire me?' Ask for advice and leads. Then ask for guidance.

7 By all means ask for leads within specific target companies, but don't rely on a contact with a particular company to get you in.

8 When you do get help, say thank you. And if you get the help verbally, follow it up in writing. The impression is indelible, and it just might get you another lead.

When you write networking letters and make the follow-up calls, you might be surprised to find out who your friends are: someone you always regarded as a real mate won't give you the time of day, and someone you never thought of as a friend will go above and beyond the call of duty on your behalf.

Names increase your options

Sometimes, to alert all the right people at a target company that you're available you might approach half a dozen different managers. For example, let's say you are a young engineer enthusiastic about a job with Last Chance Electronics. It is within the bounds of reason that you would submit a cover letter and CV to any or all of the following people, with each letter addressed by name to minimize its chances of going straight into the bin:

- Managing Director;
- Director of engineering;
- Chief engineer;
- Engineering design manager;
- Head of Human Resources;
- Technical engineering manager.

Think through all the titles likely to be of use to you, based on the above criteria, and keep all these titles in mind when you go looking for names to attach to them: the more options you have, the more results you will get.

Sending out your cover letters

E-mail and traditional mail initiatives should be integrated into every aspect of your job search. They should be a vital part of your job search strategy. Maintain a balance between the number of e-mails and letters you send out on a daily and weekly basis and the types of letters you send out. Follow them up by making telephone calls to initiate the conversations that must take place if you are to get job offers.

Do you need to compose more than one letter?

Almost certainly, there is a case for having letters targeted at all your specific needs: to headhunters, to managers referencing job postings, to managers without reference to a specific job, letters referencing a referral, and networking letters, to name but a few. The key is to do a great master version of each that you can customize as needed.

A plan for a direct approach

A professionally conducted campaign will target the employers most likely to hire you and use e-mail and traditional mail for the initial approach, followed by a phone call.

Scary I know, but it works, and I'll give you advice for doing it shortly.

As you identify target companies, create a folder for each one; the next time you need to make a strategic career move, having details of the area's desirable employers is one of the many ways you will be ahead of the game.

As you discover names to go with job titles, send a personalized cover letter and CV via e-mail and traditional mail and schedule a follow-up telephone call in your week's agenda.

Send further CVs and personalized cover letters as you find other people within that company. You might also consider bookmarking desirable companies to check their job openings.

This is not your last job search

This is probably not the first or the last job search you will ever do, so save all your job search letters in a career management folder where you can find them again when you need them.

Develop electronic documents or paper file folders containing all the relevant information for each company. You'll want a link to the website and a list of the names of the company's executives and all other management names and titles that you have identified as relevant to your job search. Whenever you find interesting information, copy it into the company folder. For instance, you might come across information on growth or shrinkage in a particular area of a company, or you might read about recent acquisitions the company has made. You can use the website, Google and Google News to track company activities.

All this information will help you target potential employers. Your knowledge will create a favourable impression when you first contact the company: that you made an effort is noticed and sets you apart from other applicants who don't bother. It says that you respect the company, the opportunity and the interviewer; these perceptions help you to stand out.

All your efforts have an obvious short-term value in helping you generate job interviews and offers. Who would you interview and subsequently hire? The person who knows nothing about your company, or the person who knows everything and shows enthusiasm with that knowledge?

Your efforts also have long-term value, because you are building a personalized reference work of your industry/speciality/profession so you can hit the ground running the next time you wish to make a job change.

Follow-up: a cautionary tale

If you sit there like Buddha waiting for the world to beat a path to your door, you may wait a long time.

A friend of mine placed an advertisement for an analyst. Within a week he had received more than 100 responses. Ten days later he'd received 50 more and was still ploughing through them when he received a follow-up call (the only one he did receive) from one of the candidates who'd tracked down his name. The candidate's CV was languishing in the pile with all the others, but the follow-up phone call got it discovered.

The job hunter was in the office by the end of the day. She returned the following morning, and was hired by lunchtime. This is not an isolated incident. It happens all the time.

Managers are always on the lookout for competent professionals in their field, BUT they hate recruiting and interviewing. They just want to find the right person, hire him or her, and get back to work. All you have to do is help them by using the tactics outlined in this book.

Follow-up calls work

You'll notice that some examples in the letter section mention that the applicant will follow up with a phone call. This allows the writer to explain to any inquisitive receptionist that Joe Smith is 'expecting my call' or that it is 'personal', or 'it's accounting/engineering/customer-service business'.

It's surprising that so many people are nervous about calling a fellow professional on the phone and talking about what they do for a living. Don't worry so much. In this unsettled world, there is an unwritten credo shared by the vast majority of professional people: you should always help one another if it isn't going to hurt you in the process. Everyone out there has been in your situation and knows it can happen at any moment. Because of this, almost everyone you speak to will be sympathetic to your cause and help you if they can.

No manager will take offence at a call from a professional colleague, and this is what you are.

Use a contact tracker

To ensure that you keep track of your mailings and the follow-up phone calls, I recommend that you create a Contact Tracker on a spreadsheet program such as Microsoft Excel. Create columns for the company name, telephone number, e-mail address and contact name. As a rule of thumb, an e-mail sent today is ripe for follow-up within 24 to 48 hours; a mailing sent today is ripe for follow-up three to five days later.

Cover letters: the key to your job search

A great cover letter will get your CV read with serious attention. It will set you apart and increase the number of interviews you get. Use the following letter examples to help you stand out at every step of the selection process.

9
Sample letters

Here's the real meat and potatoes of the book – the sample letters you can use as models for your own.

E-mail response to online job posting (technical sales representative)

From: Joan Carter [jcartersalespro@hotmail.com]
To: mbroome@palmettonetworksecurity.com
Cc:
Subject: Tech sales/key acct/new territory dev/negotiation/customer service

Dear Ms _____:

Please accept this letter as application for the Technical Sales Representative position currently available with your company, as listed on Monster.co.uk. My confidential CV is attached for your review and consideration, and I believe you will find me well qualified.

Detailed on my CV you will find a solid background in Sales and Marketing, with over two years in technical sales. In this capacity, I have developed an expertise in new and key account acquisition, new territory development and management, contract negotiation and customer service. I am confident that my experience in these areas will prove to be an asset to ABC Ltd.

Additionally, I am familiar with blueprints, part number breakdowns and the bidding process of our major accounts, which include _____, _____, _____ and _____. I have doubled my sales from £40,000/month to £80,000/month in just two years, and I am known for effectively identifying and resolving problems before they affect related areas, personnel or customers.

I would welcome the opportunity to discuss with you how I might make similar contributions to the success of ABC Ltd. I look forward to hearing from you to arrange a personal interview.

Yours sincerely,

Joan Carter
12345 678901
jcartersalespro@hotmail.com

E-mail response to online job posting (investment banker)

From: James Stratton [jsinvest@anyserver.co.uk]
To: lwilliam@teweles.com
Cc:
Subject: 'Can do' administrator

Dear Mr _____:

In response to your job posting for a _____ on your company's website, I have attached my CV for your consideration.

My experience as an administrative investment banker and assistant to a Director is, I believe, readily adaptable to your needs. I have spent five years in a position best described as 'doing whatever needs to be done' and have capitalized on my ability to undertake a large and widely varied array of projects, learn quickly, find effective solutions to problems, and maintain a sense of humour throughout.

My years as an administrative professional have also provided me with an unusual sensitivity to the needs of senior professionals. I have substantial computer experience and am fully computer literate. I have been told my verbal and written communication skills are exceptional.

I believe your firm would provide a working atmosphere to which I would be well suited, as well as one where my diverse experience would be valuable.

My salary requirements are reasonable and negotiable based on the responsibilities and opportunities presented.

Yours sincerely,

James Stratton
12345 678901
jsinvest@anyserver.co.uk

E-mail response to online job posting (legal administrator)

From: Helen Darvik [darviklegalpro@earthlink.net]
To: ggoodfellow@budownoble.com
Cc:
Subject: Administrator/mgmnt/mktg/cmptr/acctg/planning/personnel

Dear Ms _____:

I am responding to your job posting on Hotjobs.co.uk for a legal administrator of a law firm.
I wrote to you on (date) about law administrator positions in the _____ area. I have
attached another CV of my educational background and employment history. I am very interested
in this position.

I have been a legal administrator for two law firms during the past six years. In addition, I have
been a law firm consultant for over a year. Besides my law firm experience, I have been a medical
administrator for over 10 years. I believe that all of this experience will enable me to manage this
position very successfully. I possess the management, marketing, computer, accounting/
budgeting, financial planning, personnel and people-oriented skills that will have a very positive
impact on this law firm.

I will be in the _____ area later in the month and hope we can meet at that time to
discuss this position. I look forward to hearing from you, Ms _____, concerning this
position. Thank you for your time and consideration.

Yours sincerely,

Helen Darvik
12345 678901
darviklegalpro@earthlink.net

E-mail response to online job posting (manufacturing)

Murray shows loyalty, depth of experience in several positions, reliability and accomplishments, as well as his well-earned reputation.

From:	Murray Danton [manufacturerMD@mindspring.com]
To:	CVs@NexPress.com
Cc:	
Subject:	Warehouse pro committed to productivity

Dear Sir/Madam:

Please accept the attached CV in application for a position with your company that will make use of my extensive background in material handling, shipping, receiving and warehousing. Throughout my career, I have demonstrated my loyalty, commitment to excellence and solid work ethic. I am confident that I will make an immediate and long-term contribution to your company.

For the past 26 years, I have been working successfully in manufacturing and warehouse settings. I am a hard-working employee who always looks for ways to improve productivity, efficiency and accuracy. In past positions, I have identified ways to reduce downtime and waste, as well as methods to increase production.

I am dedicated to the principles of quality, continuous improvement and customer satisfaction. My supervisor has noted my record of 'excellent attendance and dependability' and praised me as 'reliable and highly motivated'.

I would like to meet you to discuss my qualifications. Please call me at the following phone number, or leave a message, to arrange an interview. Thank you for your consideration.

Yours faithfully,

Murray Danton
12345 678901
manufacturerMD@mindspring.com

E-mail response to online job posting (production supervisor)

From: Edwin Pastore [productionpro@yahoo.com]
To: hr@XYZLabs.com
Cc:
Subject: Production Super matches your exact requirements

Dear Ms _____:

In response to the job posting on your company's website, please consider my CV in your search for a Production Supervisor.

With a hi-tech background in FTSE 100 companies, I feel well qualified for the position you described. I am presently responsible for the coordination of production in three assembly and test areas that employ 35 personnel. Maintaining control of work of this magnitude and complexity requires my ability to function independently, and a willingness to make decisions quickly and effectively.

I am accustomed to a fast-paced environment where deadlines are a priority and handling multiple jobs simultaneously is the norm. I enjoy a challenge and work hard to attain my goals. Constant negotiations with all levels of management and employees have strengthened my interpersonal skills. I would very much like to discuss with you how I could contribute to your organization.

I am seeking an opportunity to excel in a more dynamic company and am looking forward to relocating to the _____ area.

Please contact me at your earliest convenience so that I can clarify my background and enthusiasm for the job. Thank you for your time and consideration.

Yours sincerely,

Edwin Pastore
12345 678901
productionpro@yahoo.com

Response to newspaper advertisement (health care management)

This applicant wants to change to an administrative position in the field of health care; thus we highlighted her leadership and administrative skills.

REBA WOODWARD

1 Any Street, Anytown AA1 1AA
12345 678901(H) • 1098765 4321 (M)
r w o o d 5 8 6 @ h o t m a i l . c o m

15 February 20–

Human Resources Coordinator
Sunny Home Nursing Service
9999 Hospital Ave
Anytown AA1 1AA

We make a living by what we get,
but we make a life by what we give.
– Winston Churchill

Re: ADMINISTRATOR OF HEALTH CARE SERVICES

Dear Human Resources Coordinator:

Your recent classified ad in the *City Journal* caught my eye. As an experienced registered nurse, I am currently investigating career opportunities in the field of management in the private health sector where my highly developed skills will be of use. The enclosed CV reflects an exceptionally suitable candidate for the above-named position.

I am a registered nurse with a background as programme director, school nurse, operating room circulator, and charge nurse in clinic, A&E and hospital floor environments. The following skills and characteristics are reason to take a closer look at my credentials. I am:

- **strong in handling multiple tasks and multifaceted situations while maintaining satisfactory interpersonal relationships with staff, physicians, patients, students and families;**

- **an expert at ensuring compliance with regulations while keeping costs within budget;**

- **talented in prioritizing issues and tasks and visualizing the 'big' picture when considering the long-term effects of my decisions;**

- **an outcome-orientated self-starter with superior organizational and administrative skills.**

After reviewing my CV, you will discover that my qualifications are a good match for this position. The opportunity for a personal interview to discuss employment possibilities further would be mutually beneficial. You can reach me on 12345 678901 to arrange an appointment. In the meantime, thank you for your time and consideration.

Yours sincerely,

Reba Woodward

Reba Woodward

Enclosure: CV

Response to newspaper advertisement (speech therapy position)

A speech therapist is looking for a position in a community college.

Harriette L Christophorous

12345 678901   1 Any Street   harrichris@anyserver.co.uk
                                Anytown AA1 1AA

12 January 20–

Ms Alexandra Kinkead
Director of Human Resources
Anytown Community College
1000 Any Avenue
Anytown AA1 1AA

Dear Ms Kinkead:

Your recent advertisement has captured my serious interest. I am confident that my 25 years' experience as a Speech Therapist at the ABC Centre provides me with the capabilities to fulfil the **Voice & Articulation** position mentioned in the ad. Accordingly, I have enclosed a CV that briefly outlines my professional history.

Some key points you may find relevant to this opportunity include:

✓ *Experience assessing needs of and providing instruction to the disabled. In my current position, I work one-on-one with students having hearing loss, emotional disorders, ADHD, autism, and other physical disabilities impacting their ability to acquire speech. I also develop IEPs and participate in the CSE process to define students' needs and implement instruction plans.*

✓ *Excellent leadership skills, with experience mentoring co-workers. Currently, I mentor speech therapists and teachers working with hearing-impaired students, as well as direct the activities of two other speech therapists.*

✓ *A master's degree in Speech Pathology, plus Certification as a Speech & Hearing Handicapped Teacher. In addition, I have attended workshops in Phonemic Awareness, Autism, and Pervasive Developmental Disorders.*

In my current role, I am accountable for addressing the needs of approximately 300 elementary and secondary school students with various speech deficiencies. I believe that my knowledge and expertise would allow me to serve your students effectively in this Voice & Articulation instructional role. I would enjoy speaking to you in person to discuss in more detail how my qualifications can fulfil your needs. Please contact me via phone or e-mail to arrange a mutually convenient date and time for us to meet.

Thank you for your time and consideration. I look forward to talking to you soon.

Yours sincerely,

Harriette L Christophorous

Harriette L Christophorous

Enclosure

Response to newspaper advertisement (hydrogeologist)

Applying for positions in a newly emerging scientific discipline, this candidate's CV requires a heavy emphasis on educational background information.

Aileen Renfro
1 Any Street, Anytown AA1 1AA
12345 678901 ▪ aileenrenfro@anyserver.co.uk

30 June 20–

Human Resources Department
ABC Ltd
111 Any Avenue
Anytown AA1 1AA

RE: Position of Hydrogeologist/Groundwater Modeler, Company Job ID: ACHZ4121-234059, AJB Reference Number: 4950495, Job ID #0000BZ/BBBB

Dear Human Resources Manager:

I learned about your position for a Hydrogeologist/Groundwater Modeller with great interest, as my qualifications match your requirements for this position. Therefore, please accept my CV for your review and allow me to explain briefly how I can contribute to the future success of ABC Ltd.

With an MSc in Hydrologic Sciences and over 7 years' research experience, I have developed a strong background in advanced theories of solute transport modelling. Consequently, I have developed effective quantitative skills and a practical understanding of the fundamental principles and concepts associated with hydrogeology.

My CV will provide additional details regarding my educational background and professional experience. Beyond these qualifications, it may be helpful for you to know that I have worked successfully in both independent and team project environments, adapt readily to rapidly changing work conditions, and enjoy the prospect of contributing to ABC's '80-year reputation as a water industry leader' in the advancement of hydrogeologic and groundwater projects.

I would welcome the opportunity to be interviewed for this position and to discuss the results you can expect from me as a member of your team. Thank you for your time and consideration.

Yours sincerely,

Aileen Renfro

Aileen Renfro

Enclosure

Response to newspaper advertisement (customer service representative)

An ad response with requested salary history.

Cassidy Stratton
1 Any Street • Anytown AA1 1AA • 12345 678901 • cassidy123@custsrv.net

4 February 20–

Mr Josh Williams
Personnel Director
ABC Financial Group
111 Any Avenue
Anytown AA1 1AA

Dear Mr Williams:

In response to your advertisement in *Newsday* for a customer service representative, I am forwarding my CV for your review and consideration. Ideally, this position will make optimal use of my experience working in capacities that require strong interpersonal communication and customer needs assessment skills, an ability to interface effectively with internal/external contacts, and a skill for ensuring the accurate, timely processing of electronic, verbal and written information.

Since 1994, I have held longstanding positions of increased responsibility for leading financial services organizations, in charge of tracking, monitoring, reviewing and processing account and market-related data. In these positions, I have proved and continue to prove myself a capable, take-charge team player with an ability to coordinate diversified departmental and customer support functions. Combined with my ability to manage and train others proficiently on the complexities of comprehensive databases and improve workflow efficiencies, I am confident that I would be an asset to your customer service organization.

I would welcome the opportunity to meet you for an in-depth interview. Thank you for your review and consideration. I look forward to hearing from you soon.

Yours sincerely,

Cassidy Stratton

Cassidy Stratton

Salary Requirement:
£36,000 – £44,000

Salary History:
XYZ Financial Group: Starting £29,000; Ending £40,000
Credit Checkers: Starting £20,000; Ending £26,000

Response to newspaper advertisement (sales associate)

An entry-level cover letter to convince the employer that he can tackle a full-time job even though he is still in college.

....**MARC LOMBARDI**

3 September 20–

Mr John Relka
Sales Manager
ABC Sports Outfitters
111 Any Avenue
Anytown AA1 1AA

Re: Sales Associate Position

Dear Mr Relka:

If you are searching for a success-driven Sales Associate who is a hard worker and an innovator, look no further. Highlights of my achievements include the following:

- Awarded end-of-year bonus and commended for exemplary sales performance.
- Started a business from scratch and increased customer base using multiple marketing methods.
- Earned most of my own college expenses for the last four years.

Although I will not graduate until December, I am eager to start work as soon as possible – either full- or part-time. I am certain that I can balance the responsibilities of a Sales Associate position with my studies, because I have successfully handled full-time employment with a full course load in the past.

My CV is enclosed for your consideration. I believe that I can make a positive contribution to ABC Sports Outfitters and look forward to discussing my qualifications in detail.

I will call you next week to arrange for a meeting at a mutually convenient time. Thank you for your consideration.

Yours sincerely,

Marc Lombardi

Enclosure

---

1 Any Street • Anytown AA1 1AA • 12345 678901 • mlombardi@dotcv.com

Response to newspaper advertisement (skilled labourer)

This cover letter had to overcome an obvious 'overqualification' barrier.

JACK **Levan**
_____

1 Any Street • Anytown AA1 1AA • jlevan555@yahoo.com • 12345 678901

Tuesday, 11 November 20–

Mr Drake Norris
ABC Ltd
111 Any Avenue
Anytown AA1 1AA

Dear Mr Norris:

When I saw your announcement for a skilled labourer at ABC Ltd, I made writing this letter my first priority. Of course, I've already applied online. But, the more I thought about this opportunity, the more it seemed a perfect match for both of us. And so I wanted you to have a good deal more than the usual, impersonal, application.

I think you deserve to see the contributions I can make to the ABC team at once. That's why you'll find my CV different from others you may have come across. In place of the usual 'objective statement', you'll read about four productivity-building capabilities I can bring to the job. And, right below them, are seven examples of the kinds of contributions I've made to my employers.

But I am concerned that you may think I am 'overqualified'. To put that in plain language, you may feel I will be bored by the job. In fact, your position fits well with my goal of getting my degree in Aerospace Engineering. I can't think of a better opportunity to see the OT&E process at work than being 'in the trenches' on a project like yours.

I do best when I can learn about my employer's special needs. May I call in a few days to explore how I might fit your team?

Yours sincerely,

Jack Levan

Jack Levan

Encl: CV

Response to newspaper advertisement (assessment coordinator)

Anna M Sanchez

111 Any Street • Anytown AA1 1AA • 12345 678901 • Mobile 1098765 4321

2 PAGES VIA FAX   11 June 20–
DEPT. HD 212-555-9999

Your advertisement in the *Times*, on 9 June 20–, for an **Assessment Coordinator** seems to match my background and experience perfectly. As the International Brand Coordinator for ABC, I coordinated meetings, prepared presentations and materials, organized a major off-site conference, and supervised an assistant. I believe that I am an excellent candidate for this position as I have illustrated below:

YOUR REQUIREMENTS	MY QUALIFICATIONS
A highly motivated, diplomatic, flexible, quality-driven professional on every project.	Successfully managed project teams involving different business units. The defined end results were achieved.
Exceptional organizational skills and attention to detail.	Planned the development and launch of the ABC Heritage Edition series. My former manager enjoyed leaving the 'details' and follow-through to me. Project management training.
Degree and minimum 3 years' relevant business experience.	BA from City University. 5+ years' business experience in productive, professional environments.
Computer literacy.	Extensive knowledge of Windows & Macintosh applications.

I'm interested in this position because it fits well with my new career focus in the human resources field. Currently, I am enrolled in City College's Adult Career Planning and Development certificate programme and working at XYZ Ltd.

I have enclosed my CV to provide more information on my strengths and career achievements. If after reviewing my material you believe that there is a match, please call me. Thank you for your consideration.

Yours sincerely,

Anna M Sanchez

Anna M Sanchez

enclosure

Response to newspaper advertisement (office administrator)

Mark Stevenson

5 May 20–
Philip _____
(title)
ABC Ltd
1 Industry Plaza
Anytown AA1 1AA

Dear Mr _____:

Your advertisement for an **Office Administrator** caught my attention because my background appears to parallel your needs. Please refer to the enclosed CV for a summary of my qualifications. I am sure you have been flooded with hundreds of qualified applicants; please allow me to explain why you would want to call me first.

I am very **self-sufficient** and able to **work independently with little supervision**. With little formal training, I have taken the initiative to learn about and remain current with my company's products, processes and expectations. I am regarded as **an information resource** and enjoy sharing my knowledge with others. I also enjoy **managing projects** and **planning meetings, trips and special events**.

I am always looking for ways to **streamline processes** and become more efficient. I have **developed systems and processes** using available software to automate production reporting, notify customers of changes and inform the field staff of company changes or initiatives. When supervising clerical staff, I always try to **plan ahead** to make the best use of their time.

I work well with executives, sales representatives, customers, vendors *and* co-workers, and demonstrate strong interpersonal communication and good judgement. I always try to listen closely and understand what others need. Then, I look for ways to help solve the problem. I have particularly found that listening, without interrupting, can diffuse a tense situation and allow the issue to be resolved more quickly with a positive outcome.

I am confident that I can deliver similar results for ABC Ltd. I would appreciate the opportunity to speak to you to arrange an appointment and provide you with more information. Thank you for your time and consideration; I look forward to speaking to you soon.

Yours sincerely,

Mark Stevenson

Mark Stevenson

enclosure

111 Any Street • Anytown AA1 1AA • 12345 678901 • officeadministrator@hotmail.com

Response to newspaper advertisement (legal secretary)

Marianne Johnston

1 Any Street / Anytown AA1 1AA
12345 678901 / 1098765 4321 (Mobile)
legalsecretary@earthlink.com

(Date)

Emily _____
(Title)
General Council of the Bar
1 Industry Plaza
Anytown AA1 1AA

RE: GENERAL COUNCIL OF THE BAR, LEGAL SECRETARY

Dear Ms _____ :

It is with continued interest and enthusiasm that I respond to your advertisement for Legal Secretary to the General Council of the Bar. I believe that my education and experience combine to create a perfect match for the position, and would appreciate careful consideration of my credentials as presented below and within my CV, enclosed.

It has long been my dream to pursue a career in the legal arena, and my goal to associate with the top professionals in the field. Where better to continue my professional development than within the heart of the organization as a provider of administrative support to members of the Bar itself.

Although a relative newcomer to the field, I have earned my HNC in Legal Studies and Paralegal certificate. With more than two years' experience after qualifying, providing administrative and clerical support in private practice, I am confident that I possess the expertise and dedication that will make an immediate and significant contribution to the efficiency and organization of the Council.

If you are looking for a legal support professional who is committed to the highest standards of performance, relates well with others, is self-directing and highly motivated, and is looking for a long-term employment relationship, please contact me to arrange an interview. I will make myself available at your earliest convenience.

Thank you for your consideration; I look forward to the opportunity to speak to you soon.

Yours sincerely,

Marianne Johnston

Marianne Johnston

enclosure (CV and Professional References)

Response to newspaper advertisement (accounting manager)

Paul Anthony

12345 678901	1 Any Street	accountingpro@anyserver.co.uk
	Anytown AA1 1AA	

(Date)

Phillip _____
(Title)
ABC Ltd
1 Industry Plaza
Anytown AA1 1AA

Dear Mr _____:

Re: File No. 213

I have six years' accounting experience and am responding to your recent advertisement for an Accounting Manager. Please allow me to highlight my skills as they relate to your stated requirements.

Your Requirements	My Experience
• A recognized accounting qualification plus several years of practical experience	• Obtained CIMA membership and have over three years' experience as an Accounting Manager.
• Excellent people skills and demonstrated ability to motivate staff	• Effectively managed a staff of 24 including two supervisors.
• Strong administrative and analytical skills	• Assisted in the development of a base reference library with Microsoft Excel for 400 clients.
• Good oral and written communication skills	• Trained four new supervisors via daily coaching sessions, communication meetings and technical skill sessions.

I believe this background provides the management skills you require for this position. I would welcome the opportunity for a personal interview to further discuss my qualifications.

Yours sincerely,

Paul Anthony

Paul Anthony

enclosure

Response to newspaper advertisement (international sales manager)

Suzanne A Kennedy
1 Any Street
Anytown AA1 1AA
12345 678901

(Date)

Phillip _____
(Title)
ABC Ltd
1 Industry Plaza
Anytown AA1 1AA

Dear Mr _____:

Re: International Sales Manager, *Globe & Mail*, – September 20–

I was recently speaking to Mr _____ from your company and he strongly recommended that I send you a copy of my CV. Knowing the requirements for the position, he felt that I would be an ideal candidate. For more than 11 years, I have been involved in international sales management, with seven years directly in the aerospace industry. My qualifications for the position include:

- establishing sales offices in France, Great Britain and Germany;
- recruiting and managing a group of 24 international sales representatives;
- providing training programmes for all of the European staff, which included full briefings on our own products as well as competitor lines;
- obtaining 42 per cent, 33 per cent and 31 per cent of the French, German and British markets, respectively, dealing with all local engine and airframe manufacturers; and
- generating more than £32 million in sales with excellent margins.

My Bachelor of Science degree in electrical engineering was obtained at the University of _____ and my languages include French and German.

I feel confident that an interview would demonstrate that my expertise in setting up rep organizations and training and managing an international sales department would be an excellent addition to your growing aerospace corporation.

I look forward to meeting you, Mr _____, and will give you a call to follow up on this letter the week of (date) _____.

Yours sincerely,

Suzanne A Kennedy

Suzanne A Kennedy

enclosure

Response to newspaper advertisement (executive assistant)

Andrew F Petersen

1 Any Street • Anytown AA1 1AA

12345 678901 • executiveassistant@localnet.com

(Date)

Box 9412
Anytown AA1 1AA

Dear _____ :

I was very pleased to learn of the need for an Executive Assistant in your company from your recent advertisement in _____ . I believe the qualities you seek are well matched by my track record:

Your Needs	My Qualifications
Independent Self-Starter	• Served as company liaison between sales representatives, controlling commissions and products.
	• Controlled cash flow, budget planning and bank reconciliation for three companies.
	• Assisted in the promotion of a restaurant within a private placement sales effort, creating sales materials and communicating with investors.
Computer Experience	• Used Lotus in preparing financial spreadsheet used in private placement memoranda and Macintosh to design brochures and flyers.
	• Have vast experience with both computer programming and the current software packages.
Compatible Background	• Spent five years overseas and speak French.
	• Served as an executive assistant to four corporate heads.

A CV is enclosed that covers my experience and qualifications in greater detail. I would appreciate the opportunity to discuss my credentials in a personal interview.

Yours sincerely,

Andrew Petersen

Andrew Petersen

enclosure

Power phrases

Consider using adaptations of these key phrases in your responses to newspaper advertisements.

I believe that I am particularly well qualified for your position and would like to have the opportunity to meet you to explore how I may be of value to your organization.

Your advertisement no. 5188 in the 25th March edition of The _____ *has piqued my interest. This position has strong appeal to me.*

I am confident that with my abilities I can make an immediate and valuable contribution to _____ .

I would be pleased if you contacted me for an interview.

I was recently speaking with Mr _____ from your company and he strongly recommended that I send you a copy of my CV. Knowing the requirements for the position, he felt that I would be an ideal candidate.

I've had both large- and small-company experience and it is my preference to work in a smaller operation where goals are measurable, results are noticeable and contributions really make a difference.

I feel confident that an interview would demonstrate that my expertise in setting up organizations, and training and managing an international sales department, would be an excellent addition to your growing _____ company.

I look forward to meeting you, Mr _____ , and will give you a call to follow up on this letter the week of 25th September.

The opportunity to work with your client is appealing to me, and I would appreciate an opportunity to discuss the position further. I look forward to hearing from you soon.

I believe this background provides the management skills you require for this position. I would welcome the opportunity for a personal interview to discuss my qualifications further.

In response to your ad, please consider my CV in your search for a Sales Service Coordinator.

I look forward to hearing from you in the near future to arrange an interview, during which I hope to learn more about your company's plans and goals and how I might contribute to the success of its service team.

I am accustomed to a fast-paced environment where deadlines are priority and handling multiple jobs simultaneously is the norm. I enjoy a challenge and work hard to attain my goals. Constant negotiations with all levels of management and employees have strengthened my interpersonal skills. I would like very much to discuss with you how I could contribute to your organization.

I am seeking an opportunity to excel in a dynamic company and am looking forward to relocating to _____ .

Please contact me at your earliest convenience so that I can clarify my background and enthusiasm for the job.

Your ad captured my attention.

My personal goal is simple: I wish to be a part of an organization that wants to excel in both _____ and _____ . I believe that if I had the opportunity of an interview with you it would be apparent that my skills are far-reaching.

Although I'm far more interested in a great company and an intriguing challenge than merely in money, you should know that in recent years my compensation has been in the range of £45,000 to £60,000.

Can we arrange a time to talk?

What you need and what I can do sound like a match.

Please find enclosed a copy of my CV for your review. I believe the combination of my _____ education and my business experience offers me the unique opportunity to make a positive contribution to your firm.

As you will note in my CV I have not only 'grown up' in and with the Operations and Warehousing area of a major (apparel) (consumer products) company; I have also established my expertise and my value to a discriminating and brilliant employer who depended upon me – on a daily basis – to represent and protect his interests and contribute significantly to his profitability... I am seeking an opportunity to replicate this situation and again use my considerable abilities to dedicate myself to the profitability of my employer.

I am available to meet you to discuss my qualifications at your convenience. I can be reached at _____ . I would like to thank you in advance for your time and any consideration you may give me. I look forward to hearing from you.

Having been born and raised in the _____ area and wishing to return to this area to work as a _____, I have been researching _____ firms that offer the type of experience for which my previous education and work experience will be of mutual benefit. Highlights of my attached CV include: _____.

Please consider my qualifications for the position of _____ which you advertised.

As you will note in the enclosed CV, the breadth of my expertise covers a wide area of responsibilities, thereby providing me with insights into the total operation.

Recently, I saw an advertisement in the _____ for a position as a Technical Trainer. My application for this position is advanced by my experience in training and support, and a technological background.

I thrive on challenge and feel that my skills and experience are easily transferable.

I would appreciate an opportunity to discuss my abilities in more depth and am available for an interview at your earliest convenience.

Is the ideal candidate for the position of _____ highly motivated, professional and knowledgeable in all functions concerning _____? Well, you may be interested to know that a person possessing these qualities, and much more, is responding to your ad in the _____ for this position.

I very much enjoy working in a team environment and the rewards associated with group contribution.

The skills you require seem to match my professional strengths.

I have a strong background in telemarketing small and medium-sized businesses in _____ and outlying areas.

I look forward to hearing from you soon to arrange an appointment. Please feel free to give me a call at my office at _____ or leave a message at my home number, _____.

As a recent MBA graduate, my professional job experience is necessarily limited. However, I believe that you will find, and previous employers will verify, that I exhibit intelligence, common sense, initiative, maturity and stability, and I am eager to make a positive contribution to your organization.

I read, with a great deal of interest, your advertisement in the 20 October _____, issue of _____.

Please allow me to highlight some of my achievements that relate to your requirements: _____.

I would greatly appreciate the opportunity to discuss this position in a personal interview. I may be contacted at _____ to arrange a meeting.

I would appreciate an opportunity to meet. At present I am working as a temp but am available at any time. I look forward to meeting you.

Thank you for taking the time recently to respond to my questions concerning a _____ position with _____.

I will be in your area Friday, 5th December, and will call you early next week to see if we might arrange a meeting at that time.

This experience has provided me with a keen appreciation for the general practice of _____.

A salary of £30,000 would be acceptable; however, my main concern is to find employment where there is potential for growth.

'Cold' cover letter to a potential employer (entry-level network admin)

Network administrator seeking entry-level opportunity highlights his certifications to emphasize recent professional development, a good idea when attempting a ground-floor position.

ANDREW J STELLS

PO Box 2146 ◆ Anytown AA1 1AA ◆ 12345 678901 ◆ ajs@hotmail.com

Dear Sir or Madam:

I have received my **MCP Certification**, and I am currently working on my **A++ Network Certification**. I am seeking an opportunity that will enable me to use my training and hands-on technical exposure in an **entry-level Network Administrator** position. A brief highlight of the skills and values I would bring to your organization include:

- Knowledge of installation, configuration, troubleshooting and repair of sophisticated, state-of-the-art software and hardware developed through recent computer operations training.

- Analytical, research, troubleshooting, interpersonal and organizational skills developed through on-the-job training within an IT environment.

- Proven success in prioritizing time, completing projects and meeting deadlines under time-sensitive circumstances, achieving stellar results.

- An energetic, enthusiastic and 'people-driven' communication style.

Since a CV can neither fully detail all my skills and accomplishments, nor predict my potential to your organization, I would welcome a personal interview to explore further the merging of my training and knowledge with your **IT** needs.

Yours faithfully,

ANDREW J STELLS

Enclosure

'Cold' cover letter to a potential employer (entry-level librarian)

Helena, who emigrated from Poland, has completed her master's in library science and is looking for her first full-time position in her career field.

Helena Swenka

12345 678901 | 1 Any Street | helenaswen@anyserver.com
| Anytown AA1 1AA |

November 15, 20–

Mr Jeffery Devine, Library Division Director
ABC Library
111 Any Avenue
Anytown AA1 1AA

Dear Mr Devine,

Does your library anticipate the need for an **Entry-Level Research or Reference Librarian or Cataloguer?** With my recent MSc in Information and Library Management from a CILIP-accredited programme, as well as internship experience in the reference department of academic and business libraries, perhaps I can be of service.

My CV is enclosed for your review. You will find evidence of my librarianship training, library database and computer skills, and work history. What you will not immediately see on my CV are my character traits and achievements – allow me to list some of them for you that I believe are relevant:

✓ *Hard-working, determined achiever – I set my sights high, whether attaining a **degree** at University of London in a demanding **MSc Degree** programme, or responding to reference requests with a high level of customer service and promptness (within 1–3 hours).*

✓ *Information technology knowledge and fast learner – My references will attest to how quickly I assimilated knowledge of library databases, computer software and integrated library automation systems. With hands-on experience using **Voyager Module, AACR2r, LC classification scheme, MARC format, and OCLC**, as well as **Lexis-Nexis, Dow-Jones, Dialog Web, and Classic**, I have worked with diverse reference materials such as legal, business, genealogy documents, as well as periodicals.*

✓ *Proactive problem-solver and team player – Using my broad foreign language skills (Polish, Russian, Slovak, German, Latin) allowed me to problem-solve with confidence and correctly catalogue foreign language materials while serving a **reference library internship** with **The Anytown County Library**. As an **intern cataloguer**, I worked cooperatively with others in serial publication cataloguing and serial control, achieving high rates of daily production.*

Providing high-level customer service and efficiency is my goal in library services and support. My knowledge and practical use of internet resources and navigational tools, combined with my experience with library databases, affords you the opportunity to hire an entry-level library professional with proven librarianship success. May we meet soon to discuss your needs? I will call your office next week to arrange a mutually convenient appointment, if that is agreeable with you. Thank you for your time and consideration.

Yours sincerely,

Helena Swenka

Helena Swenka

Enclosure

'Cold' cover letter to a potential employer (manager)

Concerned that his company is not doing well financially, William has decided to 'test the waters' for another position similar to those he has had in the past.

WILLIAM C KITE

1 Any Street   12345 678901
Anytown AA1 1AA   Wmckite@hotmail.com

12 December 20–

Mr Jacob Abernathy
Warehouse and Assembly Services
17 Industrial Way
Anytown AA1 1AA

Dear Mr Abernathy:

More than ever, good companies need proven performers who can get results in competitive industries and a tough economy, whether working independently or leading teams. If you are in need of a Warehouse Manager, Inventory Control Specialist, Production Manager or Assembly Order Fulfilment Supervisor, consider my track record:

✓ Efficiently scheduled assembly, material handlers and warehouse personnel, and closely monitored interplant transfers of raw materials from 20 warehouses. Assembly production and distribution procedures yielded high levels of productivity: 90 per cent on-time delivery, including emergency orders, of up to £1 million in SKUs per week. (Expediter/Production Dept. Scheduler, ABC Ltd)

✓ Developed cooperative relationships with field sales reps of major companies, such as ABC Ltd, DEF Healthcare, and XYZ, and served as liaison with in-house account executives and customer service reps at The GHI Group, to streamline receiving and shipping operations and upgrade quality control. (Warehouse Manager, The JKL Group)

✓ As final assembly and inspection member of four-person team, met heavy production schedule (35 to 60 complex, fabricated units per day) with 6 per cent or less error rate. (Order Fulfilment Clerk, ABC Ltd)

✓ Working as part of a team, created, tested, packaged and directed to shipping custom ship sets of complex hose assemblies, meeting deadlines 99-plus per cent of the time. Used quality assurance testing methods, including pressure testing of assembled units, to ensure highest level of customer satisfaction. (Hose Fabrication Technician, ABC Ltd)

I am confident I can deliver similar results for your company.

Page 1 of 2

William C Kite
Page 2 of 2

With well-rounded experience in assembly, expediting and scheduling, shipping and receiving, order fulfilment, customer service, sales, supervision and training, and a 15-year track record of meeting deadlines in demanding (even emergency) situations, I believe I have the proven skills that can benefit your company.

In addition, I realize it is hard-working and cooperative people who deliver results. My focus on teamwork and productivity has proven successful in my past assignments. I am confident I can convince you that I have the technical experience and knowledge that you need, as well as the intangible qualities – enthusiasm, strong work ethic, dedication and dependability – to get the job done.

May we meet soon to discuss your needs? I will contact your office next week to arrange a mutually convenient appointment, if that is agreeable with you. Thank you for your consideration.

Yours sincerely,

William C Kite

Enclosure

'Cold' cover letter to a potential employer (mental health)

An applicant seeking to advance his career.

PETER A EDGEWATERS

Dear Sir or Madam:

Throughout my career, I have held increasingly responsible positions within the Mental Health Care service, gaining extensive experience in working both with patients and in administrative functions. My particular areas of expertise are:

- Physical Medicine and Rehabilitation
- Adult Intervention
- Family Counselling
- Legal Issues
- Government Regulations
- Child Evaluation

My greatest strength lies in my ability to communicate with all types of people and different levels of professionals. Being able to work with patients, physicians, legal officers and family members has enabled me to be a highly effective therapist and an advocate for the patient and the patient's family. As an Administration official, I have been inducted into the intricacies of the Mental Health Service and have been able to gain a thorough understanding of the workings of various government agencies as they relate to mental health, including the Benefits Agency, Department of Health, Social Services and other entities.

I feel my knowledge and strengths would be best applied as a consultant or Mental Rehabilitation Therapist. Further, I desire to return to a more focused health care organization such as yours and would welcome an opportunity for an interview with you in person.

I look forward to speaking to you at your earliest convenience and appreciate your time in reviewing my credentials and qualifications. I am confident that my professional knowledge and strengths, combined with my dedication, work ethic and energy, will add measurable value to your organization. Thank you for your consideration.

Yours sincerely,

Peter A Edgewaters

PETER A EDGEWATERS

Enclosure

---

1 Any Street • Anytown AA1 1AA • 12345 678901 • xxxx@msn.com

'Cold' cover letter to a potential employer (senior customer service specialist)

This candidate's most impressive qualifications are summarized in an eye-catching bulleted list.

Maria H Berretta
1 Any Street
Anytown AA1 1AA
Home: 12345 678901
Mobile: 1098765 4321
berretta@dotcareer.com

3 March 20–

Ms Jayne Longnecker
Customer Service Manager
ABC Insurance Company
111 Any Avenue
Anytown AA1 1AA

Re: Senior Customer Service Specialist

Dear Ms Longnecker:

Are you looking for a Senior Customer Service Specialist who is:

- A consistent top performer with a strong desire to get the job done?
- A team player able to achieve results through coordination with employees in all functional areas?
- An effective communicator with excellent writing, training and telephone skills?
- Able to learn quickly, analyse complex information and find solutions to problems?
- Organized, thorough and precise?

If so, you will be interested in my qualifications. I have a bachelor's degree in business administration and seven years' experience in the insurance/financial industry, serving in diverse roles as customer relations advisor and calculations processor. For more than a year and a half, I have consistently received the highest ratings in my branch despite the fact that the difficult cases frequently find their way to my desk. I have also contributed to my team by putting in extra time to clear backlogs and analysing existing procedures to devise more efficient methods of operation.

My CV is enclosed for your review. I believe that I can make a positive contribution to ABC Insurance Company and look forward to meeting you to discuss my qualifications in detail. Thank you for your time and consideration.

Yours sincerely,

Maria H Berretta

Maria H Berretta

Enclosure

'Cold' cover letter to a potential employer (research professional)

Darrin is a data specialist working for the local government, compiling birth/death and census statistics. He wants to enter the private sector to do more consumer/product research projects.

Darrin Wilson

MARKET RESEARCH ANALYST

Dear Sir/Madam:

As a research professional, I understand that success depends on a strong commitment to *customer satisfaction*. Executing the basics and using logic and reasoning to identify the strengths and weaknesses of alternative solutions, conclusions or approaches to problems are key to increasing performance and market share. I believe that my background and education reflect a commitment and ability to find solutions to these challenges. I developed excellent skills in **project coordination and the design and development of research projects** that increased the effectiveness of my organization.

I am considered an energetic, aggressive and innovative leader who is extremely client-oriented.

My position encompasses multiple tasks and responsibilities that include:

- examining and analysing statistical data to forecast future trends and to identify potential markets;

- designing and implementing new formats for logging and transferring information while working as part of a team researching data and statistics.

Thank you for your consideration. I approach my work with a strong sense of urgency, working well under pressure and change. I look forward to meeting you personally so that we may discuss how I can make a positive contribution to your organization.

Yours faithfully,

Darrin Wilson

Darrin Wilson

Enclosure

---

1 Any Street • Anytown AA1 1AA• 12345 678901 • dWilson53@excite.com

'Cold' cover letter to a potential employer (personal trainer)

James wants to move into fitness training after a long and successful career in general management, sales and customer relationship management.

JAMES J HUTCHISEN
PO Box 901 ◆ Anytown AA1 1AA
12345 678901 ◆ jjhutch@hotmail.com

Dear Sir or Madam:

Reflecting on my professional sales and management experience within the marine industry, it is at this point in my career I am seeking to pursue a long-term personal and professional goal of a challenging opportunity as a **Personal Trainer/Strength Coach** within a health club, physical therapy and/or fitness centre. Let me briefly highlight the skills, values and contributions I will bring to your organization:

- **Certified Personal Trainer/Health Fitness Instructor at leading training centre.**

- Possess over 25 years' health club experience with most types of cardiovascular, plate and free-weight systems.

- Proven ability to plan and implement training programmes through experience as a Personal Trainer for a health club.

- Strong general management, sales, marketing and customer relationship management expertise developed through 16 years as an Owner/Operator of a marine business.

- Comprehensive experience in human relations, within the retail/service arena, has characterized me as considerate, dependable, honest, straightforward, hard-working and personable.

Since a CV can neither fully detail all my skills and accomplishments, nor predict my potential to your organization, I would welcome the opportunity to meet and discuss the possible merging of my talent and experience with your personal trainer needs.

Yours faithfully,

James J Hutchisen

JAMES J HUTCHISEN

Enclosure

'Cold' cover letter to a potential employer (registered nurse)

This applicant moving out of the Navy has gained a great deal of experience with trauma treatment and crisis management.

RICHARD P ISAACS

1 Any Street • Anytown AA1 1AA • 12345 678901 • richi@cs.com

---

12 January 20–

Ms Florence Blackwell, RN
Director of Nursing
ABC Medical Centre
1234 Hospital Row
Anytown AA1 1AA

Dear Ms Blackwell:

In anticipation of completing my naval service in April, 20–, I am seeking a civilian position that will capitalize on my experience and training as a Registered Nurse. I believe that my clinical background and specialized training in emergency response and crisis management would make me an asset to your nursing staff. With this in mind, I have enclosed a CV for your review that outlines my credentials.

Some key points you may find relevant to a nursing position with your centre include:

- Caring for a broad range of patients, ranging from infants to senior citizens, and including post-operative, medical, infectious disease, oncology and end-of-life scenarios.
- Developing rapport with diverse cultural groups, both in clinical and social settings. The patients I have dealt with cut across the full spectrum of ethnic and socioeconomic strata, from enlisted personnel to officers and their dependents. In my current assignment in Tokyo, I have had the opportunity to experience the local culture and interact with the local population.
- Completing training and engaging in field exercises that have prepared me for deployment to combat zones. This is relevant to a civilian setting because it encompasses mass casualty treatment, nuclear and biohazard treatment, and field hospital training, all of which relate to disaster response in a civilian community.

I am confident that my dedication to caring for patients and capacity to function as an integral part of a treatment team would allow me to make a significant contribution to the health and well-being of your patients. I would enjoy discussing with you how I can fulfil your needs in a clinical nursing role. Please contact me via phone or e-mail to arrange a mutually convenient date and time for an initial interview.

Thank you for your time and consideration. I look forward to speaking to you soon.

Yours sincerely,

Richard P Isaacs, RN

Enclosure

'Cold' cover letter to a potential employer (entertainment industry)

This letter begins with an attention-grabbing opening followed by statements indicating that she understands the high-energy demands and realities of the entertainment industry. She ends the letter with a call to action.

MARY MANSON
_____

1 Any Street/Anytown AA1 1AA
Home 12345 678901/ Mobile 1098765 4321
m m @ e m a i l . c o m

[Date]

[Name]
[Address]
[Town, Postcode]

Dear [Salutation]:

Perhaps your company is in search of a highly motivated recent graduate who is passionate about the entertainment industry and has the energy and drive to 'pay my dues', acquire knowledge and advance professionally. If so, then we should talk.

I offer a combination of creative talents and a strong work ethic as well as the following qualifications:

- BA in Communications from the University of London

- Hands-on experience directing, acting in and producing short independent and student films

- Realistic understanding of the demands of the entertainment industry, gained through internships for TV production company

- Operating knowledge of a variety of audio and video equipment

While my enclosed CV provides a brief overview of my background, I look forward to a personal meeting at which time we can discuss your needs and my qualifications in detail.

I will call you next week to arrange a meeting; in the meantime, you can contact me at the above numbers. Thank you in advance for your time and consideration.

Yours sincerely,

Mary Manson

Mary Manson

Enclosure

'Cold' cover letter to a potential employer (management)

Scott's recent experience with his last employer focused on IT implementation and project management. He seeks to gain a project management position with an IT consulting firm where he can make use of both his technical expertise and his management skills.

SCOTT A McFADDEN

1 Any Street • Anytown AA1 1AA
12345 678901 • sam@earthlink.com

12 January 20–

Mr Addison Elgar
Director of Client Engagement
Computer Consultants
1234 Technology Terrace
Anytown AA1 1AA

Dear Mr Elgar:

Capitalizing on a career that encompasses substantial IT project management experience and extensive sales/marketing experience, I am seeking a new professional challenge that will combine these skills in a senior account management, project management or technical leadership role. With this goal in mind, I have enclosed for your review a CV that outlines my qualifications.

Some key points that you may find relevant to a position with your firm include:

- *Managing the technical deployment of six different releases of Cannon's SalesTeamX-pert sales force automation tool over the past three years. This has involved ensuring that hardware platforms in the field are prepared to receive the latest release and resolving technical issues impacting end-user training for 6,000 users at 34 sites across the UK.*
- *Building relationships with key decision-makers at FTSE 100 firms while serving as Marketing Manager for two different firms providing end-to-end transportation solutions for firms importing and exporting materials and products.*
- *Hands-on experience providing desk-side support to end-users; configuring hardware and installing software in the field; and delivering training to end-users and IT specialists.*

I am confident that my knowledge and expertise would allow me to make a meaningful contribution to the success of your firm and its clients. I would enjoy discussing with you in person how my capabilities can match your needs, and will contact you soon to arrange an appropriate time for an initial meeting.

Thank you for your time and consideration. I look forward to speaking to you soon.

Yours sincerely,

Scott A McFadden

Scott A McFadden

Enclosure

'Cold' cover letter to a potential employer (radiation safety officer)

This highly skilled and highly educated physicist is applying for the post of Radiation Safety Officer, which is his boss's job, as the boss leaves for another opportunity. He is competing with highly qualified external candidates, and his best asset is his familiarity with the institution, based on existing experience.

Michael Z Ostrowski
1 Any Street/Anytown AA1 1AA/12345 678901
michaelzo@earthlink.com

12 January 20–

Mr Zachary P Emerson
University of London
111 Any Avenue
Anytown AA1 1AA

Dear Mr Emerson:

Please accept this letter and the enclosed CV as an expression of my interest in the Radiation Safety Officer position you are currently seeking to fill. I am confident that my education, experience and familiarity with the University of London Research Centre facilities provide me with the necessary skills to meet or exceed your expectations in this role.

For the past year, I have been a Health Physicist with the university, with responsibility for a variety of functions, including:

- Testing & Monitoring Equipment
- Training Medical Staff
- Ensuring Compliance with Regulations
- Monitoring Staff Exposure
- Achieving CRESO Certification
- Supervising Four Technicians
- Serving on Various Committees
- Consulting with Physicians
- Maintaining Updated Technical Knowledge

Earlier, I held a similar position at University of Wales' School of Medicine and Hospital. There I trained and supervised the work of a six-person technical team. I ensured that all equipment, materials and supplies were in compliance with state regulations. State inspection results were always outstanding. Throughout my career, I have built a reputation for quality, flexibility and professionalism in all areas. My commitment to health and safety has resulted in a perfect safety record.

I hold two master's degrees, one in Nuclear Engineering from City University, the other in Nuclear Physics from South West University. I have taught Biophysics at university level. In addition, I speak three languages (English, Portuguese and Russian). Having lived and worked in other countries has given me a sensitivity and understanding of diverse cultures and customs.

I have thoroughly enjoyed working at the university, and would welcome this opportunity to make an even more significant contribution to the success of its mission. I would enjoy discussing my qualifications with you in person and invite you to contact me to arrange an initial interview.

Thank you for your time and consideration. I look forward to speaking to you soon.

Yours sincerely,

Michael Z Ostrowski

Michael Z Ostrowski

Enclosure

'Cold' cover letter to a potential employer (veterinary surgeon)

This veterinary surgeon practices in an elite niche, treating only competitive horses at race courses.

PARKER DOUGLASS, DVM

1 Any Street ◆ Anytown AA1 1AA ◆ 12345 678901

12 January 20–

Dr Amber Morgenstern
ABC Equine Hospital
111 Any Avenue
Anytown AA1 1AA

Dear Dr Morgenstern:

My extensive experience addressing the health and performance needs of elite race horses at major tracks makes me a strong candidate for the opening you recently advertised on your website. Accordingly, I have attached my CV for your consideration and review.

Some key points you may find relevant include:

- **Strong capacity to function independently and make critical decisions without direct supervision. My knowledge of horses and experience at several major race courses means that I will need minimal orientation to 'hit the ground running'.**
- **An excellent track record of maintaining the health of elite thoroughbreds and quarter horses, as well as assisting trainers in enhancing the performance of horses by improving their respiratory and general health as well as dealing with lameness issues (references can be provided).**
- **The ability to effectively evaluate young horses prior to purchase, through observation and diagnostic testing. I routinely produce quality repository radiographs and review radiographs in a repository setting. I also accompany buyers to auctions to assess horses being considered.**
- **Experience assisting trainers setting up effective farm-based training programmes, as well as helping breeders address reproductive health issues.**

I believe that I can be an asset to your organization and would enjoy discussing further how my knowledge, expertise and professional dedication can address your needs. Please feel free to contact me to arrange either a phone or in-person interview at a mutually convenient date and time.

Thank you for your time and consideration. I look forward to speaking to you soon.

Yours sincerely

Parker Douglass

Parker Douglass
Enclosure

'Cold' cover letter to a potential employer (internship)

This is a cover letter to apply for a competitive internship in the financial services industry.

Carlos M Nunez

13 January 20–

Current Address
City University
1 Any Street
Anytown AA1 1AA

Karen Carmichael
XYZ Ltd
111 Any Avenue
Anytown AA1 1AA
Re: Finance Intern

Telephone: 12345 678901
Email: nunezc@cu.edu

Dear Ms Carmichael:

Permanent Address
111 Any Road
Anothertown BB1 1BB

Are you looking for a driven, high-achieving intern committed to excelling in business and finance?

Telephone: 10987 654321

As a student at City University, I am pursuing a BA in Business Administration with an emphasis on Finance. My passion for financial markets and economics has steadily increased over the last five years and I am committed to developing my career path as a business leader within a major organization.

I approach all my work with discipline and focus; as an intern with your organization, I would look forward to effectively contributing to your programme goals. City University, ABC Academy, and The ABC Club of London have acknowledged my academic and leadership achievements for excellence in academic studies, volunteering, and peer mentoring.

Please feel free to contact me at my number in London, 12345 678901. Thank you for your consideration. I am enthusiastic about working at XYZ Ltd. My background, professionalism and enthusiasm will make me an effective member of your team.

Yours sincerely,

Carlos M Nunez

Enclosure

'Cold' cover letter to a potential employer (teacher)

A cover letter sent with the CV hard copy as a follow-up to the CV submission via e-mail.

.... **JONATHAN YOUNG**

14 November 20–

Ms Jennifer Jones
Personnel Coordinator
ABC Language School
111 Any Avenue
Anytown AA1 1AA

Dear Ms Jones:

Although I recently submitted my CV to your office via e-mail, I am submitting the enclosed hard copy as a follow-up. I welcome any questions you might have.

With this letter, I would like to reiterate my sincere motivation to teach in Japan. My experience as a substitute middle school teacher has helped me to understand methods of student interaction and reach a level of comfort in the classroom. I strive to build relationships with students – as much as a substitute teacher can – to facilitate classroom activities and inspire the learners. It is something I really enjoy.

The ABC website encourages 'all outgoing, dynamic, and flexible people to apply'. In my current position as a flight attendant for XYZ Airlines, I am required to demonstrate these characteristics daily. Communication and quick-thinking skills are a must onboard an aircraft full of passengers. Flexibility is essential in the areas of customer service, in interaction with colleagues, and in work scheduling.

My motivation is indeed genuine, and I look forward to the possibility of discussing the opportunity with you. I will gladly make myself available for a telephone or videoconference interview.

Yours sincerely,

Jonathan Young

Jonathan Young

Enclosure: One-page CV

---

1 Any Street • Anytown AA1 1AA • 12345 678901 • jon@jonyoung.com

'Cold' cover letter to a potential employer (production supervisor)

Two problems to overcome: a move from automotive service manager to production supervisor and a break in employment of more than a year.

Fergus McLean
  1 Any Street
  Anytown AA1 1AA

12345 678901
FML5505@anyserver.co.uk

Tuesday, 28 October 20–

Mr Charles W Worth
Director of Operations
ABC Ltd
111 Any Avenue
Anytown AA1 1AA

Dear Mr Worth:

How big is that gap between what the ABC leadership wants from its skilled, semi-skilled and unskilled employees and what the ABC bottom line gets? If you'd like to shrink that costly mismatch, we should explore adding me to your team as your Transportation Manager.

On the next pages, you'll see more than a half-dozen contributions I have made in this area. They illustrate the five profit-building capabilities I've listed right at the top of the next page. I'd like to put those advantages to work for you right away.

Over the last year, the health of a family member made the most demands upon me and guided my relocation from Anytown to Anothertown. Now that problem is resolved and I am ready to return to my first love: helping teams want to do well.

If my approach and philosophy appeal to you, please let me suggest a next step. I would like to hear about your specific needs in your own words. May I call in a few days to arrange a time to do that?

Yours sincerely,

Fergus McLean

Fergus McLean

Encl: CV

'Cold' cover letter to a potential employer (sales professional)

George has two specific needs: to show the sales aspect of his previous career as an accountant, and to convince a new employer that his desire to leave his current company was based solely upon having to work in an oversold market.

George Williams

1 Any Street – Anytown AA1 1AA
12345 678901 – 1098765 4321 (mobile) – gwilliams102@charter.net

Thursday, 20 July 20–

Ms Laura Worth
Sales Manager
XYZ Ltd
111 Any Avenue
Anytown AA1 1AA

Dear Ms Worth:

I want you to get the credit for adding ROI to the XYZ sales team. Specifically, I'd like to become your newest sales professional. And, perhaps the best way to link those two ideas is with this graph that shows how I'm performing right now.

What I do isn't magic. I just work harder and smarter than my competition by finding some profitable way to say yes to every customer and potential customer.

My focus on your sales needs starts on the next pages. I wanted you to see a CV that offers more than the usual recitations of job titles and responsibilities. That's why you'll find six capabilities I want to put at XYZ's disposal at once. Backing them up are a dozen examples of sales that show those capabilities in action.

My company values what I do. And, if I thought our market was growing as fast as yours, I would stay with them. While I cannot control market conditions, I am interested in making even greater contributions to my employer. That's why I'm 'testing the waters' with this confidential application.

I do best using the consultative approach to sales. So, as a first step, I'd like to hear about XYZ's sales needs in your own words. May I call in a few days to arrange a time to do that?

Yours sincerely,

George Williams

George Williams

Encl: CV

'Cold' cover letter to a potential employer (credit account specialist)

Kim wants to affiliate herself with a larger company that offers a more challenging role in analysing and managing financial accounts; she also seeks to take on more responsibility to allow her to grow professionally.

KIMBERLY A CARTER

1 Any Street ▪ Anywhere, AA1 1AA ▪ 12345 678901

8 December 20–

Marcy Johnson
ABC Accounting
111 Any Avenue
Anywhere AA1 1AA

Dear Ms Johnson,

As a well-qualified credit account specialist, I demonstrate my ability to communicate effectively with clients, resolve payment issues, and collect on past-due payments. I bring over 18 years of accounts receivable experience in addition to being involved in all processing stages of collections. The scope of my experience includes, but is not limited to, commercial, automotive and manufacturing environments.

My focus is to deliver results and provide superior service by quickly identifying problem areas in accounts receivable and developing a solution strategy to ensure issues are resolved. My expertise lies in my strong ability to build rapport with clients, analyse accounts, and manage all aspects related to my appointed position and areas of responsibility. I find these qualities to be my greatest assets to offer employers.

Due to an unforeseen circumstance, I was unable to continue my employment as a cash applications analyst with a well-known automotive industry leader. Since my employment with XYZ Ltd, I have accepted a temporary position as an invoice clerk with a local company. My objective is to secure a position in accounts receivable and credit collections with an established company. As you will note, my CV exhibits a brief review of contributions I have made to my employers. I enjoy challenges.

A complete picture of my expertise and experience is very important. Therefore, I will contact you next week. I look forward to speaking to you soon to answer any questions you may have regarding my background.

Yours sincerely,

Kimberly Carter

Kimberly Carter

Enclosure

'Cold' cover letter to a potential employer (sales)

After 'playing around' with part-time and seasonal positions for six years after college, John was ready to combine his variety of sales and customer service achievements into a bid for a serious, high-paying sales career.

JOHN MICHAEL ANDERSON
1 Any Street • Anytown AA1 1AA
12345 678901 (H) • 1098765 4321 (Mobile) • gatehous@anyserver.co.uk

Dear Sales Manager:

My competitors were like flies – they kept popping up everywhere, opening with lots of glitz, taking all the customers, and then crashing and burning after six months. But during those six months they were trying to take all <u>my</u> customers! As a newly graduated student in his first real management position, these were serious challenges to which I responded with all the advertising ideas and new gimmicks I could muster – free pool playing, fruity drinks for girls; I even gave away free beer one night using three kegs we couldn't get rid of.

Today I am the same aggressive, ambitious sales professional I was then. OK… these days I wouldn't give away free beer (it might even have been illegal), but I <u>do</u> respond to sales challenges with all the competitiveness, creativity and customer concern in my heart. In my last sales position, I was quite successful selling holiday packages by telephone for several reasons:

- I qualified my targets well.

- I was very knowledgeable about the product and painted a good picture of the product in the customer's mind.

- I think well and profitably on my feet.

- I'm honest and a natural rapport-builder.

The point of my enclosed CV is that I would like to talk to you about bringing all the sales, problem-solving and customer service skills to which it refers to work for your organization. When can we meet?

Yours sincerely,

John Michael Anderson

John Michael Anderson

enc.

'Cold' cover letter to a potential employer (media)

Letting her professors speak for her and then confirming their words with her own words of commitment is a very effective strategy. The strength of the text is enhanced by the brevity of the letter.

BROOKE M WELLINGTON   brookewelli@anyserver.co.uk

1 Any Street ◆ Anytown AA1 1AA ◆ Phone: 12345 678901

'I would rank Ms Wellington's work in the top 10 per cent of students I have taught; she is not afraid to tackle tough projects; I believe she has the ability to quickly make positive contributions…'
> – John Weiss, PhD, Chairperson, Department of Communications, City College

'Brooke was an exemplary Journalism student. She took charge of the tasks given to her and performed them in a superior manner. I admire her strong enthusiasm and her attention to detail…'
> – Stephen M Ross, Assistant Director of Television Technical Operations, City College

---

Dear Selection Committee:

Tenacious and *driven* are terms my colleagues have used to describe my work habits. It is with a strong sense of career commitment that I submit my CV for your review.

Having completed classes in August, I will be granted a BA in Journalism from City College in December 20–. Sometimes holding two jobs while attending college, I will have completed my degree in three years. It is with the same passion, integrity and energy that I intend to pursue my career.

Like so many, I possess the talent and understanding of how demanding a career in media can be. But unlike most, I am willing to 'pay the price' of hard work, demanding work schedules and total availability that the industry requires.

Thanks so much for your consideration. I am eager to learn more about the challenges facing your organization and to discuss how I can make a difference.

Yours sincerely,

Brooke M Wellington

Brooke M Wellington

'Cold' cover letter to a potential employer (director)

Richard T Carpenter

1 Any Street • Anytown AA1 1AA • 12345 678901
carpenter_vp@aol.com

(Date)

Emily _____
Title
ABC Ltd
1 Industry Plaza
Anytown AA1 1AA

Dear Ms _____,

As a Chief Financial Officer, I have built a reputation for my strong ability to provide decisive leadership. For the past several years, my career as a senior-level executive has provided me with opportunities to promote high-level strategic business and financial planning goals for worldwide multimillion-pound companies. My ability to identify challenges and to capitalize upon opportunities to expand revenue growth, reduce operating costs and improve overall productivity has been one of my strongest assets to my employers.

My strengths in financial and accounting management as well as my thorough understanding of finance operations have vastly contributed to my career and success as a leader. I maintain self-confidence, credibility and stature to make things happen with colleagues inside and outside the company. Just as significant are my abilities to develop rapport among co-workers and management, build effective teams and promote team effort.

My objective is to secure a position as a CFO or Director and to pursue new opportunities with an organization providing new and exciting challenges. Having a complete picture of my expertise and experience is very important. As you will note in my CV, I have made significant contributions to my employers and take my job very seriously.

I appreciate your time and consideration and will be in contact next week to see if we are able to arrange a date for an interview. I look forward to speaking to you soon.

Yours sincerely,

Richard Carpenter

Richard Carpenter

enclosure

'Cold' cover letter to a potential employer (pharmaceutical sales)

Elana M Carter

1 Any Street • Anytown AA1 1AA

Emily _____   (Date)
(Title)
ABC Ltd
1 Industry Plaza
Anytown AA1 1AA

Dear Ms _____ :

I currently hold a sales management position for a very successful retail company. My talents to achieve high sales volume, work cooperatively with diverse personalities, and focus on providing exceptional customer service have allowed me to excel in customer relations and succeed in sales and marketing.

I have always enjoyed a challenge and have made the decision to extend my experience to the pharmaceutical sales field. Pharmaceutical sales has been an interest of mine for some time, and I am confident that my background and skills in customer service, human relations and product distribution would translate well into pursuing this change. What I may lack in specific experience in your business, I more than make up for with my dedication, energy and determination.

I thoroughly understand the importance of developing customer relations, generating revenue from sales potential within a designated territory, and maintaining accurate customer information. I have the aptitude and willingness to learn the necessary technical medical materials to promote your products. I am fully capable of projecting a positive and professional image of a company and its products, and I strongly believe I possess the necessary skills and qualifications your organization seeks to be successful in this field of work.

Your time in reviewing my confidential CV is greatly appreciated. I will follow up next week to answer any questions you may have regarding my qualifications. At that time, I would like to discuss the possibility of setting up a personal interview with you. Please contact me if you would like to speak sooner.

Yours sincerely,

Elana Carter

Elana Carter

enclosure

'Cold' cover letter to a potential employer (recruiter)

Interested in fast-track career progression, Betsy has reached her peak with her current employer. She is seeking a position in a high-growth global company.

BETSY McGILL
1 Any Street • Anytown AA1 1AA • 12345 678901

(Date)

Alice _____
(Title)
A, B&C
Executive Search Consultants
111 Any Avenue
Anytown AA1 1AA

Dear Ms _____:

Having spent several years in executive recruitment, I understand the number of CVs you receive on a daily basis. However, I remember how valuable a few always turned out to be.

The purpose of this communication is to introduce myself and then to meet you with a view to joining your organization.

When asked which business situations have been the most challenging and rewarding, my answer is the time spent in the search profession.

My background, skills and talents are in all aspects of sales and sales management. My research indicates that your expertise is in this area.

I have enclosed a CV that will highlight and support my objectives. I would appreciate the opportunity to meet you and exchange ideas. I will call you over the next few days to make an appointment. If you prefer, you may reach me in the evening or leave a message at 12345 678901.

Thank you and I look forward to our meeting.

Yours sincerely,

Betsy McGill

Betsy McGill

enclosure

'Cold' cover letter to a potential employer (project management)

Matthew A Sims
1 Any Street
Anytown AA1 1AA
12345 678901

(Date)
Mr _____
ABC Ltd
1 Industry Plaza
Anytown AA1 1AA

Dear Mr_____:

Information technology expertise, combined with visionary leadership, the ability to motivate cross-functional teams, and develop cost-effective solutions, are key to creating long-term customer satisfaction and loyalty.

As a seasoned **Project Manager** experienced in providing strategic direction in the design and deployment of technology solutions, I have:

- successfully managed customer accounts from defining project requirements through to implementation;
- engineered e-commerce business solutions for myriad organizations from start-up ventures to FTSE 100 companies;
- completed all the coursework, including specialized electives, to obtain the Microsoft Certified Systems Engineer designation;
- developed comprehensive RFIs and RFPs; selected the most qualified, cost-effective vendor; and directed cross-functional teams to ensure on-time, on-budget implementation;
- efficiently prioritized projects, developed realistic timelines and consistently met deadlines;
- compiled and driven ratification of product requirements;
- provided technical expertise to sales teams to assist them in closing the sale.

Could your company use a high achiever with a thirst for growth and new challenges? If so, I would like to discuss how my skills and experience could benefit your organization.

I look forward to speaking to you.

Yours sincerely,

Matthew Sims

Matthew Sims

enclosure

'Cold' cover letter to a potential employer (publishing)

An administrative support person who wants to break into the publishing industry. She has no actual experience but is an avid reader who volunteers time to edit community fundraising publications and newsletters.

Genevieve Stone
1 Any Street ▪ Anytown AA1 1AA ▪ 12345 678901 ▪ genstone@anyserver.co.uk

(Date)

Phillip _____
(Title)
ABC Ltd
1 Industry Plaza
Anytown AA1 1AA

Dear Mr _____:

In the interest of exploring opportunities in the publishing industry, I have enclosed my CV for your review.

Over the last two years, I have gained valuable knowledge and experience in many aspects of personnel assistance, office procedures and administrative operations. Recently I volunteered my time to edit a cookbook and have been responsible for editing the newsletter for my college. I consider myself a good writer and an avid reader and have always wanted to get into publishing. With my considerable energy, drive and ability to work long hours, I believe I could make a positive contribution to your organization, and I would appreciate the opportunity to discuss my qualifications with you.

Should any questions arise regarding the information on my CV, or if you need personal references, please do not hesitate to contact me through the address or telephone number listed above.

Thank you for your time and consideration. I look forward to meeting you.

Yours sincerely,

Genevieve Stone

Genevieve Stone

enclosure

'Cold' cover letter to a potential employer (international sales)

·· **JENNIFER DELOREAN**

(Date)

Phillip _____
(Title)
ABC Ltd
1 Industry Plaza
Anytown AA1 1AA

Dear Mr _____:

I received your name from Mr _____ last week. I spoke to him regarding career opportunities with _____ and he suggested contacting you. He assured me that he would pass my CV along to you; however, in the event that he did not, I am enclosing another.

As an avid cosmetics consumer, I understand and appreciate the high standards of quality that your firm honours. As you can see from my enclosed CV, I have had quite a bit of experience in the international arena. My past experience working overseas has brought me a greater understanding of international cultures and traditions, as well as a better understanding and appreciation of our own culture. These insights would certainly benefit a company with worldwide locations, such as your own. In addition, I have gained first hand experience in the consumer marketplace through my various sales positions. I have noticed your recent expansion into the television media and am sure that an energetic individual would surely be an asset to ABC in this, as well as other, projects.

I would very much like to discuss career opportunities with ABC. I will be calling you within the next few days to set up an interview. In the meantime, if you have any questions I may be reached at the number above. Thank you for your consideration.

Yours sincerely,

Jennifer Delorean

Jennifer Delorean

enclosure

···

1 Any Street • Anytown AA1 1AA • 12345 678901
internationalsalespro@msn.com

'Cold' e-mail to a potential employer (banking)

Having completed a one-year contract, Matthew had been offered a permanent position. However, he is interested in a position in a company that is more financially stable, and one where he could make use of his diverse technology skills.

From: Matthew Lorenzo [bankerpro@hotmail.com]
To: hr@abccareers.com
Cc:
Subject: Financial management / Sales orientation

Dear Mr _____:

Please include my name in your job search database. As requested, I have attached a copy of my current CV.

Banking today is definitely a sales environment. While my marketing skills will always be useful, my interests lead me now to seek a more distinct financial management position such as Controller, Treasurer, or Head of Finance.

Since my CIMA Part III will be completed in January 20–, my search may be somewhat premature, but my transcript and results, combined with my practical experience, should offset my temporary lack of an accounting designation. I would therefore like you to begin considering me immediately. As an Account Manager, I saw many different industries, and so would not feel constrained to any one sector.

Including a mortgage loan benefit, I am currently earning £4,500 per month plus a car allowance. This should provide you with an indication of my present job level. Your suggestions or comments would be appreciated. I am available for interviews, and can be reached at 12345 678901. Thank you.

Yours sincerely,

Matthew Lorenzo
bankerpro@hotmail.com

'Cold' e-mail to a potential employer (software development)

From: Julie Baxter [softwarespecialist@anyserver.co.uk]
To: hr@developers.net
Cc:
Subject: Developer with quality, productivity and commitment

Dear Mr _____:

ABC Ltd caught my attention recently as I began a search for a new employer in the South West area. ABC Ltd is well known in the software industry for quality products and excellent customer service; it also maintains a strong reputation as a great employer. Your organization has created an environment in which people can excel, which is why I write to you today.

I am very interested in joining your software development team. I am confident that my background and experience will meet your future needs. My current position is Application Developer for XYZ Ltd. I enjoy it very much as it has provided me with extensive hands-on training in Visual Basic and other languages. However, I am ready to get more into actual software writing, as well as return to the Bristol area. I possess a bachelor's degree in Computer Science as well as training in a variety of programming languages. I am also a fast learner, as demonstrated by my learning Visual Basic quickly after joining XYZ. Additionally, I plan to pursue my master's degree and have begun the application process.

I would appreciate the opportunity to meet you to discuss your goals and how I can help you meet them. I will call you soon to arrange a meeting. In the meantime, please feel free to call for further information on my background and experience.

Thank you for your consideration and reply. I look forward to meeting you in the near future.

Yours sincerely,

Julie Baxter
12345 678901
softwarespecialist@anyserver.co.uk

'Cold' e-mail to a potential employer (internship)

From: David Kent [internationalrelationspro@earthlink.net]
To: hr@internationaljobs.org
Cc:
Subject: Motivated International Relations Intern

Dear Ms _____:

I am interested in being considered for an internship. I am currently in my final year at the University of XYZ studying International Studies with a concentration on Latin America and Political Science.

My internships have increased my knowledge of International Relations and have enabled me to make use of my education in a professional environment. I am very serious about my International Relations education and future career and am eager to learn as much as possible throughout my internship. I am interested in working for your organization to gain practical experience and additional knowledge pertaining to my field of study.

My professional and academic background, along with my sincere interest in helping others, has enhanced my sensitivity to a diverse range of cultures. As a highly motivated professional, I enjoy the challenge of complex demanding assignments. My well-developed writing and communication skills are assets to an office environment.

I welcome the opportunity to elaborate on how I could make a substantial contribution to your organization as an intern. I look forward to talking to you soon. Thank you.

Yours sincerely,

David Kent
12345 678901
internationalrelationspro@earthlink.net

Power phrases

Consider using adaptations of these key phrases in your 'cold' letters to potential employers.

My 22-year operations management career with a multibillion-pound _____ company has been at increasing degrees of responsibility. While I have spent the last five years in top management, I am especially proud of my record – I started as a driver many years ago and, like cream, have risen to the top. I have consistently accomplished all goals assigned to me, particularly overall cost reductions, improved productivity, and customer service. Some of my achievements include:

Your recent acquisition of the _____ chain would indicate an intention to pursue South Eastern market opportunities more vigorously than you have in the past several years. I believe that my retail management background would complement your long-range strategy for _____ very effectively.

With the scarcity of qualified technical personnel that exists today, I thought that you would be interested in my qualifications as set forth in the attached CV.

In approximately three months, I am moving to _____ with my family, and am bringing with me 15 solid years of banking experience – the last eight in branch operations management. I would particularly like to use this experience with your company.

I have noticed that you conduct laser exposure testing at your facility. If there is a need for laser technicians in this endeavour, I would like to be considered for a position.

As you can see from my CV, I am a psychology graduate and was chair of our debating society in my final year. I feel both would indicate a talent for sales. I did some selling in my summer job in 20– (ABC Books), and found not only that I was successful, but that I thoroughly enjoyed it.

The position you described sounds challenging and interesting. After receiving your comments about the job requirements, I am convinced that I can make an immediate contribution toward the growth of _____ and would certainly hope that we can explore things further.

The opportunity to put to use my medical knowledge as well as my English degree would bring me great pleasure, and it would please me to know that I was bringing quality to your company.

I feel that the combination of _____'s educational environment and my desire to learn as much as possible about the data processing field could only bring about positive results.

If you think after talking to me and reading my CV that there might be an interest with your client company, I would be very interested. I have been put in many situations where I had to learn quickly, and have always enjoyed the challenge.

My accomplishments include:

As my CV indicates, I have demonstrated commitment to clients and to my employer's goals. That track record is consistent in my career endeavours as well as in my life as a whole. I dedicate myself to whatever task is at hand, marshal my resources, and stay with the project until it is completed – to my satisfaction. Since my goals and demands are even more stringent than my employers' expectations, I consistently exceed quotas and objectives.

You will notice one common thread throughout my career – I am an administrator and a problem solver.

Currently I am considering opportunities in the £65–£85K range.

My confidential CV is enclosed for your review and consideration.

My current salary requirement would range mid to high £50Ks, with specifics flexible, negotiable, and dependent upon such factors as benefit structure and advancement opportunity.

Having spent several years as a _____ , I understand the number of CVs you receive on a daily basis. However, I remember how valuable a few always turned out to be.

I would like the opportunity to discuss with you how we could mutually benefit one another. You may leave a message on my answering machine at my home and I will return the call. I look forward to hearing from you very soon.

I'm a clear communicator equally at ease with senior management, government officials and agencies, vendors and contractors. I'm a hard-driving manager who is project driven and accustomed to inspiring the best job performance possible from associates and employees.

This job seems to be the right challenge for me; I know that with my strong Java skills and manufacturing background experience I will be an asset to your company.

Hoping to meet you in person, I thank you for your time.

I will be calling you on Friday, 15 August 20–, to be sure you received my CV and to answer any questions you might have.

I have enclosed a CV that will highlight and support my objectives. I would appreciate the opportunity to meet and exchange ideas. I will call you over the next few days to make an appointment. If you prefer, you may reach me in the evening or leave a message at _____ .

'Cold' cover letter to employment industry professional (health care)

Adam has developed strong relationships with clinics, hospitals and physicians through-out his career. He wants to use this experience to gain a position with a clinic, capitalizing on his expertise in preventive health and chronic illness management programmes.

ADAM G STEVENS

1 Any Street
Anytown AA1 1AA
12345 678901
E-mail: adams@anyserver.co.uk

12 January 20–

Ms Greta Pederson
Hunter, Gatherer & Recruiter Executive Search
1234 Executive Tower
Anytown AA1 1AA

Dear Ms Pederson:

As an accomplished professional with a 20-plus-year track record in the pharmaceutical industry, I believe that I have unique talents that could benefit a clinic or a health care organization. With this in mind, I have enclosed for your review a CV that briefly outlines my professional history.

Some of the key capabilities that I can bring to a new opportunity include:

- *Design and implementation of health management programmes. I have firsthand experience developing programmes for asthma management, and direct the implementation of programmes that have delivered substantial savings to client companies.*
- *Managing the development and implementation of web-based services that are new revenue centres for my company and value-added services to its physician customer base.*
- *Exceptional account relations skills. I currently call on and maintain business relationships with key client contacts at the highest levels.*
- *Certification from the University of London in Quality Management and from the National Heart, Lung & Blood Institute.*

I am confident that my knowledge and expertise would allow me to deliver successful results for one of your clients in the health care service. I would enjoy speaking to you in person to explore potential opportunities and how I can best serve someone's needs. Please call or e-mail me to arrange a convenient time for us to meet.

Thank you for your time and consideration. I look forward to talking to you soon.

As my employer is unaware of my job search, I trust that you will hold this correspondence in strict confidence and consult with me before releasing my materials to a prospective employer.

Yours sincerely,

Adam G Stevens
Enclosure

'Cold' cover letter to employment industry professional (senior network control technician/administrator)

Peter's goal is to move from a network administrator to a senior position.

PETER M GUTIERREZ

1 Any Street, Anytown AA1 1AA • pmgutierrez@sbcglobal.net • 12345 678901

20 January 20–

I regard network downtime as unacceptable, yet realize it sometimes happens due to powers beyond my control. I always have contingency plans. – Peter Gutierrez

Placement Services Ltd
Anytown AA1 1AA

RE: SENIOR NETWORK CONTROL TECHNICIAN/ADMINISTRATOR, London

Dear Personnel Recruiter:

As I consider career options that offer new and challenging opportunities to facilitate my growth, I am excited by your job posting for Senior Network Control Technician/Administrator. My qualifications and technical background, as well as fieldwork, marketing and customer service experience, match your requirements for this position. The enclosed CV reflects the experience and technical training/expertise to provide customized network and hardware/software solutions to meet remote customer needs.

The following *key strengths* also exemplify highly marketable skills and characteristics. I possess:

- *an accommodating attitude and willingness to work hard at any level to accomplish tasks and meet deadlines;*
- *the ability to prioritize tasks and job assignments to balance customer needs with company goals;*
- *strategic planning to head off downtime and restructure company systems to realize major improvement;*
- *aptitude for troubleshooting problems, while respecting customers and explaining problems/ solutions in simple, illustrative language;*
- *consultative, straightforward communication techniques that promote development of strong and lasting rapport and trust;*
- *a work ethic that honours integrity and excellence to enhance company distinction;*
- *a persuasive, take-charge style seasoned with a sense of humour for a pleasant work environment;*
- *psychological insight and a talent for motivating others to work at higher levels to increase productivity.*

An interview to investigate your needs and my qualifications further would be mutually beneficial. I look forward to hearing from you. In the meantime, thank you for your time and consideration.

Yours sincerely,

Peter M Gutierrez

Enclosure: CV

'Cold' cover letter to employment industry professional (accountant)

THERESE E MAYSONET

1 Any Street • Anytown AA1 1AA • maysonet_accountant@email.net

Emily _____   (Date)
(Title)
ABC Ltd
1 Industry Plaza
Anytown AA1 1AA

Dear Ms _____:

As I am just completing the requirements for my MBA in Accounting at City Institute of Technology, I am exploring potential opportunities with a well-established firm that will lead to a career as an accountant. I hope to join an organization where I can learn and grow within the accounting profession and build a long-term relationship. With these goals in mind, I have enclosed for your consideration and review a CV that briefly outlines my credentials.

Some of the key experiences I can bring to an entry-level position with your company include:

- **administering Accounts Receivable and Payroll for an engineering firm that was also engaged in construction and some custom manufacturing;**

- **preparing individual tax returns as part of a volunteer programme;**

- **serving as Treasurer of a college organization, which entailed maintaining financial records and providing financial reports to the auditors and to the national organization;**

- **proficiency with basic Windows and Microsoft Office applications, as well as a keen interest in technology and high-tech businesses.**

I am confident that my education and experience to date provide me with skills that would be beneficial to your firm and its clients. I would enjoy speaking to you in person to discuss the possibilities that exist and how I can best serve the needs of your company and your clients. Please call me on 12345 678901 to arrange a convenient date and time for us to meet. I look forward to opening a dialogue with you soon.

Yours sincerely,

Therese Maysonet

Therese Maysonet

enclosure

'Cold' cover letter to employment industry professional (quality assurance)

David Jameson
1 Any Street
Anytown AA1 1AA
12345 678901 / Mobile: 1098765 4321

(Date)

Phillip _____
(Title)
ABC Ltd
1 Industry Plaza
Anytown AA1 1AA

Dear Mr _____:

Reliability. Problem Solving. Attention to Detail. Innovation. These are a few of the many qualities I have developed as a Quality Assurance Technician. If you are looking for a topnotch Quality Assurance Technician, look no further. I have over 15 years' experience in quality assurance and quality control and have not only designed more consumer-friendly products but have improved sales of existing products.

Because delivering solid productivity increases has been the norm throughout my career in the electronics field, I have achieved superior results at ABC Biomedical, DEF Technologies, WHI Electronics, JKL Healthcare, MNO Magnetic, and PQR Electronics. As a result, you get a Quality Assurance Technician who is productive from day one. My commitment to you would be the same: simplify processes, improve products, develop workforce competencies, and boost output while completing projects ahead of time and under budget.

Qualifications I can bring to your clients are outlined in the enclosed CV. Given my technical skills, familiarity with the product line, and understanding of your clients' needs, I could step into the position and be of immediate assistance.

Please contact me at my home telephone number to arrange a convenient time to meet. Thank you for your time; I look forward to speaking to you soon.

Yours sincerely,

David Jameson

David Jameson

enclosure

'Cold' cover letter to employment industry professional (executive computer specialist)

Kelly L Hillman
1 Any Street ▪ Anytown AA1 1AA ▪ 12345 678901

(Date)

Emily _____
(Title)
ABC Ltd
1 Industry Plaza
Anytown AA1 1AA

Dear Ms _____:

My experience installing and maintaining computer networks, hardware and software, along with my skills in training users and developing cost-saving applications, are the assets I would bring to the position of Executive Computer Specialist.

I am a Certified Novell Administrator. And my technical skills include expertise in Novell Netware, MS DOS and Windows, as well as experience with hardware including Cabletron, and software including the Microsoft Office Suite.

My computer expertise has saved my employers production time and costs. As a Senior Computer Specialist, I installed a Personal Computer LAN using the Novell Netware Networking System. I saved £35,000 and used the savings to upgrade the equipment installation. Also in that position I designed and implemented a system to cut printing costs. The system is projected to save the government £4 million over four years.

I have also developed software packages, including 'point of sale' software and mortgage software, which was for commercial sale.

I believe my skills and experience will make me succeed in the position of Executive Computer Specialist. Kindly review my CV, then contact me at your earliest convenience to schedule a professional interview.

Yours sincerely,

Kelly Hillman

Kelly Hillman

enclosure

'Cold' cover letter to employment industry professional (senior executive)

·· **Thomas J Flokhart**

(Date)

Mr _____
(Title)
A, B & C
Executive Search Consultants
111 Any Avenue
Anytown AA1 1AA

Dear Mr _____:

In the course of your search assignments, you may have a requirement for an organized and goal-directed Senior Executive. My present position provides me with the qualifications and experience necessary to successfully fulfil an executive position. Key strengths that I possess for the success of an administrative position include:

- direct line operations responsibility improving gross margin to 8.0 per cent;
- planning and developing over £15 million in new construction projects;
- reduction of departmental operating expenses to 1.1 per cent below budget;
- negotiating and developing contractual arrangements with vendors.

I have the ability to define problems, assess both large-scale and smaller implications of a project, and implement solutions.

The enclosed CV briefly outlines my administrative and business background. My geographic preferences are the central and South East regions of the country. Relocating to a client's location does not present a problem. Also, I possess a degree from _____ University, and a BA in Business Administration from _____ University. Depending upon location and other factors, my salary requirements would be between £130,000 and £150,000.

If it appears that my qualifications meet the needs of one of your clients, I will be happy to discuss my background further in a meeting with you or in an interview with the client. I will be contacting your office in the near future to determine the status of my application.

Yours sincerely,

Thomas Flokhart

Thomas Flokhart

enclosure

···
1 Any Street • Anytown AA1 1AA • 12345 678901

'Cold' cover letter to employment industry professional (senior manager)

Lisa K Botkin

1 Any Street   home: 12345 678901
Anytown AA1 1AA   senior manager@yahoo.com

(Date)

Mr _____
ABC Ltd
1 Industry Plaza
Anytown AA1 1AA

Dear Mr _____:

Mentored by Bob _____, founder of _____, I successfully progressed within his privately held organization for 12 years, serving on the **Board of Directors of 13 separate companies** and holding positions including **Treasurer, Head of Finance,** and ultimately **CEO**. During my tenure the company grew from seven employees to more than 1,000 while **revenues increased from £3 million to £108 million**. My enclosed CV gives further detail.

My reason for contacting you is simple. I am interested in exploring any senior management opportunities that may be available through your organization and would also be interested in interim or consulting roles. Geographically speaking, I have no limitations and am available for relocation throughout the UK and abroad. Due to the level and quality of my performance, I feel it pertinent to state that I am only willing to consider positions consistent with my current income level. I have the experience, the talent and the energy to turn around, create or develop a dynamic organization.

I have built my career on my commitment and ability to create open lines of communication between the Board of Directors and senior management to **protect the investments of my organization and to assure the attainment of the target return**.

I look forward to hearing from you in the near future to discuss any mutually beneficial opportunities. If you do not at present have a need for a professional with my experience but know of someone who may, please be so kind as to pass my letter and CV on to that individual, or simply call me.

Yours sincerely,

Lisa Botkin

Lisa Botkin

enclosure

'Cold' cover letter to employment industry professional (international operations)

Franklin Townsend
1 Any Street • Anytown AA1 1AA
Home 12345 678901 • Mobile 1098765 4321 • internationaloperations@email.com

(Date)

Ms _____
(Title)
ABC Ltd
1 Industry Plaza
Anytown AA1 1AA

Dear Ms _____:

Over the years, I have built a successful career in **international operations and project management** on my ability to assess situations quickly and accurately, identify problems and focus on strategies that obtain results. I am currently seeking a challenging opportunity with an internationally focused, growth-orientated organization. I am willing to explore interim assignments and consulting projects as well as senior management opportunities. My enclosed CV details some of my accomplishments and credentials.

I have extensive experience in **diplomacy and international public affairs** dealing with foreign government officials, Heads of State, and Ambassadors as well as FTSE 100 senior executives. Building effective teams and inspiring others to peak performance are among my strengths. I am particularly adept at living and working effectively in foreign countries and with individuals of various cultural backgrounds. As such, I am interested in opportunities in both the UK and abroad.

Feasibility studies, crisis resolution and international risk assessment are areas where I excel. Unit construction and operations, mining/drilling and industrial equipment procurement, and sales and distribution are areas where I may be of particular assistance, but my skills are transferable to virtually any industry.

I look forward to hearing from you to discuss any mutually beneficial opportunities that you may be aware of. Please feel free to send my CV to others who may have a need for a professional of my calibre.

Yours sincerely,

Franklin Townsend

Franklin Townsend

enclosure

'Cold' e-mail to employment industry professional (IT professional)

From: Jacqueline Smith [smithITpro@mindspring.com]
To: hr@corptech.com
Cc:
Subject: REF: Project management

Dear Mr _____:

Capitalizing on my success managing IT design and implementation projects for ABC Design in Anytown, I am seeking a professional opportunity where my project management, customer relations and organizational skills can benefit your clients. With this goal in mind, I have attached for your consideration a CV outlining my qualifications.

Some of the experiences I would bring to a position with your company include:

- *defining project parameters, including interviewing clients to assess goals and objectives, and developing specifications and project deliverables;*
- *serving on leadership teams that have managed project budgets of up to £10 million to consistently meet customer timeline requirements and budgetary constraints;*
- *coordinating activities of programmers, web developers, software engineers, network engineers, graphic artists and customer representatives to meet project goals;*
- *testing and validating applications during development stages and upon completion to ensure client objectives are met.*

I am open to relocation anywhere in the United Kingdom and would eagerly accept either contract assignments or permanent employment. I believe that my capabilities would allow me to serve your needs and benefit your clients. I would enjoy meeting you to discuss my qualifications in greater detail. Please contact me via phone or e-mail to arrange an initial interview.

Thank you for your time and consideration. I look forward to speaking to you soon.

Yours sincerely,

Jacqueline Smith
12345 678901
smithITpro@mindspring.com

'Cold' e-mail to employment industry professional (computer professional)

From: Sally Winston [computerpro@earthlink.net]
To: mcooper@isculptors.com
Cc:
Subject: Technology guru, plus global experience

Dear Ms _____:

My broad background in all aspects of computers, from design and installation to user training and maintenance, coupled with my business operations expertise, are the assets I would bring to a position with one of your clients.

I currently hold a management level position with ABC Graphics, a firm that designs and builds flight simulators for UK and foreign governments. I provide the electronics expertise in completing approximately 12 major projects annually, which means I conceptualize the simulators' computerized mechanisms, direct the design and manufacturing processes, then install and test the systems at clients' sites around the globe.

In addition to providing technical expertise, the other major aspect of my job involves aggressively targeting new business. At a point when ABC was facing an essentially saturated UK market, I designed and implemented an internet website, then had it translated into several languages to target international clientele. The site generated 80 per cent of our new business within one year.

Other assets I would bring to this position include skill in relocating entire company computer systems from existing facilities to new or expanded sites, as well as experience servicing all major brands of PCs. I am extremely familiar with nearly every computer-associated component, program or operating system on today's market.

Thank you in advance for taking a few moments to review my CV. I am confident that the experience you'll find outlined therein will be valuable to your company. Kindly contact me at your earliest convenience to schedule a professional interview.

Yours sincerely,

Sally Winston
12345 678901
computerpro@earthlink.net

'Cold' e-mail to employment industry professional (programmer/analyst)

From: Suresh Gupta [certifiedprogrammer@yahoo.com]
To: hr@techvibes.com
Cc:
Subject: REF: Programming assignments

Dear Ms _____:

My certification in computer programming, along with my professional background in electro-mechanical engineering, are among the primary assets I would bring to a programmer/analyst position with one of your clients.

As part of my training at the Computer Institute in South London, I was required to design, write, code, edit and modify an e-commerce website. The project succeeded not only because of my skill in applying my technical knowledge, but also because of my strict attention to detail.

Currently I'm employed at ABC Pharmaceuticals in Lincoln, executing experiments on electrical/mechanical equipment I was involved in manufacturing to ensure conformance to customers' specifications.

I am also committed to furthering my professional education, which is key for success in this field. I plan to augment my knowledge by attending and completing relevant courses.

I am confident this background equips me well for success with one of your clients. Kindly review my CV, then please contact me at your earliest convenience to arrange an interview.

Yours sincerely,

Suresh Gupta
12345 678910
certifiedprogrammer@yahoo.com

'Cold' e-mail to employment industry professional (IT management)

From: Maria Costas [ITexpert@anyserver.co.uk]
To: cfloyd@mtechit.com
Cc:
Subject: Top productivity enhancement professional

Dear Mr/Ms _____:

Leading information technology projects for high-growth companies is my area of expertise. Throughout my career I have been successful in identifying organizational needs and leading the development and implementation of industry-specific technologies to improve productivity, quality, operating performance and profitability.

In my current position at XYZ Company, I have initiated and managed the technological advances, administrative infrastructures, training programmes, and customization initiatives that have enabled the company to generate over £3 million in additional profits in the past year. The scope of my responsibilities has included the entire project management cycle, from initial needs assessment and technology evaluations through vendor selection, internal systems development, beta testing, quality review, technical and user documentation, and full-scale, multi-site implementation.

My technological and management talents are complemented by my strong training, leadership and customer service skills. I am accustomed to providing ongoing support and relate well with employers at all levels of an organization, including senior executives. Most notable are my strengths in facilitating cooperation among cross-functional project teams to ensure that all projects are delivered on time, within budget, and as per specifications.

Originally hired for a one-year contract at XYZ Company, I have been offered a permanent position within the company. However, I am interested in greater challenges and would welcome the opportunity to meet you to determine the contributions I can make to your client. I will call you next week to set up an appointment.

Yours sincerely,

Maria Costas
12345 678910
ITexpert@anyserver.co.uk

'Cold' e-mail to employment industry professional (systems integration)

From: Michael Wilson [systemsintegrationpro@hotmail.com]
To: hr@sap-si.com
Cc:
Subject: Onstar engineer plus more

Dear Company Representative:

My solid background in electrical engineering supported by extensive management and product development experience are key assets that I can contribute to your client's future success.

Throughout my career I have worked with cutting-edge technologies, including **embedded microprocessors, RF, telecommunications,** and **wireless,** in the development and manufacture of products for varied industries. In all my positions, integrating software, firmware and hardware to create unique applications has been a key strength. Some of these applications that proved quite marketable include development of custom instrumentation and a PC-based network for tracking vehicles in transit. In addition, I have also played an important role in both the sales and customer support process, helping ABC win its largest municipal contract with the City of London.

Currently, I am exploring opportunities in the telecommunications industry where I can contribute significant expertise in systems integration. I welcome the opportunity to meet you to explore areas of mutual benefit. Attached is my CV for your review.

In order to present my credentials more fully, I will follow up with a call to you to answer any questions you may have. Thank you for your consideration.

Yours sincerely,

Michael Wilson
12345 678910
systemsintegrationpro@hotmail.com

'Cold' e-mail to employment industry professional (systems administrator)

From: Dae Sung Kwan [systemsspecialist@mindspring.com]
To: gdawson@abc.com
Cc:
Subject: Sys admin/people skills/military background

Dear Ms _____:

If you seek a new Systems Administrator who is more than just technically orientated, but also people orientated, then we have good reason to meet. As you'll find in my attached CV, I possess extensive technical skills and experience. What is more difficult to portray in a brief CV are my people skills.

Several colleagues, supervisors, subordinates and end-users have commended me for my interpersonal skills. I am dedicated to helping others with their technical issues and sharing my knowledge to help them complete their work more efficiently. My job is to serve as a support person, there to keep the system operating smoothly for end-users, as well as to provide them with training. I also understand that most technical projects are a team effort. Again, I have been recognized for my abilities as a team player as well as a team leader. I have a proven track record of taking projects and running with them, but the successes are a result of the combined efforts of the whole team. Whether it's a matter of motivating others, coordinating tasks, or just doing my part, I can do it.

My technical skills speak for themselves. My primary focus has been on Windows NT. In fact, I am currently pursuing my Microsoft Certified Systems Engineer designation. My plans are to attain this at about the time I leave the army. I will be able to bring this added expertise to an employer.

A meeting with you would be greatly appreciated. Please feel free to contact me to arrange a time or to gain further information on my background. I am sure you will agree that I am right for the job after reviewing my CV and meeting me in person.

Thank you for your time and prompt reply. I look forward to meeting you in the near future.

Yours sincerely,

Dae Sung Kwan
12345 678910
systemsspecialist@mindspring.com

Power phrases

Consider using adaptations of these key phrases in your 'cold' letters to employment service professionals.

I am an optimist, thrive on challenges, lead by example, and readily adapt to situations. If your client – international or domestic – would benefit from these kinds of qualities, we should meet each other. If you would like to call or write, I look forward to telling you more about my background.

As a dedicated listener, I am usually assigned to client/customer relations and produce notable results in client/customer retention – even under the least favourable conditions.

An industry association referred to _____ as an active and selective executive search firm, and mentioned your name because of your work in logistics. I liked that referral and think our meeting would be mutually beneficial.

I would like to talk to you personally to discuss our meeting further. I suggest next week, the week of 13th October, when you have a free minute. I have asked my staff to forward your message immediately in case I am unavailable when you call. I look forward to hearing from you.

Please include my name in your job search database.

Including a mortgage loan benefit, I am currently earning £4,500 per month plus a car allowance. This should provide you with an indication of my present job level. Your suggestions or comments would be appreciated.

For 25 years, my family operated one of the most prestigious landmark restaurants in Oxford. From the age of six, I was a part of the family workforce – I couldn't wait to 'help'. That attitude pervades my work ethic, and I'm grateful for the training that helped me to develop an attitude of service, teamwork and pride in performance and product.

One of your clients is looking for me, if not today then sometime in the near future. I know good people are hard to find because I've had to find them myself.

I have the depth of experience it takes to make a positive contribution.

Income is in the mid-five figures, but the right opportunity is the motivating factor. References and CV are available. With my well-rounded professional background, I look forward to a new and interesting career opportunity through your agency.

Because my enthusiasm is contagious and I personally project credibility, people are inclined to (1) cooperate and participate wholeheartedly on projects with which I'm involved, (2) consider products I recommend favourably, and (3) be open to my efforts on their behalf when they experience problems or dissatisfaction.

The following are some highlights of my track record for your consideration:

I understand your clients frequently ask you to locate senior operating executives with much higher than average ability to accomplish difficult jobs quickly and profitably.

It is my goal to play an integral part in the development, operation and success of a small to mid-sized company where the diversity of my experience and the level of my commitment can be used to their fullest advantage and I can have the satisfaction of seeing the results of my efforts… really *impacting profitability!*

Please call this week so we can explore potential opportunities more fully. Use the home number, please; our company's uncertain financial status is stirring up the office rumour mill. Thank you for your time and attention.

I am a motivated and dedicated leader. Many of my staff have worked for me from 10 to 30 years. My enthusiasm for meeting goals and accomplishing objectives has been contagious, and I know how to reward outstanding performance without disturbing a profit and loss balance. My employees and I thrive on a 'family' environment with no loss of respect or production.

As a former business owner, I am well aware of the needs, concerns and challenges facing management. By the same token, I am accustomed to operating with the best interests of the total business in mind and at heart, as well. I operate expeditiously, constantly seeking the best use of time, effort, resources and money… for my staff and myself.

My experience as an entrepreneur as well as an employee of a demanding employer gives me the unique ability to empathize with the needs of management as well as the assertiveness necessary to represent management effectively.

I'm seeking an opportunity to join an employer who can benefit from my expertise and experience while offering me the opportunity for challenge, continued professional growth, as well as commensurate compensation.

I'm a dedicated listener and an accomplished problem solver, always seeking to assist clients to accomplish their mission. My clients express a sense of trust and confidence in me and my recommendations because my sincerity and my efforts invested on their behalf are evident and consistent. They never have a doubt that I really care and will operate in their best interests.

Broadcast letter (teaching position)

This instructor was awarded the position she aspired to.

SARA ANNE STEEL

1 Any Street • Anytown AA1 1AA • 12345 678910 • sasteel55@mindspring.com

3 May 20–

Human Resources Office
City University
111 Any Avenue
Anytown AA1 1AA

I am interested in ideas,
not merely visual products.
– Marcel Duchamp

Dear Human Resources Coordinator:

An instructor in good standing at ABC College, I am very interested in moving from painting, design and art appreciation instructor to your recently posted **Jewellery Repair and Design Tutor position**. I was thrilled to discover an **exceptional match between your requirements for this opening and my skills and qualifications**. The enclosed CV reflects a progressive career path and a credible applicant for this position. Qualifications follow:

Your Requirements:	My Qualifications:
Diploma in metal working	Diploma in Jewellery/Metalsmithing from XYZ School of Art, 20–.
Bench work/experience with jewellery repair practices	Jewellery repair and bench work for local retail jeweller. Experience includes stone setting, soldering, pearl stringing, ring sizing, jewellery designing, and riveting. Valuation and maintenance.
Teaching, jewellery design education, and curriculum development	Two years' teaching experience. Comprehensive knowledge of casting gained through education, freelance and contract work includes wax carving, wax chasing, and mould making.
Excellent communication skills	Excellent oral and written self-expression. Give clear instructions and relate well to students. Relaxed communication style fosters encouragement and support. Subscribe to open-door policy.
Commitment to working with a diverse population	Successfully teach and interact with physically and mentally challenged individuals, as well as people of all ages from varied backgrounds and cultures.
Ability to manage projects and set specific objectives.	Extremely goal-orientated, giving particular attention to planning and follow-up for positive results. Day planner and 'to-do' lists spark productivity. Experience coordinating special events such as art shows, parties and dinners.

Page 1 of 2

Sara Anne Steel
Page 2 of 2

Besides these qualifications, I am an avid photographer, have an interest in gemology, and produce an average of one large art object a month. Personal qualities include a cheerful, energetic demeanour, positive attitude, dedication, self-sufficiency and creative/innovative idea generation. I am passionate about art, teaching, and mentoring, and enjoy the twofold return of the enthusiasm I bring to class.

Additionally, positive feedback from both peers and students includes:

- 'I have never seen painting so strong from the art department,' and 'you are raising the bar.'
- 'I got more from this class (Painting I) than most others I've had.'
- 'This was the most exciting/stimulating class I've taken in 1½ years.'
- 'It was nice to see your work and know that it came from someone as normal as the rest of the world.'
- 'Your help contributed most to my learning. You were not afraid to help in any way you could.'

Comments like these are especially fulfilling. Other job satisfaction comes from observing facial expressions when students finally comprehend a theory or concept and helping students discover and expand their creativity.

I am willing to handle the responsibility and safety issues involved in running a jewellery/metals studio and believe properly taught techniques and procedures are of vital importance. The prospect of teaching in my field and being on the ground floor of future jewellery department development energizes me. I am confident I will continue to offer a fresh perspective to course and curriculum development at ABC College and look forward to a personal interview to further discuss your needs. Thank you for your time and consideration.

Yours sincerely,

Sara Anne Steel

Sara Anne Steel

Enclosure: CV

Broadcast letter (assistant director of student accommodation)

BRENDA YOUNG

1 Any Street • Anytown AA1 1AA • 12345 678901 • studentlife@college.edu

Miss Christine Timmons   12 January 20–
Assistant Director for Student Accommodation
University of London
111 Any Avenue
Anytown AA1 1AA

Re: Reference Code: TC-E-5556E2

Dear Miss Timmons:

In response to your ad for an Assistant Director of Student Accommodation advertised in Sunday's *Newsday*, I have enclosed my CV for your review. To illustrate my qualifications further, the following outlines the scope of my experience as it pertains to the position's requirements.

Your requirements	My qualifications
• Bachelor's degree or four years' experience in lieu of degree.	• Master's degree in Clinical Counselling • Eight years' combined experience in hall of residence administration and counselling capacities.
• Promote and develop educational programming and maintain extensive budget.	• Plan, develop and implement educational programmes, and manage an operational budget.
• Administration of three to five halls of residence housing approximately 1,000 students.	• Administration of halls of residence housing up to 500 students.
• Supervise, develop and evaluate three to five full-time halls of residence directors.	• Supervise, develop and evaluate 26 Resident Advisors with direct responsibility for four RAs and a Head Resident Advisor (HRA).
• Develop departmental policies and procedures, manage area office including rent, occupancy and facilities records.	• Direct all aspects of front desk management and facilities maintenance operations.
• Assist in the development and leadership of departmental committees, and serve as manager for student conduct cases.	• One year as chair of Committees and Organizations for the Student body.

Thank you for your review and consideration. I look forward to hearing from you soon.

Yours sincerely,

Brenda Young

Brenda Young

Broadcast letter (financial planning professional)

The employer was so impressed with the detail of the cover letter that he offered a position to this applicant at the initial interview.

David Meyers
1 Any Street ▪ Anytown AA1 1AA
Phone: 12345 678910 ▪ Mobile: 1098765 4321 ▪ E-mail: meyerstown@juno.com

19 September 20–

David Borgrum
ABC Financial Manager
111 Any Avenue
Anytown AA1 1AA

Dear Mr Borgrum,

The Rock. ABC is known internationally by this symbol of security and permanence, the assurance to their clients the company will always be there. The corporate slogan 'Increasing and Protecting Your Wealth' can only be accomplished through principled management, effective investment strategies and ethical financial planning.

The relationship. With corporate scandal and financial malfeasance perceived to be the norm, now, more than ever, a relationship built on integrity and mutual respect is paramount to success in the financial services industry. As a goal-orientated financial planning professional who possesses strong marketing and communication skills, I am confident that upon review of my qualifications you will find I have the solid combination of experience and achievement that ABC looks for in its representatives.

My qualifications include:

- Registered Investment Advisor.
- BA in Economics.
- Commitment to client satisfaction and quality service through needs assessments.
- Demonstrated results in business development and execution of marketing strategies.
- Effective communication and presentation skills necessary to articulate product benefits clearly and accurately to clients.
- Outstanding time management and organizational ability.
- A willingness to 'go the extra mile' for client and corporation.

The consultation. Inherent to every successful consultation is my obligation to obtain a comprehensive financial background in order to meet the clients' future needs and objectives. Performing an effective client needs assessment gives me the decisive edge when the client makes their financial planning decisions. Furthermore, I am skilled at new business development, cold calling and seminar presentations. Employers and colleagues have consistently praised my attention to detail, hard work ethic and ability to deal with the most complex client engagements.

Please contact me at your earliest convenience to set up an interview concerning employment opportunities within your company. I look forward to hearing from you.

Yours sincerely,

David Meyers

David Meyers

Broadcast letter (heavy equipment operator)

Relocating to Scotland, Jack wants to secure a position that could capitalize on his diverse range of skills.

·· **JACK L CROUTHER**

Dear Sir or Madam:

Please accept the enclosed CV in application for your Heavy Equipment Operator position advertised in *The Times Journal*.

My diverse range of experience includes over 10 years' experience operating and maintaining heavy equipment. In my current position, I operate backhoes, loaders, lulls, Gallion cranes, Ditch Witch trenchers (large and walk-behind), fork lifts, street sweepers and bucket trucks. In addition, I supervise the troubleshooting, maintenance and repair of all of the department's equipment.

Of equal importance are my supervisory and leadership skills where I have managed multiple crews of up to 40 employees. Being extremely diligent, I have assumed responsibility for overseeing and monitoring various projects and issues that affect the daily operations, efficiency and profitability of the company. I am recognized by senior management for consistently completing projects on time and within budget.

Working in several trades during my career has developed my strong multitasking abilities which have proven to be an asset in my current position. Additional areas of experience include plumbing, irrigation, landscaping, electrical work, fibre optics and carpentry. In each of these areas, I have received training and have worked independently.

If you are in need of a person with my skills, I would welcome the opportunity to meet you to determine the contributions I can make to your company.

Thank you for your consideration.

Yours faithfully,

Jack L Crouther

Jack L Crouther

---

1 Any Street • Anytown AA1 1AA
Phone: 12345 678910 • Mobile: 1098765 4321• jlcrouther@yahoo.com

Broadcast letter (chef / hotel / restaurant manager)

Michael started as a chef and went into the management side of the restaurant. He is now hoping to work for a multi-restaurant chain in a management capacity.

Michael J Fisher

1 Any Street
Anytown AA1 1AA
12345 678910

Dear Sir/Madam:

I am confident that my extensive experience as a chef and hotel/restaurant manager would serve as an asset to a position in your organization. My career began 23 years ago as an apprentice training under several notable internationally known chefs. Since that time I have been involved extensively in the area of food services management and marketing.

I am currently General Manager and Corporate Executive Chef of ABC London. In 20–, I was hired to start up this 225-seat restaurant. The casual dining establishment is part of XYZ Brands Ltd. I am responsible for all financial reporting and instituted key control systems to meet the standards of the parent company. Additional achievements include gaining excellent media publicity, creative menu development, and directing on- and off-site catering for many city events. I was asked to coordinate all aspects of our new construction and assist in the design aspects of the kitchen.

As Director of Operations for DEF Catering and the DEF Restaurant in Oxford, my staff and I expanded the business to accommodate parties ranging from 10 to 4,000 people and grossed over £1.5 million in sales.

Working as Director of Operations and Executive Chef for JKL Hotels, I oversaw all profit and loss functions for a 165-seat à la carte restaurant and a 1,000-seat banquet facility. The hotel had an 18-hole Championship Golf Course that I managed, with an active membership of 1,000 members.

I gained extensive international experience working as Executive Chef for MNO, a five-star-rated restaurant in New Zealand. I prepared food for the Prime Minister, various heads of state, and visiting dignitaries. I obtained my New Zealand Master Chef's Certification. In addition, I served as an Executive Pastry Chef and Chef for a Hawaiian hotel owned and operated by the Sheraton Corporation.

Thank you for your consideration. I look forward to speaking to you personally regarding my qualifications and how I can contribute positively as a member of your management staff.

Yours faithfully,

Michael J Fisher

Michael J Fisher

Broadcast letter (maintenance mechanic)

Elizabeth was a bus driver who changed to a warehouse position, and eventually to a higher-paying maintenance mechanic position. After redundancy, she wishes to continue her career as a mechanic.

ELIZABETH DENTON

1 Any Street ~ Anytown AA1 1AA

12345 678910 (H) ~ 1098765 4321 (M) ~ E-mail: lizdent3@msn.com

RE: Maintenance Mechanic

Dear Sir/Madam:

As a professional **Facilities** and **Maintenance Mechanic**, I understand that success depends on several factors. These include timely upkeep of machinery maintenance and repair, supervision of maintenance programmes, and monitoring outside contractors. My extensive hands-on experience as a mechanic has allowed me to ensure the efficient completion of projects and adherence to company safety requirements.

Throughout my career I have been promoted and have acquired increasing responsibilities within every position. In my latest position as a Mechanic for ABC Foods, I had the reputation for excellent machinery knowledge and a keen attention to detail.

ABC Foods is downsizing the factory in Anytown, and I have accepted a voluntary redundancy from the company. I would like to continue my career with a new company offering me new challenges.

Thank you for your consideration. I possess excellent hands-on knowledge as well as supervisory expertise, and I look forward to meeting you personally so that we can discuss how I can make a positive contribution to your team.

Yours faithfully,

Elizabeth Denton

Elizabeth Denton

Enclosure

Broadcast letter (database engineer)

Edward Kumamoto
kumamotoed@islandnet.com

1 Any Street
Anytown AA1 1AA

Home: 12345 687910
Mobile: 1098765 4321

(Date)
Phillip _____
(Title)
ABC Ltd
1 Industry Plaza
Anytown AA1 1AA

Dear Mr _____:

Empowering your employees with the information and tools necessary to make better strategic business decisions is very likely to improve your company's competitive advantage and profitability. I can do this through insightful strategic planning and the delivery of superior data warehouse and decision support systems.

My extensive career experience in data warehousing, database administration and business systems development, coupled with my commitment to exceed customer expectations and my focus on achieving sustainable strategic competitive advantage, are the primary assets I would bring to your Director of Database Engineering position. I have successfully delivered numerous data warehouse projects that were effectively aligned with company strategic objectives. I am also highly skilled at directing teams on complex initiatives and improving processes, communication, teamwork and quality.

As a senior-level employee of Information Technology Ltd, I have established an excellent track record of successfully managing large complex projects. Notably, I managed a £10 million development project for XYZ Ltd, building and implementing their first enterprise data warehouse and certain downstream divisional data marts. So successful was this project that within three months of implementation it established itself as the recognized supreme source of accurate company data for all of XYZ's business units. Additionally, it met tight service level commitments over 97 per cent of the time and experienced no downtime due to programming error.

As a Project Leader/Manager for DEF Business Systems, I also managed the development of a large data warehouse. I led the design and development efforts for this data warehouse of sales information for their Speciality Products division. This was the first data warehouse developed at DEF that successfully met user expectations.

An additional asset I would bring to your organization is competency in correlating data warehousing functions with overall company goals. I am skilled in providing counsel to senior managers and executives and adept at monitoring data warehouse systems to ensure their value and usefulness to an organization as a whole.

I am confident that this experience equips me for success as your Director of Database Engineering. Kindly review my CV, then please contact me at your earliest convenience to arrange a professional interview.

Yours sincerely,

Edward Kumamoto

Broadcast letter (senior technical sales)

STEPHANIE PAIGE NEWMAN
1 Any Street ▪ Anytown AA1 1AA ▪ 12345 678910
techsales@anyserver.co.uk

Emily _____   (Date)
(Title)
ABC Ltd
1 Industry Plaza
Anytown AA1 1AA

Dear Ms _____:

As a seasoned Technical Sales and Marketing Consultant, I've generated considerable new business for my previous employers, and now I'd like to do the same for you. For the past 15 years I have pursued an increasingly successful career in telecommunications sales and marketing. Among my accomplishments are:

SALES
Qualified to spearhead the entire sales management process, from initial client consultation and needs assessment through to product demonstration, price and service negotiations, and final sales closings.

MARKETING
Success in orchestrating all aspects of developing a gainful marketing strategy, from competitive market intelligence and trend analysis, product development, launch and positioning to distribution management and customer care.

TELECOMMUNICATIONS & NETWORK SOLUTIONS
Recognized for pioneering technology solutions that meet the needs of complex customer service, logistics, and distribution operations. Able to test operations to ensure optimum systems functionality and availability, guide systems implementation across multiple platforms and deliver user training and support programmes that outpace the competition.

I hope you will contact me in the very near future. You'll find my address and telephone number above. I would welcome the opportunity to contribute my skills to the success of your marketing team and look forward to learning about any available opportunities in your organization.

Yours sincerely,

Stephanie Newman

Stephanie Newman

enclosure

Broadcast letter (telecommunications)

Tom Clancy
....
1 Any Street • Anytown AA1 1AA • telecompro@anyserver.co.uk
Home: 12345 678901 • Work: 55555 555555 • Mobile: 1098765 4321

(Date)

Emily _____
(Title)
ABC Ltd
1 Industry Plaza
Anytown AA1 1AA

Dear Ms _____:

If you need someone with proven international success who will really listen to your clients'
needs and has leaped over cultural barriers to forge some of the most profitable technical
opportunities in the telecommunications field, I am your number 1 choice for any opportunity in
international or domestic sales or marketing.

For the last 10 years, my work in strategic partnering, developing alliances, creating new
opportunities and exceeding multinational clients' expectations has helped my employers to more
than double their sales. However, follow-up, tenacious attention to detail, and my ability to listen
have solidified longstanding relationships with major players worldwide.

With a global leader in telecommunications, I received three promotions in four years due to my
success in managing contacts, motivating staff and implementing marketing campaigns that
delivered ROI threefold.

Since 20, I have:

- Marketed a full range of data and voice communication services to multinational corporations
  and Internet service providers in Japan, Southeast Asia, Canada and Western Europe.
- Brought in 28 new global accounts representing up to a 250 per cent increase in business –
  currently handle brand management efforts for XYZ on track to exceed annual goal; managed
  20 accounts requiring broadband connectivity to international locations.
- Created the first transcontinental ATM circuit and earned one of the most prestigious awards
  in the company.
- Trained technical associates in ATM and employed knowledge of DWDM, SONET, SDMS, and
  TCP/IP technology to create some of the most cost-effective networks on the planet.

Page 1 of 2

Tom Clancy
Page 2 of 2

If these proven successes sound like the work of a go-getter you need on board:

- Consider that, in just two years with a system software developer, I added £1.5M in new business, trained an all-Japanese staff in direct marketing principles, and launched direct sales campaigns that increased client awareness of our services.

Additionally, my efforts with an international contractor:

- Partnered the parent company with Japan-based joint venture interests that enabled the first UK-built airport in Japan.
- Kept Japanese executives and high-ranking government officials apprised of progress – and landed two additional opportunities for a total of £10M in business in just a year.

Technically speaking:

- I have worked with ATM, Frame Relay, Private Line, SONET, DWDM, SNA/SDLE, SDMS, and IP, and managed networks and a diverse array of hardware and software packages – in addition to holding numerous Novell and Windows specialized certifications.

I love calling on clients who have been let down by other reps, because I know my negotiating skills, ability to cross cultural barriers and generate win–win opportunities will get the decision-maker to sign every time.

Reviewing my attached CV, you will note doctoral, master's and bachelor's degrees – and a host of quantifiable results and technical training that serve only to enhance my drive and enthusiasm. I will gladly set aside time to meet you and discuss how my knowledge of technology, client relations and strategic partnering can become your biggest asset.

I will take the liberty of contacting you on Monday at 10 am. If you need to reach me, please feel free to contact me at 12345 678901. Thanking you in advance for the opportunity to meet you,

Yours sincerely,

Tom Clancy

Tom Clancy

enclosure

Broadcast letter (senior R&D engineer)

Samantha Robinson

1 Any Street • Anytown AA1 1AA
12345 678910 • R&Dpro@email.com

SENIOR R&D ENGINEER... patent holder... launched x no. new products... recognized worldwide... created win–win alliances... cornered global markets...

(Date)

Phillip _____
(Title)
ABC Ltd
1 Industry Plaza
Anytown AA1 1AA

Dear Mr _____:

If your R&D-to-market time needs a sense of urgency, creativity and a seasoned coordinator of people and priorities, I am one individual you need to discuss the ABC POSITION with. Here's why:

- STRATEGIC PLANNING: Etched long- and short-term technological plans that kept a £2B manufacturer ahead of its competition since 20–

- COORDINATED RESOURCES: 20+ years in planning, reviewing and benchmarking technical performance, meeting budgetary goals, and coordinating interlaboratory and interdepartmental efforts

- IGNITED STAFFS' CREATIVITY: Led efforts and piqued an in-house multidisciplinary R&D staff's synergy; got x no. new products to market

- ENRICHED KNOWLEDGE: Trained sales, marketing, and technical staffs since 19–; well-known for abilities to communicate new ideas, selected for numerous assignments in product training worldwide

- MOVED THE MARKET TO OUR PRODUCT: Recognized expert – created the need for cutting-edge technology in the cutting-tool market by featuring results in technical articles for leading publications

- INTEGRATED OPERATIONS: one of two individuals to integrate a newly acquired company's R&D with parent company's

- IGNORED STIGMAS: First person to involve marketing with R&D-created pathway between R&D and marketing, bringing projects to market in record time; landed £10 million+ in new accounts – only non-salesperson to get a one-of-a-kind annual sales award

-MORE -

- IMPECCABLE RECORD: Achieved 70 to 80 per cent first-time success rate in field testing for all products developed; hold x no. UK patents; consulted worldwide by engineers and scientists; published; presenter at technical conferences since post-doctoral fellowship

Reviewing my credentials and past results, you will note they occurred in the XYZ field. However, I am confident the core *technical, interpersonal and organizational expertise I bring to your staff and customers would easily fit* at ABC LTD.

If you need *a driven problem solver who can get your people moving*, I am readily available to discuss how I can channel my more than two decades of success to your POSITION at ABC LTD. I will be in the area next month, and would appreciate meeting you then.

I am in a position to move to the London area, and *am ready to demonstrate how I can reignite your R&D efforts and create a flurry of opportunity*. Should you need added information, please do not hesitate to contact me at 12345 678910 or R&Dpro@email.com.

Yours sincerely,

Samantha Robinson

Samantha Robinson

enclosure

Broadcast letter (multilingual sales manager)

Robert Rodriguez

---

1 Any Street ~ Anytown AA1 1AA
Mobile: 1098765 4321 ~ Pager: 123456 7890 ~ E-mail: robrodriguez@hotmail.com

Fluent in Spanish... time management skills... eight years' front-line experience... service-orientated positions... trainer... presentation expertise...

(Date)

Emily _____
(Title)
ABC Ltd
1 Industry Plaza
Anytown AA1 1AA

Dear Ms _____:

If you know your *customers and operations deserve attention to detail*, as well as a high-energy individual who is *fluent in Spanish and makes people a number 1 priority*, I am one individual you need to interview for a ZYX position at ABC Ltd.

Reviewing my credentials, you will note that I have taught in a secondary school for the past eight years. This exposure to *daily planning, keeping people motivated and moving* ahead can be an immediate asset at ABC, and here are some areas that align with your needs:

– SUCCESS IN DIRECT COMMUNICATION: Whether with students, decision-makers or the general public, my presentation skills kept people interested, involved and properly served...

– MULTILINGUAL ABILITIES: Fluent in Spanish, Japanese and Russian – despite having a Spanish-only background, mastered the dialects of Russian and Japanese and was teaching classes...

– ALWAYS LOOKING FOR IMPROVEMENTS: Successfully integrated technology with additional conversational strategies... working for a distributor as an undergraduate, took initiative to revamp routing – increased productivity and service... increased a student's competency from 31 per cent to 100 per cent while a student...

– FOCUS ON SERVICE: Made individual needs a priority as a teacher – adept at varying approach to suit individual personalities and priorities...

– MOTIVATED: Worked up to 30 hours weekly while pursuing degree... proven abilities to juggle diverse assignments opened door for additional assignments and leadership roles...

Page 1 of 2

Robert Rodriguez
Page 2 of 2

I want to channel my communication, presentation, customer service, training and organizational skills, and the ZYX opportunity at ABC Ltd matches my goal for a transferable opportunity. *You would benefit from someone with a proven track record in front-line positions, and your customers and operations will have a team player who knows how to set goals, meet goals and keep customers' needs at the forefront.*

I will take the liberty of contacting you on _____ at _____ to confirm your receipt of my information and briefly discuss how my energy and talents could be your asset. I would also like to arrange a meeting at that time. Should you need to reach me sooner, I can be contacted at 12345 678910 or robrodriguez@hotmail.com.

Yours sincerely,

Robert Rodriguez

Robert Rodriguez

enclosure

Broadcast letter (management)

LORI PAULEY

1 Any Street • Anytown AA1 1AA • 12345 678910

(Date)
Phillip _____
(Title)
ABC Ltd
1 Industry Plaza
Anytown AA1 1AA

Dear Mr _____:

People will only give you what you're willing to accept. That's why my staff employed the Golden Rule every day, treating customers the way they themselves would like to be treated.

If you need someone with a technical background who has hired and kept top talent challenged and on their toes delivering exemplary service, then consider that in 20+ years:

– I turned my knowledge of physics and business into profits and operational success – for my staff, my employers, and myself.

– I took on the lead engineering position in my second year with an industry giant, skipping over the traditional 12-year career path – I simply outworked everyone and never said I couldn't do something or get it done on time or within budget.

– I earned full latitude in decision making after proving my team's understanding of a new target market's needs – I introduced more products than my successors, improved processes, and cut manufacturing and warranty costs by roughly £1M the first year.

– Operations I had an impact on experienced extremely low employee turnover – and employees met or exceeded customer expectations 100 per cent of the time.

I've made sure my staff are so service-oriented that the customer doesn't have to ask for warranty repairs or 'the next step' – they have the answers or have already performed the warranty work.

And when my name is on a project, it is always on schedule, within budget – and is a winner:

– When a relationship with a speciality manufacturer ended, I spearheaded development of an intake manifold line, analysed and negotiated manufacturing costs, and selected vendors – and launched an 18-unit product line in 18 months that led the industry.

Page 1 of 2

Lori Pauley
Page 2 of 2

–   The first race manifold we developed took the first five finishes in the 19– motorsport race without prior testing by participating teams.

If you seek someone with the work ethic of a business partner, then I am your top choice for the _____ opportunity with ABC Ltd. I fully understand the nuts-and-bolts of customer service, and can certainly combine my financial know-how with proven success in the field at ABC.

Right now I'm ready to step down from entrepreneurial management, simplify my role, and do 'one or three things' well for an organization that values integrity, hard work and creativity.

If I sound like the person you need at ABC, then contact me right away to discuss the _____ opportunity. I can be reached on 12345 678910 after 6 pm Monday to Friday, or at my place of business on 10987 654321 during regular business hours. I will take the liberty of contacting you on Monday at 10 am to briefly screen my qualifications and see if we can arrange an interview.

Yours sincerely,

Lori Pauley

Lori Pauley

enclosure

Broadcast letter (HR generalist)

Elliott Davidson
1 Any Street
Anytown AA1 1AA
12345 678910 • davidsonhrpro@msn.com

HR GENERALIST
9 years advising senior decision-makers on employee matters…
5 years in pension administration for £1B company and 5 affiliates…
15 years delivering HR presentations…
Open enrolment/pension processing for professional employees…
13 years' grievance/disciplinary meeting involvement…
10+ years' training/development, entry through professional levels…
Worked through mergers and reorganizations…
Created award-winning concept for enrolment booklet…
Earned highest ratings throughout career…

(Date)

Phillip _____
(Title)
ABC Ltd
1 Industry Plaza
Anytown AA1 1AA

Dear Mr _____:

If your organization seeks someone to advance your human resource programmes, consider my proven track record. I am ready for a challenge with ABC Ltd, as your recent growth needs someone used to working with new subsidiaries and maintaining the bottom line. I am absolutely ready to step in as your Human Resource Director at ABC Ltd, as my commitment extends to all areas you seek to address.

I bring you and your employees objectivity, knowledge of policy/procedure implementation and interpretation, and hands-on work in an ever-emerging climate. Here are some highlighted abilities that can be put to work immediately at ABC Ltd:

MET THE CHALLENGE: With little notification, stepped in and was an asset in a HR Directorship capacity; administered £20M in pension benefits; initiated multi-tier health plan to better suit regional product needs

Page 1 of 2

ELLIOTT DAVIDSON
2 of 2

BENEFITS: Five years working with open enrolment for all levels of employees – restructured pensions during three internal reorganizations

REMAINED FLEXIBLE: Adapted to the needs of entrepreneurial organizations while continuing a career with major utility company

LEADERSHIP: Entrusted to step in for superiors due to track record in HR; number 1 person consulted by senior managers of a £1B parent company and its five affiliates regarding HR or pensions; negotiated with union leadership, discussed and resolved grievances and complaints

COMMUNITY INVOLVEMENT: Accepted leadership role in major charity organization, keynote speaker for regional fundraising appearances

TRAINING/DEVELOPMENT: Delivered HR and pensions presentations since 1995, safety training, two years

OVER/ABOVE: Travelled over three-year period to help a newly formed company whose explosive growth took it to 2,000 employees in three years (coordinated staffing and pension enrolment while maintaining existing workload); singled out for HR support for special finance division structure, took on policy making/interpretation and HR

If you need someone seasoned in policy making who can interface with decision-makers and keep you 100 per cent compliant with regulations, I am one individual awaiting your call for an interview.

I will call on Monday at 10 am to see if you agree that my background could be an immediate asset, and to arrange a meeting. I can forward a CV for your review immediately. Should you need to reach me sooner, I am on 12345 678910.

Yours sincerely,

Elliott Davidson

Elliott Davidson

~ Pensions ~ Multi-tier Coverage ~ Labour Relations ~ Grievances ~ Arbitration ~
Job Bidding ~ CPP, CRS, PDS ~ Redundancy Compensation ~ Sexual Harassment ~
Safety Training ~ Background Investigations ~

Broadcast letter (operations manager)

A redundant environmental operations manager is trying to get back into a tight job market.

Diane Baldwin
1 Any Street ▪ Anytown AA1 1AA
12345 678910 ▪ operationsmanager@alphone.net

(Date)

ABD Ltd
1 Industry Plaza
Anytown AA1 1AA
Attention Ms Emily_____

Dear Ms_____:

Do you need an experienced, versatile individual who can improve bottom-line profits? I can bring innovative ideas to the position of Operations Manager – ideas that can benefit a service-driven, quality-orientated company like yours. No one has money to burn in a tough economy, which is why adding a ready skilled manager to your staff can reduce time and money.

The match between your needs and my talents is ideal. Why? Because my strengths lie in understanding the labour and manufacturing operations that design, build, install and manage equipment for environmental and production improvements. I am a leader both by example and through effective management of individuals and teams. In short, I have the drive and vision to make a positive difference in any organization.

Dozens of proposed projects have been successfully implemented due to my established reputation for the quality of work completed. The work performed under my direction has come in at, or below, budget and we meet project deadlines.

The enclosed CV summarizes my qualifications and achievements. I would be glad to discuss any of this information with you as an opportunity for employment. Because 'proven skills' are best explained in person, I look forward to our conversation and will call early next week to arrange a meeting. Thank you for taking the time to review my CV and for your consideration.

Yours sincerely,

Diane Baldwin

Diane Baldwin

enclosure

Broadcast letter (pharmaceutical sales)

··**Rebecca Marks**

(Date)

ABC Laboratories
1 Industry Plaza
Anytown AA1 1AA

Dear_____:

ABC Laboratories is one of the fastest-growing companies in the United Kingdom. Your achievements are impressive, and I am eager to make a contribution to your professional team as a Pharmaceutical Sales Representative. Given a chance, based on my enthusiasm and desire to excel, **I can make a positive difference in your company.**

As a recent graduate, my professional experience is limited. However, I believe that you will find that I exhibit intelligence, common sense, initiative, maturity and stability. Various jobs over the last 10 years have required a good attitude and keen interpersonal skills. These jobs, along with my education, life experience and extensive travels, have not only enlightened me intellectually, but have also given me a totally different paradigm compared with other applicants.

Analysing an audience is of utmost importance as a sales representative. As the daughter of a physician, I had extensive exposure to the medical environment. I strongly believe this gives me insight into the way physicians think – that patients' needs come first. Therefore, effective presentations of products must be made in a timely, succinct, and caring manner for successful sales in this industry. My desire is to stay close to the medical field, and working in a pharmaceutical company is exactly where I aspire to be.

After reviewing the enclosed CV, please contact me on 12345 678910 to arrange an interview. Because 'proven skills' are best explained in person, I look forward to discussing how my qualifications can meet your personnel needs and contribute to your company's important mission.

Yours sincerely,

Rebecca Marks

Rebecca Marks

enclosure

···
1 Any Street • Anytown AA1 1AA • 12345 678910

Broadcast letter (information technology programme manager)

DARRYL C WARREN

1 Any Street   12345 678910
Anytown AA1 1AA   ITpro@yahoo.com

(Date)

Mr Philip _____
CEO
ABC
1 Industry Plaza
Anytown AA1 1AA

Dear Mr _____:

May I ask your advice and assistance?

As a result of XYZ's merger with DEF Bank, I am confidentially exploring my opportunities. Although I am confident that I will be offered a role in the new organization, I am currently assessing where I can make the optimal contribution.

I am an Information Technology Programme Manager. In this role, I have led the development of key financial systems and strategic business plans, co-managed the seamless migration of two divisions to another region and founded the GHI Networking Group – delivering noteworthy cost savings and productivity gains. For the past 11 years, I've had dream jobs with leading firms like XYZ and JKL Consulting. I have been entrusted with the direction of large-scale global projects. Many times I learned 'on my feet' – to implement new systems, design testing methods, manage resources, repair damaged vendor relations for mutual gain, and to meet a wide array of challenges. My career has accelerated based on the results, as you'll note from the accomplishments in my enclosed CV.

I'm considering transferring my skills and experience to an organization where I can continue to be a team player and visionary leader for state-of-the-art technology programmes, and where I'll also continue to learn new functional and technical areas. My expertise and interests are in the financial service industry.

I would greatly appreciate a few minutes of your time to discuss my options and glean any suggestions you can offer. I'll phone you in a few days to see if we can arrange a brief meeting.

Thanks very much.

Yours sincerely,

Darryl Warren

Darryl Warren

enclosure

Broadcast letter (director of operations)

A retiree in his late fifties, Barry is still interested in full-time employment and wants to communicate this to his contacts without giving the impression that he is 'old' and 'set in his ways'. The tone of the letter is intended to be energetic and full of youthful enthusiasm.

Barry D Hargrove

1 Any Street • Anytown AA1 1AA • 12345 678910 • operationsvp@yahoo.com

(Date)

Philip _____, (Title)
ABC Equipment
1 Industry Plaza
Anytown AA1 1AA

Dear Mr _____:

Problem – Action – Results. It is a simple formula, and one that I have implemented successfully throughout my long career in manufacturing. A former business associate passed your name on to me after commenting that my business philosophy and style reminded him of a CEO he had heard speak at a conference in Luton. That CEO was you.

It has been several years since I took my first job as a machinist back in Birmingham, but I have never lost my enthusiasm for finding faster and better ways to accomplish goals while cutting costs. I have worked my way up through the ranks from Foreman, to Supervisor, to Manufacturing Engineer, to Operations Manager, and finally Director of Operations. Taking a shot at every new idea that came my way, I may have missed a few, but overall my success rate has been good:

- led a £340M manufacturing firm to earning ISO9002 certification on first attempt;
- revitalized operations at a plant site in Romania by implementing a comprehensive employee training programme;
- increased profits by 200 per cent by identifying and rectifying problems with production and delivery at a Romanian manufacturing facility.

I believe strongly in teams and am comfortable working with R&D, engineering and marketing professionals. My colleagues have expressed appreciation for my direct and honest approach to people and problems.

Between jobs now, I am planning a fishing excursion in Ireland. I will be arriving in London on 20th March and would like to get together with you to explore potential opportunities with ABC Equipment. It would be great to meet over lunch. I will give you a call the morning of the 22nd to see if that can be arranged.

I'm sending you my CV to lay a foundation for our meeting. I look forward to meeting you and exchanging ideas.

Yours sincerely,

Barry Hargrove

enclosure

Broadcast letter (consultant)

A retired executive wants to approach companies directly and offer her unique expertise on a contract or consulting basis.

Elizabeth H Jameson

1 Any Street ◆ Anytown AA1 1AA ◆ Home: 12345 678901

(Date)

Philip _____, (Title)
ABC Company
1 Industry Plaza
Anytown AA1 1AA

Dear Mr _____:

- **Is your organization fully prepared to safeguard its technology services, information and facilities in the event of a disaster?**

- **Are you taking full advantage of high-value and cost-effective vendor agreements?**

- **Do you benefit from high team performance and low turnover?**

If you have answered 'No' to any of the above questions, then allow me to introduce myself and the expertise I can offer your organization. With a proven and award-winning track record of achievement, I offer a unique combination of expertise in disaster recovery/business continuity planning, vendor management/negotiations and team leadership. I am currently offering my services to organizations within the Durham region, and would like to draw your attention to the value I offer.

Put simply, my expertise is delivering results. In previous positions, I have designed, implemented and optimized comprehensive enterprise-class disaster recovery and information security procedures, saved millions in vendor negotiations and third-party service agreements, and led a variety of cross-functional teams to consistently achieve and exceed organizational mandates.

If the following interests you, I invite you to review the attached CV which further illustrates my experience, achievements and expertise:

- **Expert in Disaster Recovery, Information Security and Business Continuity** – expertise includes planning, protection and off-site recovery of technology services, databases and facilities

Page 1 of 2

Elizabeth Jameson
Page 2 of 2

- **Superior contract procurement, negotiation and vendor management capabilities** – proven record for negotiating agreements that improve service quality and save millions in vendor costs

- **Strong, decisive and motivating leader** – reputation for building and leading high-performance teams to breakthrough achievement

- Available for **full-time, part-time, contract and consulting opportunities**

If you believe that you could benefit from a highly motivated and talented professional with a reputation for generating results, then I would welcome the opportunity to meet and discuss the specific value I can offer your organization.

I thank you for your consideration and I look forward to speaking to you soon.

Yours sincerely,

Elizabeth Jameson

Elizabeth Jameson

enclosure: CV

Broadcast letter (project manager)

MICHAEL J SALINGER

1 Any Street • Anytown AA1 1AA • 12345 678910

(Date)

Dear Employer:

Because of current market conditions and high unemployment, I am sure you have many applicants and few **Project or Training Manager** positions to fill. With this letter and CV, please allow me to add to the list; but, may I also give a few reasons why you might want to call me ahead of other qualified candidates should an appropriate position become available?

You will note that my educational and professional **background is broad** and includes experience in post-secondary organizations, community colleges, business and the army. Because of this range of experience, I am able to bring **insight and the ability to relate well to individuals at all levels and from diverse backgrounds**.

Working within for-profit organizations has enabled me to develop an **eye for the bottom line**. Whether it be budgetary or profit-enhancing, I am continually evaluating systems and methods to make them more efficient and productive.

Incredible as it may sound, I appreciate and welcome change. I am **known for my abilities as a change agent**. However, while I may embrace change – technologically or otherwise – I recognize that many do not. Therefore, from a management standpoint, I look for ways to make transitions more tolerable for the people in my charge.

While my CV is comprehensive, it does not fully demonstrate the manner in which I have achieved success. My character, personality and the ability to lead a project or team effectively could be evidenced in a personal meeting. Therefore, I would welcome an interview to discuss your needs and my qualifications further. Thank you for your time and consideration.

Yours sincerely,

Michael Salinger

Michael Salinger

enclosure

Broadcast e-mail (senior buyer / purchasing agent / purchasing manager)

From: Kalista Jabert [purchasingpro@earthlink.net]
To: humanres@aeiu.com
Cc:
Subject: Smart Purchasing Choice

Mr/Ms _____ :

SENIOR BUYER * PURCHASING AGENT * PURCHASING MANAGER

Do you cringe at the high costs your company incurs for goods and services?

Do you need someone who will maximize vendor resources, working hard to secure lower-cost, longer-term contracts?

Do you need someone on board who will immediately slash supply costs and streamline purchasing operations?

With more than 20 years in purchasing, retail sales management, store expansions and new product research and market launch, I believe I may offer just what you're missing.

In my career with Major Company, a premier auto parts and accessories distributor, I have:

- directed procurement of over £200M of goods and services, accounting for 60 per cent of MC's total purchasing budget;
- launched three private label programmes, garnering £500K in additional profits during the first year of distribution;
- recouped £300K in stolen merchandise and prosecuted the employees responsible;
- generated £3M in savings by cultivating partnerships and negotiating long-term contracts with key suppliers.

With the right opportunity, I'd be perfectly willing to relocate. With regard to salary, I understand that flexibility is essential and would consider a salary package appropriate for a person with my outstanding qualifications and dynamic track record of accomplishments. If you're tired of seeing your company's profits slip through your fingers, call me today to arrange a business meeting. I can't wait to discuss how I can benefit your purchasing operation right away. I can be reached at 12345 678910 to arrange our interview.

Yours sincerely,

Kalista Jabert
12345 678910
purchasingpro@earthlink.net

Broadcast e-mail (new product marketing)

From: Elizabeth Stettin [marketingexpert@aol.com]
To: bmathis@planetrecruit.com
Cc:
Subject: Real Marketing Savvy

Dear Mr _____:

If you are looking for a successful executive to take charge of new product marketing, you will be interested in talking to me.

Ten years' experience in every aspect of marketing and sales in different industries gives me the confidence to be open to opportunities in almost any field. My search is focused on companies that innovate, because I am particularly effective at new product marketing. I have successfully managed new product-marketing research, launch planning, advertising, product training and sales support, as well as direct sales. In my current position with XYZ Company, I created several products and marketing approaches on which other operating divisions in the company based their programmes.

My business education includes a Marketing MBA from _____ University's School of Management, and provides me with a variety of useful analytical tools in managing problems and maximizing opportunities. My superior sales track record guarantees that I bring the reality of the marketplace to each business situation; I know what sells and why.

Currently, my total salary package is in the low seventies. I am looking for a company that rewards performance consistently.

Since I am currently weighing up several interesting opportunities, please contact me immediately if you are conducting any searches that might be a good fit. Relocation is no problem.

Thank you in advance for your consideration.

Yours sincerely,

Elizabeth Stettin
12345 678910
marketingexpert@aol.com

Broadcast e-mail (senior marketing executive)

From: Joshua Michaels [marketingexec@yahoo.com]
To: hr@abc.com
Cc:
Subject: Ref: Your Marketing Executive Search

Dear Mr _____:

I recently learned of your firm's excellent record of matching senior marketing executives with top companies. I also have learned that you have an officer-level marketing assignment in process now – I am a serious candidate for your client's vacancy. Please consider some successes:

- After joining _____ as Marketing Director, I revitalized a declining processed-meats product category in less than a year, introducing better-tasting formulas and actually reducing product costs by over £100,000. Dramatic new packaging enhanced appetite appeal, and fresh promotion strategies doubled previous sales records.

- I have carefully crafted and fine-tuned many new product introductions and line extensions, such as _____ turkey, _____ processed meats, and _____'s deodorant.

- My sales/marketing experience dates from 199–, when I formed a direct sales company to pay for my _____ MBA. Much of my subsequent success springs from strong working relationships with sales management and joint sales calls with field reps and marketing executives. I have designed events like the _____ programme, and _____'s sponsorship of the motorsports racing team.

- I have a strong personal and professional interest in consumer electronics. I consult professionally and have successfully adapted marketing techniques for home and commercial satellite systems, 'high-tech' audio/video, and radio communications equipment.

Please inform your client that I am fluent in French and I quickly absorb other languages. If your client challenges executives with the greatest of responsibilities and rewards them for remarkable performance, please contact me as soon as possible. I'll quickly repeat my past successes.

Yours sincerely,

Joshua Michaels
12345 678910
marketingexec@yahoo.com

Broadcast e-mail (logistics)

From: Leonard Curtis [logisticspro@earthlink.net]
To: careers@abc.com
Cc:
Subject: A logical choice for your client

Dear Mr _____:

An industry association referred to your organization as an active and selective executive search firm, and mentioned your name because of your work in logistics. I liked that referral and think our meeting would be mutually beneficial.

I have a successful career of using logistics to cut costs and improve profits, usually in concert with other parts of the business. For example:

- I supervised the start-up of several remote offices to assist our plants in improving their distribution operations. By offering customized service, and through sharp negotiations, we saved over £500 million in various operations and warehouse costs.

- I directed the efforts of sizable computer resources in the design and installation of a major application that saved £2.5 million in carrier costs. The application became the standard throughout the company's 46 locations.

- Working with International Sales, I have established various Quality Control programmes that have improved the timeliness and accuracy of product and paperwork delivery. Customer complaints plummeted to virtually zero, and remain there today.

A recent reorganization has reduced the number of senior management positions available within my company. I have concluded that another firm may offer a position and career advancement more in line with my personal expectations.

I would like to talk to you further. I suggest next week, the week of 29 October, if you have a free minute. I have asked my staff to forward your message immediately in case I am unavailable when you call. I look forward to hearing from you.

Yours sincerely,

Leonard Curtis
12345 678910
logisticspro@earthlink.net

Broadcast e-mail (head of asset liquidation)

From: Gene Harrison [assetliquidationpro@mindspring.com]
To: cklause@abc.com
Cc:
Subject: Asset liquidation challenge? Get this guy!

Dear Mr _____:

In recent years, as the Head of Lease Asset Liquidation with XYZ Ltd, I successfully engineered the recovery of £23 million in assets, almost three times the original buyout offer of £8 million. Throughout my career I have been instrumental in developing and implementing workout and liquidation strategies and as such I have earned a strong reputation as a professional who gets the job done.

My reason for contacting you is simple. I am interested in project opportunities that will serve both to challenge and to use my abilities in asset liquidation management. My current project will be completed within the next four to six weeks. I am currently considering offers and intend to make a decision by 1st February.

The attached summary details some of my accomplishments. I look forward to hearing from you to discuss any mutually beneficial opportunities. Please feel free to pass my CV to others who may have a need for my professional assistance.

Yours sincerely,

Gene Harrison
12345 678910
assetliquidationpro@mindspring.com

Power phrases

Consider using adaptations of these key phrases in your broadcast letters.

I hope this summary describes my experience and provides you with a better understanding of my capabilities. Thank you for your help.

If you feel that any of the strengths outlined in my CV could make a valuable contribution to your organization, please contact me to let me know of your interest.

*Recently I read about the expansion of your company in the _____.
As the _____ industry is of great interest to me, I was excited to learn of the new developments within ABC Ltd.*

I feel confident that a short conversation about my experience and your growth plans would be mutually beneficial. I will be calling you early next week to follow up this letter.

Currently, my total salary package is in the low seventies; and I am looking for a company that rewards performance consistently.

I'm a responsive and responsible listener, maintaining an empathetic attitude, creatively troubleshooting, thoroughly researching options and making well-thought-out recommendations designed to establish and enhance customer/client relationships.

I am available for relocation and travel and am targeting a salary in the £50K range.

I fervently request more than your cursory consideration; I request your time to verify my claims, believing that your time will not be wasted.

Superior recommendations from industry leaders as well as a verifiable salary history is available.

I hope you will not think me presumptuous in writing directly to you; however, in view of your position, I am led to believe that you are more aware of your organization's telecommunications personnel requirements than anyone else.

I am confident that with my experience I can make a significant contribution to your organization.

Throughout my career, I've been fortunate to represent quality merchandise and services and have learned just how to present them in their most favourable aspects. I know how to evaluate competition, assess consumer/market needs, exploit a market niche, maximize profit margins and create and maintain a reputation for dependability and excellent service.

I am a self-starter looking to join a reputable firm, one that could benefit from an individual who is ready to give 110 per cent. With over three years of sales experience, I have developed excellent interpersonal, organizational and communication skills. I am a hard-working individual who is motivated by the knowledge that my earnings are directly related to the time, energy and effort that I commit to my position.

I am personable, present a highly professional image, and deal effectively with both peers and clientele. I am confident you will agree that I should be representing your firm and not your competition. My salary requirements are negotiable. I will call you this week to set up a mutually convenient time for an interview.

Since beginning with ABC Company, my average commission has progressed from £400 to £650 weekly. My current salary or commission requirement would range upward of the mid-£20Ks, with specifics flexible and negotiable.

I look forward to hearing from you in the near future to arrange an interview, during which I hope to learn more about the position, your company's plans and goals, and how I can contribute to the success of your team.

I am grateful for that environment and the faith that was demonstrated in my capabilities. I automatically moved into the role of Executive Assistant, constantly seeking ways to limit expenses, cut costs and generate additional profit for the company. I was exceptionally successful in that endeavour – while managing five operations, three warehouses, six Warehouse Managers and a staff of 60.

I am appreciative of the time you've spent reviewing this letter (and the accompanying material). I hope to hear from you in the very near future to arrange to meet in person and discuss just how my qualifications may be of value to your organization.

Networking letter (managerial/administrative position)

A colleague to whom Maurice hasn't spoken in several months has been nominated for a prestigious award. He decides to capitalize on an opportunity to renew the acquaintance and enlist her help in his job search.

Maurice DuMaurier
1 Any Street
Anytown AA1 1AA
12345 678901

12 January 20–

Ms Philippa Consodine
ABC Ltd
111 Any Avenue
Anytown AA1 1AA

Dear Philippa,

Congratulations on your nomination for the XYZ Award. Even though you were not the ultimate winner, the nomination itself demonstrates the high degree of professional excellence you have achieved.

It's been a while since we've chatted, and I wanted to bring you up-to-date on what I've been doing. After leaving DEF, I explored several options before accepting a position as Director of Human Resources for GHI. Unfortunately, the daily drive to Anothertown, among other factors, proved to be untenable – particularly during the winter months – and I have left that position.

This puts me back in the job market, and I am writing to inquire if you are aware of any managerial/administrative positions that would capitalize on my skills. I have enclosed for your reference an updated CV that includes my recent experience.

Reiterating some of the key capabilities that I can bring to a position, consider the following:

+ **excellent team building and leadership skills;**
+ **superb interpersonal skills and supervisory experience;**
+ **developing and implementing human resource policies;**
+ **extensive knowledge and experience in the healthcare arena.**

I am convinced that my experience and professional diligence could be an asset, and would appreciate any referrals you might be able to give me for potential employment opportunities. I will contact you to arrange a convenient date and time when we might renew acquaintances. In the meantime, feel free to pass my CV on to anyone who may have an appropriate opportunity, or give me a call on 12345 678901.

Thank you in advance for your assistance. I look forward to talking to you soon.

Yours sincerely,

Maurice DuMaurier

Enclosure

Networking letter (administrative assistant)

This 'insider' networking letter works well for an administrative assistant, especially since this firm values foreign language proficiency in German and French.

Susan Jacobsen
1 Any Street, Anytown AA1 1AA ▪ 12345 678910

26 April 20–

Mr Tom O'Kane
Head of Human Resources
ABC Ltd
111 Any Avenue
Anytown AA1 1AA

Dear Mr O'Kane:

Kirsten Alexander of Human Resources suggested that I contact you in regard to applying for a position as an Administrative Assistant. If you have need of a well-qualified professional with German and French language skills and experience in office administration, customer service, sales, training and marketing, then we have good reason to meet.

My CV is enclosed for your review. Highlights include:

- Over eight years' experience in organization, coordination, communication and customer service. Consistent focus on creating and maintaining excellent client relationships, and training others in successful techniques to do the same.

- A resourceful problem-solver with a track record of getting positive results, such as a 75 per cent collection rate on accounts 90 days past due.

- Ability to build confidence and trust at all levels, and demonstrated experience in supporting cooperative, results-oriented environments.

- Proven communication skills, including fluency in French and German.

My career success has been due in large part to supporting teams, as well as internal and external customer relationships, and tackling persistent problem areas with creative approaches. I am seeking the opportunity to develop my experience, skills and enthusiasm in a new organization where I can continue to contribute to bottom-line results while growing professionally.

Should my qualifications meet your needs, I would be available to arrange a meeting immediately. I will call your office next week to answer any questions you may have and to set up a mutually convenient appointment. Thank you for your consideration.

Yours sincerely,

Susan Jacobsen

Susan Jacobsen

Enc. CV

Networking letter (internship/employment)

This letter is from a Japanese exchange student pursuing either an internship or employment.

---

14 November 20–

Ms Deborah Marks
Creative Media Academy
University of the North West
111 Any Avenue
Anytown AA1 1AA

Dear Ms Marks:

Since meeting you earlier this year at the Korean Film Festival we have exchanged e-mails and met several times. We have discussed our mutual interest in the Japanese film industry and its future in the global entertainment business. You know well my vision of integrating Japanese gaming and animation technologies into filmmaking.

Over the course of our conversations, you have mentioned that there might be an opportunity for an internship or, possibly, employment in the Creative Media Academy. I am very interested.

I offer negotiation, persuasion and liaison abilities and management, leadership and communication skills. I have also proven that I can use my bilingual proficiency to enhance international relations. Please see my CV for examples of how I have used these abilities in the past.

I believe that my unique strengths can contribute to the growth of the Creative Media programme, particularly if you are able to secure departmental status. I welcome the opportunity to discuss my continued involvement in your programme.

Yours sincerely,

Motoshi Mori

Motoshi Mori

Enclosures: 2-page CV
             Addendum of Completed Coursework

---

1 Any Street • Anytown AA1 1AA • 12345 678901 • motoshi@hotmail.com

Networking letter (computer and information systems manager)

This letter was sent to follow up a meeting with a medical school dean.

DAVID KENT

1 Any Street • Anytown AA1 1AA
12345 678910 • dkent@alohanet.com

14 January 20–

John Jones, MD
Dean, Faculty of Medicine
University of London
111 Any Avenue
Anytown AA1 1AA

Dear Dr Jones:

Perhaps you remember our chance meeting at the Bio Asia-Pacific Conference at the Sheraton Waikiki on 18 and 19 August, 20–. In our brief conversation, I shared with you the idea of using Web Development as an administrative tool. You expressed interest in the possibility of implementing such a system within the School of Medicine.

May I suggest a formal meeting to explore the idea?

I have some exciting and creative ideas, which may encourage you to take the next step toward realizing the positive impact a content management system would have in the School of Medicine. This would also be a great opportunity for us to discuss your goals and how an administrative intranet would help you reach them in a more efficient and cost-effective manner.

In addition, there has recently been spirited discussion within the IT community on the topic of organizational continuity and its potential vulnerability due to advances in technology. I think you'll find the specific strategies I have to share with you worthy of consideration.

If you recall, my background is in Web Planning and Development, with specific skills in developing administrative intranets and public websites, and designing web-based software to address the internal and external reporting needs of organizations.

Enclosed is my CV attesting to my experience and specialities. I will contact you within the next few days to discuss the possibility of meeting you.

Yours sincerely,

David Kent

David Kent
Computer and Information Systems Manager

Enclosure: CV

Networking letter (management)

SHARI T MALSCH

1098765 4321 (Mobile) • 12345 678910 (Home) • managementpro@email.com
1 Any Street • Anytown AA1 1AA

(Date)

Philip _____, (Title)
ABC Company
1 Industry Plaza
Anytown AA1 1AA

Dear Mr Harmond:

It has been said that *'in today's world there are two kinds of companies – the quick and the dead'.* I propose the same is true of managers. I am a dynamic management professional with extraordinary team building and interpersonal skills, and thrive in a fast-paced environment that is constantly moving and producing solid bottom line results. I relish a challenge and will never run from a difficult situation. In fact, if you want a successful completion, you can count on it, accurately, quickly and right the first time.

In addition to solid people skills, I posses an extensive management background in International Affairs. While living in Germany for five years, I had the opportunity to study the language and culture. I am bilingual with excellent comprehension of both German and English, and my translation skills are strong in both languages. I also have conversational knowledge of French. Having held direct responsibility for commercial dealings with the UK, Ireland and Germany, my knack for capturing key client relations with diverse cultures and people is intense. I would like to bring my business savvy and management/marketing skills to your firm.

My experience spans industries such as Property Development, International Affairs, and Procurement; however, I am an ideal candidate for a company that values well-rounded staff who can step in wherever needed and aren't afraid to learn. Dedicated to doing whatever it takes to achieve outstanding results, I will lead your team to meet tight deadlines. In short, I will not let you down.

My CV is enclosed for your consideration. I look forward to meeting you to discuss your needs and the immediate impact I will make to your organization.

Yours sincerely,

Shari Malsch

Shari Malsch

Enclosure

Networking letter (chief financial officer)

Primarily a treasury executive, Paul was seeking a broad-based senior finance assignment and was offered a CFO position.

PAUL A GERARDI

1 Any Street • Anytown AA1 1AA • 12345 678910

Dear _____:

Perhaps your company could benefit from a strong chief financial officer with a record of major contributions to business and profit growth.

The scope of my expertise is extensive and includes the full complement of corporate finance, accounting, budgeting, banking, tax, treasury, internal controls, and reporting functions. Equally important are my qualifications in business planning, operations, MIS technology, administration, and general management.

A business partner to management, I have been effective in working with all departments, linking finance with operations to improve productivity, efficiency, and bottom-line results. Recruited at The XYZ Company to provide finance and systems technology expertise, I created a solid infrastructure to support growth as the company changed from a wholesale-retail distributor to a retail operator. Recent accomplishments include:

- **Significant contributor to the increase in operating profits from under £400K to more than £4M.**

- **Key member of due diligence team in the acquisition of 25 operating units that increased market penetration 27 per cent and gross sales 32 per cent.**

- **Spearheaded leading-edge MIS design and implementation, streamlining systems and procedures that dramatically enhanced productivity while cutting costs.**

A 'hands-on' manager effective at building teamwork and cultivating strong internal/external relationships, I am flexible and responsive to the quickly changing demands of the business, industry, and marketplace. If you are seeking a talented and proactive finance executive to complement your management team, I would welcome a personal interview. Thank you for your consideration.

Yours sincerely,

Paul Gerardi

Paul Gerardi

Enclosure

Networking letter (general)

Linda Brown
1 Any Street
Anytown AA1 1AA
12345 678910

(date)

Mr Philip _____
1 Industry Plaza
Anytown AA1 1AA

Dear Philip,

Congratulations on your re-election. I hope this letter finds you and your family well and that you have an enjoyable holiday.

I am writing to update you on my job search. You may recall from our last discussion that I am now focusing on obtaining a position that will sustain me until such time as I am ready for retirement (in three to five years).

As you recommended, I have applications on file with ABC for various positions and have corresponded with various department heads, in each case indicating my flexibility and strong interest in making a meaningful contribution to smooth operations within one of their departments.

Philip, I genuinely appreciate the advice and assistance you have offered to date. Once again, I am requesting that if you are aware of any other avenues I should be pursuing, please let me know. I believe I have skills and experience to offer and can be an asset to someone in just about any position requiring maturity, reliability and dedication.

Thank you, again, for all your help.

Yours sincerely,

Linda Brown

Linda Brown

Networking letter (accounting)

ROBERT A DOWNEY
1 Any Street ▪ Anytown AA1 1AA ▪ 12345 678910
accountingpro@anyserver.co.uk

(date)

Mr Philip _____
ABC Manufacturing
1 Industry Plaza
Anytown AA1 1AA

Dear Mr _____:

As a motivated accounting professional with proven capabilities in financial analysis and accounting management, I believe that my education and experience could benefit your company. For this reason, I have enclosed a CV for your review, which outlines my relevant experiences.

Some key qualifications that may be of interest to your firm include:

- Extensive experience in providing timely and accurate financial reports using a variety of applications and procedures. I have managed accounting functions for a manufacturing firm with over £100 million in sales. I advanced quickly in the finance department and have gained a wide range of experiences, primarily focusing my efforts on analysing, reporting and planning.

- Absolute reliability and dedication to efficiency. As key financial analyst, I have worked closely with controllers and managers in monitoring financial input/output, streamlining financial reporting processes, and meeting aggressive deadlines for delivering information and analyses. I am also knowledgeable and current on legislative and regulatory requirements.

- Long-term vision. I have participated in both strategic planning for long-term marketing and in annual budget preparation. My analyses and input have contributed to the successful outcomes of external audits, annual reviews, and budgeting processes in domestic operations.

- Proficiency in current business applications, including CODA, DCS, 4TH Shift, FAS1000, MP 2, FOCUS and Microsoft Office.

I have a strong desire to move into a business environment where my skills can be fully employed in effectively furthering a leading firm's business objectives. I am confident that my knowledge and expertise, along with my dedicated professionalism, would allow me to make a significant contribution to your company's ongoing success. I would enjoy meeting you to discuss the possibilities further. Please contact me to arrange a convenient date and time for an interview.

Thank you for your time and consideration. I look forward to speaking to you soon.

Yours sincerely,

Robert Downey

Enclosure

Networking e-mail (HR administration)

From: Angela Sullivan [hrspecialist@hotmail.com]
To: awilliams@tcm.com/hr-careers/
Cc:
Subject: Great to talk to you again!

Dear _____:

It was a pleasure to speak to you on the telephone recently and, even more so, to be remembered after all these years.

As mentioned during our conversation, I have recently re-entered the job market and have 10 years' experience with a 3,000-employee retail organization in the area of human resources administration. My experience includes recruitment and selection, human resources planning and employee relations. I have been responsible for all facets of management of company personnel, including development and training, and liaison with both staff and training providers.

My goal is to become an HR Manager in a larger organization with the possibility of advancement in other Human Resources areas. My preference is to remain in the _____ area.

For your information, my CV is attached. If any situations come to mind where you think my skills and background would fit or if you have any suggestions as to others with whom it might be beneficial for me to speak, I would appreciate hearing from you. I can be reached on the telephone number shown below.

Again, I very much enjoyed our conversation.

Yours sincerely,

Angela Sullivan
12345 678910
hrspecialist@hotmail.com

Networking e-mail (publishing)

From: Robert Render [publishingpro@anyserver.co.uk]
To: hr@pennwell.com
Cc:
Subject: Thanks for all the help ;-)

Dear _____:

It was a pleasure to meet you for lunch today. I am grateful for the time you took out of your busy schedule to assist me in my job search.

It was fascinating to learn about the new technology that is beginning to play a major role in the publishing field today. I have already been to the bookshop to purchase the book by _____ which you highly recommended. I look forward to reading about his 'space age' ideas.

I will be contacting _____ within the next few days to set up an appointment. I will let you know how things are progressing once I have met her.

Thanks again for your help. You will be hearing from me soon.

Yours sincerely,

Robert Render
12345 678910
publishingpro@anyserver.co.uk

Power phrases

Consider using adaptations of these key phrases in your networking letters.

As promised, I am enclosing a copy of my CV for your information. If any appropriate opportunities come to your attention, I would appreciate it if you would keep me in mind.

After you have had a chance to look at my CV, please give me a call.

I am beginning to put out some 'feelers' in advance of the completion of my degree in December.

I do not intend to target any specific type of job. I am open to almost anything that my qualifications will fit. My only criteria are the following:

I would appreciate any advice and/or referrals you might be able to give me.

I am looking for a position in management and would appreciate any assistance you could provide.

As always, it was good to talk to you. Your positive outlook is catching. I've been called the eternal optimist, but I always feel more upbeat after a conversation with you.

Many thanks for the words of encouragement and for taking the time from your busy schedule to help me. It truly is appreciated. I have never faced an unemployment situation like this before.

It was a pleasure to speak to you on the telephone recently and, even more so, to be remembered after all these years.

For your information, my CV is enclosed. If any situations come to mind where you think my skills and background would fit, or if you have any suggestions as to others with whom it might be beneficial for me to speak, I would appreciate hearing from you. I can be reached on the telephone numbers above.

He assured me that he would pass my CV to you; however, in the event that it has not reached you yet, I am enclosing another.

Perhaps you know of a company that could use this range of experience. In this regard, I enclose a copy of my CV outlining a few of my more significant accomplishments.

My objective is to find a _____ level position at a marketing driven company where my skills can contribute to the company's growth and profitability.

I am not limited by location and would consider the opportunity wherever it presents itself.

First of all, let me sincerely thank you for taking the time and trouble to return my call last Monday. I found our conversation informative, entertaining, and (alas) a little scary. Needless to say, I genuinely appreciate your prompt response and generous, helpful advice.

Again, a thousand thanks for your time and consideration. If I might ask you one last favour, could you please give me your opinion of the revision? A copy is, as usual, enclosed.

I am writing to you in response to our recent conversation over the telephone. I thank you for your time and your advice. It was most generous of you and sincerely appreciated. Please accept my apologies for invading your privacy. I anticipated an address for written correspondence from an answering service.

I look forward to hearing from you on your next visit to _____.

I hope you'll keep me in mind if you hear of anything that's up my street.

I recently learned that your company is well connected with manufacturers in the _____ area and does quality work. We should meet soon, since it's very likely we can help each other. I'll be in the office all next week and look forward to hearing from you. I have alerted my secretary; she'll put your call straight through.

_____ suggested that I contact you regarding employment opportunities.

After many years in the _____ community, I have decided that a career change is due in order to use my interpersonal skills to their fullest.

Follow-up letter (after telephone contact) (fundraising consultant)

From an applicant who has had too many jobs in too few years, this letter was designed to get two competing 'partners' to bring her on board.

.... **Lanina Crowne**

Wednesday, 02 May 20–

Ms Patty Martineau
Director
ABC & Associates
111 Any Avenue
Anytown AA1 1AA

Dear Ms Martineau:

Thank you for making time to explore how I could help ABC & Associates as your newest Fundraising Consultant.

I've already started thinking about how I might be most productive – right from the start. Of course, my ideas must be preliminary; I don't know exactly how your organization works. Nevertheless, I would value your reactions to the preliminary thoughts you'll find in the next paragraphs.

I want each of your clients to see the tailored solutions we provide as a rapid, seamless, continuing operation that guides them through the complex world of modern fundraising. In fact, I want them to think of us as their 'sole source' for the resources they must have to grow financially and operationally. If we are to speak with the one voice the clients should demand, then our business model requires close teamwork between Ms O'Neill, you, and me.

In the meantime, I am modifying my own continuing professional development programme to concentrate on fundraising from a consultant's perspective. I've begun to look through the literature and contact professional organizations to hear about the latest trends directly from industry leaders. Later, I'll use what I learn to re-evaluate my own successes in campaigns done with and without consultants.

I appreciate your vote of confidence in recommending that I meet Ms O'Neill. I want to make that interview just as useful for her as possible. Toward that end, may I call in a few days to get your reactions to the preliminary thoughts I've outlined above?

With many thanks for all your help…

Yours sincerely,

Lanina Crowne

Lanina Crowne

---

1 Any Street • Anytown AA1 1AA • 12345 678910 (Home) • lcc@randomc.com

Follow-up letter (after telephone contact) (adult educator)

STEPHANIE A MONACO

---

1 Any Street
Anytown AA1 1AA
12345 678910

EDUCATOR/ADVOCATE/MENTOR
'Every leader a teacher, every teacher a leader, every student a success.'

Emily _____   (Date)
(Title)
ABC Community College
1 Industry Plaza
Anytown AA1 1AA

Dear Ms _____:

I enclose my CV in follow-up to our conversation last week regarding the adult education position currently available at Anytown Community College. I appreciate very much your offer to forward my credentials to the appropriate individual.

With a master's degree in Education Administration, plus four years' cumulative experience in the classroom, I believe I possess the expertise and qualifications that are critical to leading your organization's adult students to achieve their educational goals successfully.

What do I offer your students?

- Effective listening and communication skills – a demonstrated ability to provide individualized instruction based on students' interests and needs.
- Encouragement and motivation – a creative, inviting atmosphere of interaction and participation.
- Sincere desire to reach them on a level they can understand, no matter what age, skill level or cultural background.

I am excited at the opportunity to work with adult students because I recognize that they are in that classroom because they want to be there. The adult population brings a unique flavour of enthusiasm and motivation that energizes and inspires me as an instructor and makes me eager to go above and beyond expectations to help them reach their goals.

In terms of salary, I realize that flexibility is essential and am therefore open to discussing your organization's compensation package for an individual with my distinctive talents. If you believe that I could play an important role on your educational team, please call me on 12345 678910 to arrange for an interview.

Yours sincerely,

Stephanie Monaco

Stephanie Monaco

enclosure

Follow-up letter (after telephone contact) (legal secretary)

JAMES PENSON

1 Any Street, Anytown AA1 1AA

12345 678910 legalpro@anyserver.co.uk

(Date)

Phillip _____
(Title)
ABC Ltd
1 Industry Plaza
Anytown AA1 1AA

Dear Mr _____:

Thank you for returning my telephone call yesterday. It was a pleasure speaking to you, and as promised, a copy of my CV is enclosed. As I mentioned, I have been working in law firms since the end of February, as well as working at weekends and in the evenings for over one year. At present, I am looking for a second or third shift to continue developing my word-processing and legal skills.

Although the majority of my positions have been more managerial and less secretarial, I have developed strong office skills over the years. While I was attending college, I worked as Administrative Assistant to the Department Head, in addition to working in other professional capacities.

_____ speaks very highly of me, and if you need to confirm a reference with him, please feel free to contact him at _____. In addition, I would be happy to furnish you with names of people I have worked for in law firms over the past year.

Within the next few days, I will be contacting you to arrange a convenient meeting time to discuss the position you now have available. However, if you would like to speak to me, feel free to contact me on 12345 678910.

Thank you again for calling yesterday. I look forward to speaking to you on the telephone, and meeting you in person.

Yours sincerely,

James Penson

James Penson

enclosure

Follow-up letter (after telephone contact) (purchasing)

CHERYL BLOOM
1 Any Street • Anytown AA1 1AA • 12345 678910

(Date)

Bob _____ (Title)
A,B&C
Executive Search Consultants
111 Any Avenue
Anytown AA1 1AA

Dear Mr _____:

In reference to our telephone conversation, my CV is enclosed. I believe the one you have is written for a sales and marketing position.

Since we last spoke I have been working as a business consultant for the _____ group of companies on projects in a number of different areas outlined below.

- Spearheaded and supervised upgrading of the _____ companies' communications systems, including printing and copy machines, telecommunications systems, computer hardware and software systems, computer scanning system, computer filing system, and fax and modem transmission systems.

- Set up and implemented an auto and entry floor-mat marketing programme for _____ including pricing and product displays for retail sales outlets.

- Researched, purchased and installed a bar code labelling programme for the companies' products, including label setup and printing systems to allow them to sell their products to _____.

- Participated in the design and layout of a new logo for _____ division including specifications for all letterheads, forms and printed communications materials.

- Provided major input for a factory-paid _____ point-of-sale system to display custom automotive floor mats.

Most of my projects should be wrapped up by the end of November, and so I will be looking for another company that could use my broad range of experience. Please let me know if you think you might have something for me.

Yours sincerely,

Cheryl Bloom

enclosure

Follow-up letter (after telephone contact) (manager)

Andrew T Bestwick
1 Any Street
Anytown AA1 1AA
12345 678910
managerpro@anyserver.co.uk

(Date)

Bob _____
(Title)
A,B&C
Executive Search Consultants
111 Any Avenue
Anytown AA1 1AA

Dear Mr _____:

THANK YOU for allowing me to tell you a little about myself. I have just completed my MBA (December, 20–) and would appreciate the opportunity to talk to your client companies that are in need of an experienced and seasoned manager. Whether the need is for general (operational) management, products, marketing, or sales, my substantial background in management, marketing, and technical products should be very valuable to your clients.

I have enclosed two CVs (marketing-orientated and operational-orientated) with some other information that you may find useful. With eyes firmly on the bottom line, I offer: the ABILITY to manage, build, and quickly understand their business; EXPERIENCE in domestic and international corporate cultures; INTELLIGENCE and the capacity to grasp essential elements; and the WILLINGNESS to work hard, travel and relocate.

Realizing that most of your clients aren't looking for Directors, I'm not necessarily looking for fancy titles (but I am promotable). What I am looking for is that special position that will offer not only a challenge but a career opportunity with long-range potential. I know my successes will bring them (and me) rewards.

CVs and letters are brief by their very nature and cannot tell the whole story. I will be happy to discuss with your client and yourself how my commitment to them will help solve their needs or problems and will definitely make good things happen. After all, isn't that the bottom line?

May we work together?

Yours sincerely,

Andrew Bestwick

Andrew Bestwick

enclosures

Follow-up e-mail (after telephone contact) (general)

From: James Young [jyoung@earthlink.net]
To: hr@abc.com
Cc:
Subject: Glad we finally caught up

Dear Ms _____:

I appreciate the time you took yesterday to discuss the position at _____.
I recognize that timing and awareness of interest are very important in searches of this type.
Your comment regarding an attempt to contact me earlier this summer is a case in point.

Attached, as you requested, you will find an outline CV. I also believe that my experiences as
a director of client services are readily transferable to a new environment. I believe that I can
contribute a great deal to the satisfaction of your client's needs.

Realizing that letters and CVs are not an entirely satisfactory means of judging a person's ability
or personality, I suggest a personal interview to discuss further your client's needs and my
qualifications. I can be reached directly or via message on 12345 678910, so that we can
arrange a mutually convenient time to meet. I look forward to hearing from you. Thank you for
your time and consideration.

Yours sincerely,

James Young
12345 678910
jyoung@earthlink.net

Follow-up e-mail (after telephone contact) (arts management)

From: Jasmine Morgan [promotionspro@yahoo.com]
To: ewoods@abc.com
Cc:
Subject: Thanks from a motivated fanatic

Dear Ms _____:

Following yesterday's conversation, I am forwarding a copy of my CV and am looking forward to our meeting in the very near future.

As we discussed, the positions that interest me are as follows:

Event/Arts Management
Promotions/Advertising/Public Relations
Corporate Training

I am a fanatic about image, excellence and attention to quality and detail. As my academic and career background reveal, I have the tenacity of a terrier when it comes to task accomplishment.

I have never held a 'nine-to-five' job and would most likely be bored to death if I had one. Therefore, I am looking for something fast-paced and challenging to my grey matter that will allow growth and advancement and an opportunity to learn. I am in my element when I am in a position to organize… the more details the better!

I'll give you a buzz on Tuesday, 14th March to try to set an appointment for further discussion.

Yours sincerely,

Jasmine Morgan
12345 678910
promotionspro@yahoo.com

Power phrases

Consider using adaptations of these key phrases in your follow-up letters after phone calls.

As you requested in our telephone conversation this morning, I am enclosing a copy of my CV for your review.

As you can see from my CV, I have some excellent secretarial experience.

I'll give you a buzz on Tuesday, 15th March, to set an appointment for further discussion.

With reference to our telephone conversation, enclosed is my sales and marketing CV. I believe the one you have is written for a purchasing position.

I am a bright, articulate, and well-groomed professional with excellent telemarketing skills, sales instincts, and closing abilities. I am seeking a dynamic position with a reputable firm. I would like to meet you in person to discuss how I could contribute to the effectiveness of your clients' operations.

Please remember me if something arises that would tie in with my background.

My many long-term professional relationships would benefit any employer in this area.

I'd like to meet you to tell you more about my background and to show you some of the training and marketing materials I've developed. This would give you a better picture of my capabilities.

As you suggested when we spoke last week, I have enclosed my CV for your review and consideration. I contacted you on the recommendation of _____ of _____, who thought that you may have an interest in my qualifications for a position in the near future.

I have long admired _____ for its innovations in the industry, and I would consider it a tremendous career opportunity to be associated with your organization.

Follow-up letter (after face-to-face meeting) (library system director)

Victoria was genuinely impressed with the facility she visited, but also recognized she could help them improve by applying her management experience.

Victoria Leung
1 Any Street ▪ Anytown AA1 1AA ▪ 12345 678910

---

12 January 20–

Ms Louisa May Prescott
County Library Services
West View Library
111 Any Avenue
Anytown AA1 1AA

Dear Ms Prescott:

Thank you for the opportunity to visit your facilities and discuss the Director's position with you. I enjoyed meeting you and the other trustees, as well as Sylvia Morrison and members of the library staff. I was impressed with your outline of the position and believe that I possess the capabilities to successfully lead the County Library system well into the 21st century.

My tour of three of your branches and my conversations with several staff members made it easy for me to understand how you have achieved your success. As someone with over 20 years in the library field, and experience visiting literally hundreds of library branches in the course of a year, I was favourably impressed with the design of your branches. The cordiality of your staff members and the excellent way in which the facilities are maintained are also quite impressive. Your 'Friends' organization also appears to be a real asset to the library.

Some key talents that I can bring to this leadership position include:

- *Establishing a strategic vision and motivating staff to pursue that vision.*
- *Maintaining productive rapport with advisory boards, and successfully interacting with government agencies and the community at-large to achieve goals.*
- *Developing information technology plans that have prepared libraries for the 21st century and that anticipate the changing technological landscape.*

I remain very interested in this position and am confident that my knowledge and expertise would allow me to exceed your expectations in this leadership role. I look forward to discussing my application with you soon.

Yours sincerely,

Victoria Leung

Victoria Leung

Follow-up letter (after face-to-face meeting) (sales)

This two-point letter (1) reinforces the point that he was successful in sales, even though he hadn't ever worked in pharmaceutical sales, and (2) nudges the employer to make a decision.

·· **NORMAN CORNFELD**
1 Any Street • Anytown AA1 1AA • 12345 678910 • ncorn72@anyserver.co.uk

Friday, 20 July 20–

Mark Pugh
Area Manager
ABC Pharmaceuticals
111 Any Avenue
Anytown AA1 1AA

Dear Mr Pugh:

Thank you for making time to meet me this morning. Even during our interview, it struck me how good a match I think I am for ABC. And on the way home, I began to formulate a plan to be productive for you from the first day, based on how I might meet your specific needs. Here's what I've come up with so far:

Your needs	My capabilities
• Good track record	• Bringing in twice my sales quotas for four consecutive years. • Being my organization's top producer in those same four years.
• Communication skills that build sales	• Capturing sales with presentations before busy decision-makers.
• Good work ethic	• Turning around a market that had been stagnant for 15 years. • Regularly overcoming strong sales resistance.

I can offer everything you see above because I show the benefit of what I sell – not just to the end user, but to the people who deliver those benefits. That's a direct parallel with an ABC strength.

I've already spoken with your Anytown representative, and I'm looking forward to my 'ride along'.

At this point, most applicants would ask you to contact them if you have questions. I want to do something different. Please consider this question: What additional information do you need from me to choose me as the best applicant for the position?

Yours sincerely,

Norman Cornfeld

Follow-up letter (after face-to-face meeting) (loan processor)

Richard had to overcome the effects of a prolonged slowdown in his industry – portfolio management – and convince the decision-maker that his skills were transferable and he could master the intricacies of new product lines he had never worked with before.

RICHARD WEIGMAN

1 Any Street   12345 678910 (Home)
Anytown AA1 1AA   01234 567890 (Office)
                                                               rweigman@hotmail.com

Wednesday, 13 June 20–

Malcolm S McLeod
Managing Director
ABC Mortgage Lending
111 Any Avenue
Anytown AA1 1AA

Dear Mr McLeod:

Thank you for meeting me this afternoon. I think ABC Mortgage Lending and I are a good match if I can be your newest loan processor.

In fact, as I was driving back to Anytown, I began to plan how I might be productive for you right from the start. My ideas are, of course, preliminary. But I would value your reactions to this tentative plan:

- I would start by introducing myself to every client. I want them to think of me as ABC Mortgage Lending, and I want to find out what their special needs are before any rush requirements come up. When they need answers, I want them to remember two things: my name and my phone number.

- I have already started my plan to master your requirements. As a first step, I'm jotting down the kinds of questions I must have the answers to so I can process loans quickly and right the first time. I want ABC Mortgage to be the 'provider of choice' in the eyes of buyers and agents – in short, anyone who wants quality loan processing services. If I am successful, I hope our percentage of revenue for mortgage loan processing grows steadily.

As you asked me to, I plan to call you on Friday. I've already thought of the question I would most like to ask. Here it is: Will the plan I've outlined above work for ABC Mortgage faster and better than any plan suggested by the other candidates you've interviewed?

Yours sincerely,

Richard Weigman

Follow-up letter (after face-to-face meeting) (hospitality manager)

Lacking professional experience as a concierge, Olivia was sure to remind her interviewers of her related volunteer work, enthusiasm, education, international travel experience and multilingual communication skills. Notice how she copied ('cc') her interviewers.

Olivia Beth Copperfield

1 Any Street
Anytown AA1 1AA
12345 678910
worldtraveller@sky.net

19 February 20–

Ms Janet Berlinger
Human Resources
ABC
111 Any Avenue
Anytown AA1 1AA

Dear Ms Berlinger:

Thank you for the opportunity to participate in a follow-up interview with you and your supervising managers, Mr Sean Johnson and Mrs Rita Bronson, to discuss further the possibility of my joining your hospitality team as Hospitality Manager.

As discussed during our meeting, ABC Hotel is the ideal work environment for me to express my enthusiasm for working with people as well as put to use my education in psychology and business administration. I feel strongly that my volunteer work experience at XYZ and my personal experience acquired over the years while travelling worldwide will prove especially valuable in this highly visible position. Combined with an ability to communicate effectively in Spanish, French and Italian, I feel I would make a significant contribution to ABC Hotel.

Please note that my availability is immediate. If you need to contact me, I can be reached at the above telephone number. Thank you again for your time and consideration. I hope to speak to you soon.

Yours sincerely,

Olivia Beth Copperfield

Olivia Beth Copperfield

cc: Mr Sean Johnson
        Mrs Rita Bronson

Follow-up letter (after face-to-face meeting) (merchandise manager)

This thank-you letter capitalizes on reinforcing the 'fit' between the potential job and her qualifications, as well as introducing some areas overlooked in the interview.

DEBORAH DEVEREAUX

1 Any Street, Anytown AA1 1AA • 12345 678910 Home • E-mail: ddeve@bol.com

9 November 20–

Ms Melinda Newby, Director
Human Resources
ABC Stores
111 Any Avenue
Anytown AA1 1AA

Dear Ms Newby:

Thank you for the opportunity to be interviewed for the **Merchandise Manager** position. You were extremely generous with your time and I was impressed with the warmth and efficiency of your office, and your genuine interest in acquainting me with the company's concepts and goals.

My background is unique – it does not fit into a traditional career mould – yet it encompasses a very diverse exposure in Home Furnishings and Ready-to-Wear. As we discussed, my extensive experience with the type of clientele your company targets has prepared me to 'come on board' your team. My sales record of £279,000 (20–) demonstrates that I can produce immediate value, as well as train new sales reps in highly effective merchandising and closing techniques.

What I did not stress is that I also have built an arsenal of skills around quantitative, technical processes involved in merchandising and planning. For example, I have developed six-month merchandising plans for the London division of XYZ Apparel, and classification planning that established the focus on merchandise categories, prices, styles, sizes and colours.

I have always striven to achieve high-quality results by knowing the customer well, anticipating profitable market trends and never forgetting the store image. Offering wide, but well-edited, assortments of multiple classifications so that one-stop shopping can easily occur has been my hallmark. Such high standards have been central in all of my work, whether with a major retail department store, wholesale showroom or upmarket home furnishings boutique. Your corporate environment and company goals appear to reflect those same high standards, and I am eager to join your team.

I am very interested in this position and would like to contact you next week to check on the progress of your search. Thanks again for the opportunity to attend the interview.

Yours sincerely,

Deborah Devereaux

Follow-up letter (after face-to-face meeting) (manufacturer representative)

Anthony Ruggerio

1 Any Street   **Anytown AA1 1AA**

Home Phone: 12345 678910 • Mobile: 0198765 4321

28 February 20–

Ms Kathleen McMann
General Manager
ABC Imaging
111 Any Avenue
Anytown AA1 1AA

Dear Ms McMann:

Thank you for the interview with you on Friday, 23rd February, for the Manufacturer's Representative position. Everything I learned from you about ABC Imaging leads me to believe that this is a progressive company where I could fully use my skills and make a valuable contribution. In fact, I have not been this determined or excited about a job since I started my business 25 years ago.

As I mentioned to you, I am sales orientated and have a solid technical background in printing. I relate well to printers at any level, from pressmen to owners. In my sales activities with John Watkins when he was a printing buyer at XYZ Industries, I found him to be very demanding and hard to please. One of the reasons why I was successful in acquiring and retaining his business was my constant commitment to customer service. Whenever there were any questions, I never failed to answer them promptly.

During our discussion, you seemed to express a concern about my lack of experience with dealers. Although I had not mentioned it at the time we spoke, I have had long-term relationships with dealers like DEF, and have bought approximately £1 million worth of equipment from them, starting with my first press and expanding to 20 over the years. I am certain that with my persistence and follow-through I can handle dealers at the sales and service end. Rest assured that I would keep you informed of my progress on a daily basis. Nothing would be done without you knowing about it.

Among my major strengths, I am goal-driven, self-motivated, have a strong work ethic and an ability to learn quickly. My training period would be brief, and I would use my own time to familiarize myself with your equipment and product line. In addition, I am accustomed to long hours and have no objection to the travel requirements or being away from home four days a week.

Coming from a medium-sized company, it would be an honour to work at ABC Imaging, and I am hopeful that I would have the chance to be a member of your team. Please do not hesitate to call me if you have any further questions or need additional information from me.

I look forward to your positive decision about my application.

Yours sincerely,

Anthony Ruggerio

Follow-up letter (after face-to-face meeting) (general)

MARCY SMITH
1 Any Street – Anytown AA1 1AA
12345 678910 – marcysmith@msn.com

(Date)

Phillip _____
(Title)
ABC Ltd
1 Industry Plaza
Anytown AA1 1AA

Dear Mr _____:

Thank you very much for taking the time to meet me today. I enjoyed our discussion, and I'm now even more excited about the possibility of working for ABC and with your team.

It was great to learn that you are embracing technology as it relates to your business – both in terms of day-to-day operations and the future delivery of ABC's programmes (eg, on-the-spot training). I am very interested in, and have an affinity for, computer technology and would love to be a part of your efforts in this area.

I am confident that I could make a strong contribution to the continued growth of ABC. As we discussed, I have related experience in all of the required areas for the position. In addition, I look forward to taking a project management approach to establishing the new system for the delivery of the assessment workshops to your key client. This process would allow me to ensure that I am meeting your objectives and getting a system 'up and running' within an established time-frame. Having done this, I would continually review with regard to improvement and focus on managing the enhancement of customer service.

I remain very interested in the position, and I look forward to hearing from you soon. If you require additional information in the meantime, I can be reached on 12345 678910.

Yours sincerely,

Marcy Smith

Marcy Smith

Follow-up letter (after face-to-face meeting) (librarian)

The interview in this case was by a committee and very structured, leaving the applicant with the feeling that there was more she would have liked to have said. This thank-you letter conveys some of these ideas. The result: the applicant was hired for this high-level position.

Mary Kelner

(date)

Mr Philip _____
(Title)
ABC Library Service
111 Any Avenue
Anytown AA1 1AA

Dear Philip:

Thank you for the opportunity to meet you and the selection committee on Monday. I enjoyed our discussion of the Director of Library Development opening. I was impressed with your vision for this individual's role.

Based on our conversation, I believe that I possess the capabilities to meet your expectations for this key position with the Library Service.

To reiterate the experiences I bring to this opportunity, please note the following:

- Promoting programmes and fostering working relationships with over 1,000 member libraries in all major segments of the field. These activities also encompass extensive community outreach.
- Providing strategic vision and mission, and motivating staff to pursue visionary goals. In two leadership assignments, I have recognized staff for their efforts and given them the guidance and direction that has delivered exceptional programme results.
- Managing capital projects and spearheading information technology initiatives. These encompassed upgrades to comply with access requirements, renovations that improved the use of space, and leading efforts to incorporate technology into library settings.
- Supervising departments in urban and suburban settings to address a broad range of competing priorities. Among these experiences was the supervision of an Interlibrary Loan department serving 100 individual branches in a five-county area.

I am most interested in this position and am confident that my track record at XYZ demonstrates my capacity to 'hit the ground running', and apply my leadership, enthusiasm and expertise to furthering the mission of the Library Service in this development role. I look forward to continuing our discussions in the near future.

Yours sincerely,

Mary Kelner

Mary Kelner

---

1 Any Street, Anytown AA1 1AA • 12345 678910 Home • librarianspecialist@optonline.com

Follow-up letter (after face-to-face meeting) (construction manager)

Leonard Curtis
_____

1 Any Street • Anytown AA1 1AA
12345 678910 • constructionmanager@msn.com

Emily _____   (Date)
(Title)
ABC Ltd
1 Industry Plaza
Anytown AA1 1AA

Dear Ms _____:

We had the opportunity to speak briefly at last week's Chamber of Commerce meeting concerning the Construction Management position you are seeking to fill in Birmingham. I appreciate you filling me in on the details of the project and have enclosed my CV as you suggested.

As we discussed, I am well acquainted with ABC Ltd's brand and store concept, and I am excited to learn of the company's expansion plans over the coming decade. With my background in construction, maintenance, and project management as well as operations and strategic leadership, I believe I am primed to play a key role in this growth.

As Chief Executive Officer of Superior Landscape Design, I have been instrumental in leading the company to phenomenal success within a very short time, building the organization from start-up into a solid revenue generator known throughout the UK as an aggressive competitor in markets crowded by multimillion-pound, nationally recognized companies.

I am currently in the process of selling the company and have been exploring opportunities with dynamic, growth-orientated organizations like yours that could benefit from my broad-based expertise in operations, organizational management, finance and business development. Complementing my diverse leadership background is expertise in all the fundamentals of construction management, including the ability to see projects through to completion while exceeding quality standards.

Perhaps one of my strongest assets is my ability to cultivate long-lasting relationships with clients through attentive, direct communication. I have been highly successful at defining complex project plans, establishing budgets, outlining scope of work and directly soliciting qualified contractors using the bid process. I also offer extensive experience navigating through the paperwork and bureaucracy, forging productive alliances with key regulatory agencies to streamline permits and licencing and to facilitate project starts.

I would enjoy the opportunity to speak to you again in greater detail. Could we meet for lunch on Friday? I'll call your assistant in a few days to confirm the appointment.

Yours sincerely,

Leonard Curtis

Leonard Curtis

Follow-up letter (after face-to-face meeting) (executive assistant)

Janice Moss

1 Any Street
Anytown AA1 1AA
12345 678910

(Date)

Phillip _____
(Title)
ABC Ltd
1 Industry Plaza
Anytown AA1 1AA

Dear Phillip _____:

The time I spent being interviewed by you and Sandra gave me a clear picture of your company's operation as well as your corporate environment. I want to thank you, in particular, Phillip, for the thorough picture you painted of your CEO's needs and work style.

I left our meeting feeling very enthusiastic about the scope of the position as well as its close match to my abilities and work style. After reviewing your comments, Phillip, I think the key strengths that I can offer your CEO in achieving his agenda are:

- experience in effectively dealing with senior level staff in a manner that facilitates decision making;

- proven ability to anticipate an executive's needs and present viable options to consider;

- excellent communication skills – particularly, the ability to gain feedback from staff and summarize succinctly.

Whether the needs at hand involve meeting planning, office administration, scheduling or just serving as a sounding board, I bring a combination of highly effective 'people skills' and diversified business experience to deal with changing situations.

With my energetic work style, I believe that I am an excellent match for this unique position. I welcome an additional meeting to elaborate on my background and how I can assist your CEO.

Yours sincerely,

Janice Moss

Janice Moss

Follow-up letter (after face-to-face meeting) (management information systems)

CHRISTOPHER FALK

1 Any Street • Anytown AA1 1AA • 12345 678910

(Date)

Bob _____
(Title)
A,B&C
Executive Search Consultants
1 Any Avenue
Anytown AA1 1AA

Dear Mr _____:

Thank you for meeting me this morning. Our associate, _____, assured me that a meeting with you would be productive, and it was. I sincerely appreciate your counsel, insight and advice.

I have attached my CV for your review. I would appreciate any feedback you might have regarding effectiveness and strength. I understand you may not have any searches under way that would be suitable for me at this time, but I would appreciate any future considerations.

As we reviewed this morning, I seek and am qualified for senior MIS positions in a medium to large high-tech manufacturing or services business. I seek a salary in the £150,000-and-above range and look to report directly to the business CEO. These requirements are somewhat flexible depending on a number of factors, especially potential, of a new position. My family and I are willing to relocate to any area.

Please consider any associates, customers or friends who may have contacts that would be useful for me to meet. I have learned how important networking is, and will really appreciate some assistance from a professional like you.

Thanks again, Mr _____, and please let me know if I can be of service to you. I wish you and your colleagues continued success and look forward to a business relationship in the future.

Yours sincerely,

Christopher Falk

Christopher Falk

enclosure

Follow-up letter (after face-to-face meeting) (assistant)

MELANIE SHREVE
1 Any Street
Anytown AA1 1AA
12345 678910

(Date)

Emily _____
(Title)
ABC Ltd
1 Industry Plaza
Anytown AA1 1AA

Dear Ms _____:

Thank you for the opportunity to discuss the position of Assistant.

ABC Ltd is involved in one of the most pressing concerns of today: environmentally safe methods of disposing of solid waste materials. The challenge of creating proper disposal systems is paramount. I look forward to being a part of an organization that is focusing on furthering the technology needed to enhance our environment.

At ABC Ltd I would be able to:

- be a productive assistant to management;
- be a part of a technologically developing industry;
- be in a position to learn and grow with the opportunities presented by your company;
- be involved in the excitement of a new, expanding company.

The skills that I have to offer ABC Ltd are:

- professionalism, organization and maturity;
- excellent office skills;
- ability to work independently;
- a creative work attitude;
- research and writing skills;
- varied business background;
- willingness to learn.

Again, thank you for considering my qualifications to become a part of your organization.

Yours sincerely,

Melanie Shreve

Melanie Shreve

Follow-up letter (after face-to-face meeting) (sales)

This letter is a follow-up to a meeting Carol arranged with a targeted employer. While there was no position currently available, she nevertheless wants to 'sell' her suitability.

CAROL ANN CONASTA
1 Any Street, Anytown AA1 1AA
12345 678910 ~ salespro@comcast.net

(Date)

Philip _____
(title)
ABC Company
1 Industry Plaza
Anytown AA1 1AA

Philip,

First of all, thank you. I thoroughly enjoyed our meeting last Wednesday, and greatly appreciate your insight and the time taken to discuss where I might best fit in to the ABC team. Your professionalism and willingness to share what you know put me instantly at ease, and I am now even more motivated to be part of ABC's success.

Let me begin by restating how flattered I am that you saw such potential in me. I likewise feel confident that I have the management and leadership expertise, marketing skills, and business development experience to be successful, and I see tremendous opportunities for ABC in the future.

However, as we discussed, I understand that my first step is to make my mark as a member of the Road Crew and am equally excited at the opportunity to make an impact on the front line. I realize that you are not currently in the position to make such an offer, but I want to re-emphasize my enthusiasm to join the ABC team wherever you feel I could add value.

If you allow, I'd like to take a moment of your time to re-state a few key points:

- I possess the drive, commitment and strong people skills required to make an impact in this industry.
- I offer proven business development, sales and revenue-building experience.
- I know what it takes to get results, both from myself and from others, and have proven again and again to be the 'go to' person when results are expected.

I hope that you and I have the opportunity to continue our discussions and, once again, I appreciate the time you spent meeting me. I wish you continued success in all your efforts and look forward to seeing you at the Sales Excellence seminar at the end of July.

Yours sincerely,

Carol Ann Conasta

Carol Ann Conasta

Follow-up e-mail (after face-to-face meeting) (general)

From: William Long [w_long@hotmail.com]
To: jones@abc.com
Cc:
Subject: Great meeting! May we talk again Tuesday?

Dear Mr _____ :

I appreciate the time you took today interviewing me for the position. I hope our two-hour meeting did not throw off the rest of the day's timetable. I trust you will agree that it was time well spent, as I sensed we connected on every major point discussed.

Your insight on e-commerce was intriguing. My history in hi-tech, manufacturing and biomedical industries and background in technology solutions seems to be a good match with the opportunities available in your company. As I mentioned, at XYZ Biomedical I initiated the marketing strategies that opened our markets to South America. What I failed to mention is that I also have contacts with some e-commerce investors developing online portals targeted at South Americans.

I am very interested in the position and would like to contact you on Tuesday to see where we stand.

Yours sincerely,

William Long
12345 678910
w_long@hotmail.com

Follow-up e-mail (after face-to-face meeting) (sales manager)

From: Damien Chavez [salespro@aol.com]
To: mgabor@lds.com
Cc:
Subject: Thanks for an exciting meeting. Next steps?

(date)

Mr Philip _____
(title)
ABC Ltd
1 Industry Plaza
Anytown AA1 1AA

Dear Mr _____:

I thoroughly enjoyed our meeting on Wednesday. After learning more about ABC Ltd and its goals, the prospect of joining the organization as the Western Region Sales Manager is even more exciting.

One of the most important things I have learned in my 20+ years in sales is to listen to what the customer needs. I have always taken pride in designing customized solutions that not only meet the clients' objectives, but are also competitive in price. This philosophy has enabled me to exceed corporate expectations for 17 consecutive years. In addition, I have managed to convert about 65 per cent of my clients to 'repeat order' accounts, an objective you indicated was a high priority for your sales team in ensuring the company's continued growth.

ABC Ltd's Western Region Sales Manager position is an important cornerstone in the company's overall growth plans for the new fiscal year. The company is poised to make significant strides to gain ground on the competition and the territory will be instrumental in making the corporate goals a reality. I am excited about contributing my expertise, meeting ABC's customers and building long-term client relationships.

Thanks again for your time. I am certain that I can be a valuable asset to your sales team, and I look forward to having the opportunity to contribute to ABC's growth.

Yours sincerely,

Damien Chavez
12345 678910
salespro@aol.com

Follow-up e-mail (after face-to-face meeting) (senior counsellor)

This e-mail shows how her skills and experience in counselling matched this particular job opening and would be an asset to the agency and its clients.

From: Susan Goodman [skilledcounsellor@earthlink.net]
To: cpatterson@couns.edu.com
Cc:
Subject: Looking forward to next week

Dear Ms _____:

I would like to thank you for affording me the opportunity to meet you to discuss the Senior Counsellor position with your organization. I have long been an admirer of your services and commitment to the community. I am very confident that my education, experience and counselling skills will enable me to make an immediate and long-term contribution to your mental health programme.

The position we discussed seems well suited to my strengths and skills. My counselling and teaching background includes an emphasis on the family unit and its influence and relationship to each client's needs and therapy.

I am looking forward to seeing you, again, next week. If you require any additional information before then, please feel free to call. Thank you for your time and consideration.

Yours sincerely,

Susan Goodman
12345 678910
skilledcounsellor@earthlink.net

Follow-up e-mail (after face-to-face meeting) (management)

From: Henry Jacobs [hjacobs@yahoo.com]
To: jjordan@forman.com
Cc:
Subject: The right choice for programme development

Dear Mr _____:

The position we discussed on Friday is a tremendously challenging one. After reviewing your comments about the job requirements, I am convinced that I can make an immediate contribution toward the growth and profitability of ABC Ltd.

Since you are going to reach a decision quickly, I would like to mention the following points, which I feel qualify me for the job we discussed:

1 Proven ability to generate fresh ideas and creative solutions to difficult problems
2 Experience in the area of programme planning and development
3 Ability to successfully manage many projects at the same time
4 A facility for working effectively with people at all levels of management
5 Experience in administration, general management and presentations
6 An intense desire to do an outstanding job in anything I undertake

Thank you for the time and courtesy extended to me. I look forward to hearing from you.

Yours sincerely,

Henry Jacobs
12345 678910
hjacobs@yahoo.com

Follow-up e-mail (after face-to-face meeting) (graphic design)

From: Melissa Harris [graphicdesignpro@earthlink.net]
To: rmatthews@redgraphic.com
Cc:
Subject: Let's keep in touch

Dear Mr _____:

It was a pleasure speaking to you regarding my search for a position in Corporate Graphic Design. Thank you for your initial interest.

The position I am looking for is usually found in a marketing or public relations department. The titles vary; Graphic Design Manager, Advertising Manager, and Publications Director are a few. In almost every case the job description includes management and coordination of the company's printed marketing materials, whether they are produced by in-house designers or by an outside advertising agency or design firm.

I would like to stay in the _____ area; at least, I would like to search this area first. My salary requirement currently is in the £_____ range.

My professional experience, education, activities and skills uniquely qualify me for a position in Graphic Design. My portfolio documents over eight years' experience in the business, and includes design, project consultation and supervision of quality printed material for a wide range of clients.

I hope you will keep me on your files for future reference. I will telephone your office next week to discuss my situation further.

Yours sincerely,

Melissa Harris
12345 678910
graphicdesignpro@earthlink.net

Follow-up e-mail (after face-to-face meeting) (general)

From: Joseph Winger [jwinger@hotmail.com]
To: hr@abc.com
Cc:
Subject: I listened… here's the result!

Dear Ms _____:

It was a pleasure meeting you in your office last week. I appreciate the time you spent with me, as well as the valuable information you offered. As we discussed, I have adjusted my CV in regard to my position with _____. I have attached the new CV with this e-mail so that your files can be updated.

_____, please allow me to thank you again for the compliment on my ability to present a strong interview. Please keep this in mind when considering me for placement with one of your clients.

Yours sincerely,

Joseph Winger
12345 678910
jwinger@hotmail.com

Follow-up e-mail (after face-to-face meeting) (entry-level)

From: Dana Sorrensen [dsorrensen@mindspring.com]
To: djackson@abc.com
Cc:
Subject: Thanks

Dear Mr _____:

I would like to take this opportunity to thank you for the interview on Wednesday morning at
_____, and to confirm my strong interest in an entry-level position with your
company.

As we discussed, I feel that my education and background have provided me with an
understanding of business operations that will prove to be an asset to your company. Additionally,
I have always been considered a hard worker and a dependable, loyal employee. I am confident
that I can make a valuable contribution to your Group Pension Fund area.

I look forward to meeting you again in the near future to discuss your needs further.

Yours sincerely,

Dana Sorrensen
12345 678910
dsorrensen@mindspring.com

Follow-up e-mail (after face-to-face meeting) (auditing)

From: Alex Davis [auditpro@earthlink.net]
To: hr@abc.com
Cc:
Subject: Very motivated by meeting you

Mr _____:

Thank you for allowing me the opportunity to meet you to discuss the IT Audit position currently available at ABC. The position sounds very challenging and rewarding, with ample room for growth. I feel my background and qualifications have prepared me well for the IT Audit position we discussed.

I am committed to the ongoing development of my audit skills and feel I could work well with your focused audit staff at ABC. I look forward to hearing from you.

Yours sincerely,

Alex Davis
12345 678910
auditpro@earthlink.net

Power phrases

Consider using adaptations of these key phrases in your follow-up letters after face-to-face meetings.

Thank you for meeting me this morning. Our associate, _____, assured me that a meeting with you would be productive, and it was. I sincerely appreciate your counsel, insight, and advice.

I have attached my CV for your review. I would appreciate any feedback you may have regarding effectiveness and strength. I understand you may not have any searches under way that would be suitable for me at this time, but I would appreciate any future considerations.

Please consider any associates, customers or friends who may have contacts who would be useful for me to meet. I have learned how important 'networking' is and would really appreciate some assistance from a professional like yourself.

Thanks again, _____, and please let me know if I can be of service to you. I wish you and your colleagues continued success and look forward to a business relationship in the future.

In addition to experiencing a very enjoyable and informative interview, I came away very enthusiastic about the position you are seeking to fill.

I hope _____'s consideration of candidates will result in our being together again soon.

During my drive home I savoured the possibility of working for _____ in the _____ area, and I must say it was an extremely pleasing thought.

I look forward to meeting you again and hope our discussion will precede a long-term working relationship.

I am looking forward to meeting _____ on 16 August at 10.00 am, at which time I will convince her of my abilities and prove I am the most qualified person for the position.

It was a pleasure meeting you in your office last week. I appreciate the time you spent with me, as well as the valuable information you offered.

I hope you will take a few moments to review my CV and place it in your files for future reference. I will telephone your office next week to discuss my situation further.

Gone but not forgotten…

Thank you for our time together this afternoon. What I lack in specific experience of your business I more than make up for with my people skills and my proven record of achievement, energy and pure tenacity.

Given the opportunity, I can succeed in your office. That makes you and me both successes. Is that worth the investment in training me?

I would like to take this opportunity to thank you for the interview this morning, and to express my strong interest in the position with _____ .

I would welcome the opportunity to apply and to further develop my talents within your company.

Throughout my conversations with you and Mr _____ , I felt that the company provides exactly the type of career opportunity that I am seeking, and I am confident that I will prove to be an asset to your organization.

I trust our meeting this morning helped you further define the position. First and foremost, however, I hope that you came away from our meeting with a vision that includes me filling one of the many offices in _____ . I certainly did.

I would like to take this opportunity to thank you for the interview on Thursday morning. I was very impressed with the operation, and I am enthusiastic about the prospects of joining your team.

Since we spent so much time discussing the subject, I have enclosed…

I look forward to hearing from you again to discuss the position further. Throughout my conversations with you and _____ , I felt…

After reviewing your comments about the job requirements, I am convinced that I can make an immediate contribution toward the growth and profitability of _____ .

Since you are going to reach a decision quickly, I would like to mention the following points, which I feel qualify me for the job we discussed:

The position in the _____ area is very attractive to me.

The interview confirmed that I want this career opportunity. Specifically, I want to work in the _____ department for you and _____ . That is the simplest way to say it. I will call you this week to see what the next step is in the process.

Again, thank you for your time and interest.

It was indeed a pleasure to meet you after working with you by telephone several years ago.

Thank you for taking time out of your busy schedule to meet me on Tuesday, 10 December 20–. I left the interview with an extremely favourable impression of your company.

I would like to take this opportunity to thank you for the interview on Friday morning, and to confirm my strong interest in the _____ position.

A career opportunity with _____ is particularly appealing because of its solid reputation and track record in research and development. I am confident that the training programme and continued sales support will provide me with the background that I need to succeed in a _____ career.

I look forward to discussing my background and the position with you in greater detail.

I want to take this opportunity to thank you for the interview on Tuesday afternoon, and to confirm my strong interest in the position of _____ with XYZ Health Care.

From our conversation, I feel confident of my ability to reach and exceed your expectations.

I am looking forward to spending a day in the field with a _____ representative. I will telephone you later this week to set up an appointment for my second interview.

Thank you for the time during my visit to _____ yesterday. I enjoyed our conversation at lunch and learned more about personal trust and investment services.

Thank you for your time and interest today. As I indicated, I am very new to this game of searching for employment and it is nice to start this effort on a positive note.

I am eager to hear from you concerning your decision. I know that you have several other candidates to meet, so I will wait patiently. Good luck in your interview process; I know it must be difficult. Again, thank you so much for your time and consideration. I would welcome the opportunity to work for your company.

_____, the visit to you left me feeling positive about the possibility of working for _____. I would appreciate an opportunity to join your staff, and look forward to hearing from you.

'Resurrection' letter (HR position)

Kenyon knows this decision-maker personally. Although he didn't get the job, he wants to keep the lines of communication open and hopes to be considered for other positions.

KENYON P STEWART

13 January 20–

Mr Eric Pedersen
ABC
111 Any Avenue
Anytown AA1 1AA

Dear Eric:

Congratulations on the selection of your new Director of Human Resources! I hope this new person meets your expectations and I wish you every success.

I appreciate the chance to apply for the position and am grateful for the consideration you have given me throughout this process. Although I am obviously disappointed at not being the successful applicant, I remain interested in potential opportunities with ABC. If for any reason you decide it is necessary to reopen the search at any time, please be aware that I am still interested in the position on either an interim or permanent basis.

In the meantime, should there be openings for support positions within the HR Department, or positions in other departments, I would like to be considered for such opportunities.

Eric, as we have discussed in the past, I am a team player and believe that I have a contribution to make. At this stage of my career, I would be happy to accept something other than a managerial position and am convinced that my organizational skills, communication skills and flexibility would make me an asset to any organization. If you know of other openings I would be most appreciative if you could pass that information on to me.

Thank you for all your time and consideration. I look forward to speaking to you again soon.

Yours sincerely,

Kenyon

---

1 Any Street • Anytown AA1 1AA • 12345 678910

'Resurrection' letter (team director position)

Another applicant was selected for the position that Madison was interviewed for. Because he hopes for other opportunities, he wants to both thank ABC for the interview and keep his name (and qualifications) at the top of their mind for future consideration.

Madison P Aldridge

1 Any Street
Anytown AA1 1AA
12345 678910

12 January 20–

Michael Anderson
ABC Ltd
111 Any Avenue
Anytown AA1 1AA

Dear Mr Anderson:

Thank you for the opportunity to attend the interview for the Team Director position. I genuinely appreciated the chance to discuss your vision for the DEF programme.

Although another candidate was ultimately selected for this important position, I was pleased to be among the short list of applicants under consideration.

As we have discussed, I believe that my nine years' experience with XYZ provides me with a wealth of knowledge and expertise that can be beneficial to ABC. I continue to be committed to the mission of the DEF programme, but also wish to offer myself as a candidate for other roles where my capabilities can further the objectives of ABC.

To briefly reiterate, some of the qualities that I can bring to a new position include:

- **strategic vision, creative energy and strong leadership skills;**
- **capacity to build collaborative teams across public, private and government sectors;**
- **excellent project management capabilities;**
- **ability to build employee morale and inspire team members to strive for excellence;**
- **innovative problem-solving skills.**

Please keep me in mind if other opportunities should arise where my talents would be an asset, particularly as you move ahead with implementation of the DEF project. I would enjoy speaking to you further to discuss how I can best serve ABC's needs.

Thank you, again, for your consideration.

Yours sincerely,

Madison P Aldridge

Madison P Aldridge

'Resurrection' letter (stevedore)

This is a follow-up letter to several telephone conversations with the best contact within the target company, the company director.

CASEY SMITH

1 Any Street • Anytown AA1 1AA • Home: 12345 678910 • Mobile: 0198765 4321

14 November 20–

Mr Gregory Roberts
Director, ABC Ltd
111 Any Avenue
Anytown AA1 1AA

Dear Mr Roberts:

First, I want to thank you for the time you spent with me in recent telephone conversations. I know you are a very busy person.

On 4 August I attended the recruiting event at the Convention Centre. I submitted my CV and spoke very briefly with a representative. In the short time I chatted with her I did my best to communicate my interest in, and qualifications for, the job. However, due to the overwhelming number of applicants there just wasn't sufficient time to convey how qualified I really am.

With that in mind, I have enclosed my brief CV for your review. To summarize:

- I have an extensive history of working safely around heavy equipment.
- I am in outstanding physical condition.
- I am a very reliable and dedicated employee.
- I have received first aid, CPR and terrorism awareness training.

This CV is only a hint of who I am – words on paper cannot replace a personal conversation. Therefore, would you please consider my request for a face-to-face interview so that you may evaluate my qualifications, abilities, drive and enthusiasm for yourself?

I will make myself available for any time that you can take out of your schedule. Thank you for your consideration, and I look forward to meeting you if possible in the near future.

Yours sincerely,

Casey Smith

Casey Smith

Enclosure: CV

'Resurrection' letter (social worker)

Having already been interviewed by Mr Thornson, Beth started the letter in an upbeat, informal manner to re-establish a rapport. The indication that he thought she was well suited at the time of their initial interview was an effective way to sell herself.

BETH ANDERSEN
1 Any Street
Anytown AA1 1AA
12345 678910
BAndersen@4kidsake.net

16 February 20–

Mr William Thornson
Foster Care and Adoption Coordinator
BAAF
111 Any Avenue
Anytown AA1 1AA

Dear Mr Thornson:

Talk about small coincidences. I bumped into Mr O'Brien and learned that St Mary's is opening a new foster care division this coming March. One thing led to another, and he informed me that BAAF is in desperate need of social workers and foster/adoptive care counsellors to fill several positions.

You might not recall my name, but I hope I can help you to remember our meeting. I participated in an interview with you in early May of 20– for the position of Foster Care Counsellor with BAAF's Brentwood facility. We discussed my involvement with St John's Youth & Family Counselling Programme at great length, and agreed I would be well suited to a similar position with BAAF as an Adoptive Care Counsellor. Unfortunately, funding was reduced that month leaving BAAF with no other choice but to put a freeze on hiring.

As you can imagine, I am thrilled to learn of BAAF's new foster care programme, and would welcome the opportunity to meet again to pick up where we left off. For your convenience, I am enclosing my updated CV for your review.

Thank you for your reconsideration. I look forward to hearing from you soon.

Yours sincerely,

Beth Andersen

Beth Andersen

'Resurrection' letter (bank position)

Leanne K Boardman
1 Any Street ▪ Anytown AA1 1AA ▪ 12345 678910 ▪ marketmanager@email.com

(Date)

Phillip _____
(Title)
ABC Bank
1 Industry Plaza
Anytown AA1 1AA

Dear Mr _____:

I understand from _____ of _____ that the search is continuing for the Wholesale Market Manager position at _____ ABC Bank. As you continue your search, I would like to ask that you keep in mind the following accomplishments and experiences that I would bring to the job:

1   Maximized relationships and increased balances through the sale of trust and cash management products.

2   Captured largest share of public funds market in _____ within three years and captured a disproportionate market share of insurance companies in _____.

3   Developed cash management and trust products tailored to the needs of my target market.

4   Marketed services through mass mailings and brochures, through planning and conducting industry-specific seminars, and through active participation in target markets' industry professional organization.

5   Direct experience in all phases of wholesale commercial banking, including: market segmentation, prospecting, building and maintaining customer relationships, lending, and the sale of non-credit products and services.

Yours sincerely,

Leanne Boardman

Leanne Boardman

'Resurrection' letter (construction manager)

.... **Eric L Ross**

(Date)

Alice _____
(Title)
A,B&C
Executive Search Consultants
111 Any Avenue
Anytown AA1 1AA

Dear Ms _____:

I am writing to you to follow up the initial inquiry I wrote to you on 11th July 20–. At that time I forwarded you a cover letter and CV. I am in the construction management and business management fields. Since I have not had a response I can only assume that you do not have any currently active searches that meet my qualifications in process or that my file has been deactivated.

I am still in the market for an executive position that matches my qualifications and abilities. I am open to relocating throughout the United Kingdom and overseas. If any positions become available, I would be interested in hearing from you. If you need an updated CV, please write or call me and I would be most happy to forward you any information required.

Yours sincerely,

Eric L Ross

Eric L Ross

PS I'll call in a couple of days to follow up this letter.

....
1 Any Street • Anytown AA1 1AA • 12345 678910 • constructionmanager@email.com

'Resurrection' letter (entry level)

Elizabeth A Andrews

1 Any Street • Anytown AA1 1AA

(Date)

Bob _____
(Title)
A,B&C
Executive Search Consultants
111 Any Avenue
Anytown AA1 1AA

Dear Mr _____:

I feel I should explain more thoroughly why I am willing to take even an entry-level position considering all my past experience. And that's just it – past experience.

For the past three years I ran my own small business, which, of course, kept me out of the job market. Meanwhile, computers took over the world! Fortunately, since moving here and doing temp jobs, I have gained hands-on experience in data entry. I have also taken and finished a private course in Microsoft Word. So I believe that makes me computer literate, if not entirely experienced.

Nevertheless, I'm in no position to be disdainful of clerical jobs, as I realize I must start somewhere. Fortunately, I enjoy all facets of office work (even filing), so that would not be a problem. I have enough faith in myself and my ability to learn quickly to know that some form of upper movement would be possible for me… eventually.

Incidentally, even though I am on a temp job this week and possibly next, I do have an answering machine I check every couple of hours during the day. So please leave a message and I'll return your call soon after.

Thank you, and I look forward to hearing from you. I have enclosed another copy of my CV for you.

Yours sincerely,

Elizabeth Andrews

Elizabeth Andrews

enclosure

'Resurrection' e-mail (account executive)

From: Katherine Knockwood [accountexecutive@aol.com]
To: hr@abc.com
Cc:
Subject: Thanks from Katherine, I'll be the next one

Mr _____:

I wanted to thank you for the interview we had on 13 March 20–. The position that was being offered sounds like something I would be interested in. However, I do understand your reasons for not choosing me for the position, and I thank you very much for your honesty.

Perhaps when you are looking for an account executive with five years' experience instead of ten, you will bear me in mind. I am determined to be your choice. I hope the fact that I came a close second to someone with twice my chronological experience will help you remember me.

I look forward to hearing from you, and thank you again for your time. With your permission I will stay in touch.

Yours sincerely,

Katherine Knockwood
12345 678910
accountexecutive@aol.com

'Resurrection' e-mail (programmer)

From: Robert Zelinski [programmerpro@yahoo.com]
To: hr@jitmfg.com
Cc:
Subject: Oh, the software we could create!

Dear Ms _____:

I must have been one of the first people you spoke to about the job posting, because at the time you seemed very interested in me. However, when I called you back, you had received so many calls for the position, you didn't know one from the other. That's understandable, so I hope I can stir your memory and, more important, your interest.

When I spoke to you I got the feeling we could both benefit from working together. I am a computer enthusiast, always looking for new applications and ideas to implement on the computer. I have a solid programming and project development background in both the Windows and Macintosh worlds. What's even better is my hobby: my work. I spend countless hours in one way or another doing things that concern computing.

You had asked if I had children and I do: a four-and-a-half-year-old daughter and a four-and-a-half-month-old daughter. You had some ideas for children's software and thought having kids would help when working on such software. My oldest uses _____ on my Macintosh at home and double-clicks away without any assistance from my wife or myself. She has learned a great deal from 'playing' with it and is already more computer literate than I ever expected. We need more software like _____ to help stir the minds of our children.

I have attached a CV for your perusal. But in case you don't want to read all the details, here it is in short:

- I have six years' programming and development experience in Windows.
- I have three years' programming and development experience on the Macintosh.
- I am currently the Senior Developer for Macintosh programming here at _____ Ltd.

I look forward to speaking to you again, so please don't hesitate to call me, either at home (12345 678910) or at work (109876 54321) anytime.

Regards,

Robert Zelinski
12345 678910
programmerpro@yahoo.com

'Resurrection' e-mail (product manager)

From: Amanda Jones [ajones@hotmail.com]
To: jkline@activeproducts.com
Cc:
Subject: We will work together!

Dear Ms _____ :

Four months ago you and I discussed an opportunity at Active Products, and you were kind
enough to set up meetings with _____ and _____. Shortly thereafter,
as you know, I accepted a position with _____, where I am now.

For reasons I will go into when we meet, I would like to reopen our discussions. If you think such
a conversation would be mutually beneficial, I hope we can get together. I'll call next week to see
when you have a half hour or so of free time.

Yours sincerely,

Amanda Jones
12345 678910
ajones@hotmail.com

Power phrases

Consider using adaptations of these key phrases in your 'resurrection' letters.

I turned down your job, but for reasons I will go into when we meet, I would like to reopen our discussions. If you think such a conversation would be mutually beneficial, I hope we can get together. I'll call next week to see when you have a half hour or so of free time.

As you continue your search, I would like to ask that you keep in mind the following accomplishments and experiences that I would bring to the job:

I am still in the market for an executive position that matches my qualifications and abilities. I am open to relocating throughout the United Kingdom and overseas. If any positions become available, I would be interested in hearing from you.

I look forward to hearing from you, and thank you again for your time. With your permission I will stay in touch.

I hope I can stir your memory and, more important, your interest.

I look forward to speaking to you again, so please don't hesitate to call me either at home or at work any time.

Rejection of offer letter (head librarian)

Tamara has decided to take another position. As a courtesy, she wants to tell Anytown Library that she's no longer interested in the position, while keeping her name alive for any future opportunities.

Tamara L Salinger

1 Any Street • Anytown AA1 1AA • 12345 678910

12 January 20–

Mr Henry O Felix
Anytown Library Services
111 Any Avenue
Anytown AA1 1AA

Dear Mr Hastings:

Thank you for taking the time to meet me recently to discuss the position of Head Librarian. I genuinely appreciated the opportunity to meet the Committee to learn about the position. I was very favourably impressed with the Anytown Library System and believe that if selected, my contributions would have significantly enhanced your organization's success.

However, I am writing to ask that my name be withdrawn from further consideration for the position at this time. I have recently been offered another challenging and rewarding opportunity. The relative time-frames involved have made it necessary for me to make a decision without further delay, and I have chosen to accept the offer.

Had circumstances permitted, I believe that it would have been productive to continue our discussions and am confident that we could have arrived at a mutually beneficial arrangement. I would be most interested in applying for the position should there ever be another search for a Head Librarian at some future date.

I wish you the best of luck in your current search, and much success in the future. Thank you, again, for your time and consideration.

Yours sincerely,

Tamara L Salinger

Tamara L Salinger

Rejection of offer letter (team supervisor)

This candidate was interviewed for a position that turned out to be below his level of experience and at a salary well below his expectations. He didn't want to slam the door shut on other opportunities but couldn't accept the position offered.

Ms Lucretia A Selander
Programme Director
ABC Ltd
111 Any Avenue
Anytown AA1 1AA

Dear Ms Selander:

Thank you for your e-mail message updating me on the status of the telecommunications project we discussed in our recent telephone conversation.

Although I genuinely appreciate your consideration for the Team Supervisor position, at this time, I feel it is in my best interest to seek a position more closely aligned with my level of experience and demonstrated managerial skills.

I remain most interested in opportunities with ABC, and ask that you keep my name under consideration for other positions that would more fully capitalize on my knowledge and expertise.

Thank you for your time and interest.

Yours sincerely,

Christopher J Franz

Christopher J Franz

Rejection of offer letter (general)

AUDREY M LAURENCE
1 Any Street • Anytown AA1 1AA
12345 678910 • alaurence@rochester.rr.com

(Date)

Phillip _____
(Title)
ABC Ltd
1 Industry Plaza
Anytown AA1 1AA

Dear Mr _____:

It was indeed a pleasure meeting you and your staff to discuss your needs for a
_____. Our time together was most enjoyable and informative.

As we have discussed during our meetings, I believe the purpose of preliminary interviews is to explore areas of mutual interest and to assess the fit between the individual and the position. After careful thought, I have decided to withdraw from consideration for the position.

My decision is based upon the fact that I have accepted a position elsewhere that is very suited to my qualifications and experiences.

I want to thank you for interviewing me and giving me the opportunity to learn more about your company. You have a fine team, and I would have enjoyed working with you.

Best wishes to you and your staff.

Yours sincerely,

Audrey Laurence

Audrey Laurence

Rejection of offer e-mail (department manager)

From: Allen Meriden [managementpro@earthlink.net]
To: hr@abc.com
Cc:
Subject: With regret for the present and sincere hope for the future

Dear Ms _____:

I would like to take this opportunity to thank you for the interview on Thursday morning, and to express my strong interest in future employment with your organization.

While I appreciate very much your offer for the position of Department Manager, I feel that at this stage of my career I am seeking greater challenges and advancement than the Department level is able to provide. Having worked in _____ management for over four years, I am confident that my skills will be best applied in a position with more responsibility and accountability.

As we discussed, I look forward to talking to you again in January about how I might contribute to ABC in the capacity of Unit Manager.

Yours sincerely,

Allen Meriden
12345 678910
managementpro@earthlink.net

Power phrases

Consider using adaptations of these key phrases in your rejection-of-offer letters.

It was indeed a pleasure meeting with you and your staff to discuss your needs for a

_____.

Our time together was most enjoyable and informative.

After careful thought, I have decided to withdraw from consideration for the position.

As we discussed, I look forward to talking to you again in _____ about how I might contribute to _____ in the capacity of _____.

Acceptance letter (marketing research manager)

JULIE GREGORIO
1 Any Street
Anytown AA1 1AA
12345 678910

(Date)

Ms Emily _____
ABC Financial Services Group
1 Industry Plaza
Anytown AA1 1AA

Dear Ms _____:

Thank you for your positive response to the Marketing Research Manager position. I am delighted to accept your offer of employment and look forward to 'jumping in head first' into the various projects we discussed during our meetings, especially sales forecasting and strategic market planning for ABC's core product line.

I am honoured that your organization feels that I am the right person to lead your marketing research efforts, and I am confident that I can deliver the results ABC wants. As I mentioned in our telephone conversation yesterday, I am constantly in touch with what the competition is doing with the goal of placing my team's effort higher in the marketplace to yield maximum results.

As you request, I will contact Mary Smith, Human Resources Manager, on Monday morning to arrange an orientation appointment. I look forward to meeting you after that to discuss in detail my ideas for meeting the objectives we explored in our interviews.

Yours sincerely,

Julie Gregorio

Julie Gregorio

Acceptance letter (managing consultant)

Jacqueline Mains
1 Any Street ▪ Anytown AA1 1AA
12345 678910 Home ▪ managingconsultant@comcast.com

(Date)

Dear Philip,

I want to thank you for the privilege of joining your staff as Managing Consultant. Your flexibility and cooperation in the counter negotiations was encouraging. Thank you for making every effort to make the pending transition a smooth one.

As you request, I am providing this letter, for my official file.

'In that your organization is a competitor of my previous employer, and in that this organization seeks to maintain goodwill and high levels of integrity within the industry, it should be duly noted, that neither you nor any representative of your organization, sought me as a prospective employee. It was my identification of a possible position, and solely my pursuits toward your company, that resulted in my resignation as Senior Director, to join your firm as Managing Consultant.'

If I can provide additional clarification on this matter, or assist in protecting the ethics of your company, please notify me. I look forward to starting with your team on the 15th of July.

Yours sincerely,

Jacqueline Mains

Jacqueline Mains

Acceptance letter (director)

Victor L Williams
1 Any Street
Anytown AA1 1AA

(Date)

Emily _____
(Title)
ABC Ltd
1 Industry Plaza
Anytown AA1 1AA

Dear Ms _____:

This letter will serve as my formal acceptance of your offer to join your firm as Director of _____. I understand and accept the conditions of employment that you explained in your recent letter.

I will contact your personnel department this week to request any paperwork I might complete for their records prior to my starting date. Also, I will arrange a physical examination for insurance purposes. I would appreciate your forwarding any reading material you feel might hasten my initiation into the affairs of _____.

Yesterday I tendered my resignation at _____ and worked out a mutually acceptable notice time of four weeks, which should allow me ample time to finalize my business and personal affairs here and be ready for work at _____ on schedule.

You, your board and your staff have been most professional and helpful throughout this hiring process. I eagerly anticipate joining the ABC team and look forward to many new challenges. Thank you for your confidence and support.

Yours sincerely,

Victor L Williams

Victor L Williams

JS

Acceptance e-mail (general)

From: George Keller [gkeller@mindspring.com]
To: pwalters@abc.com
Cc:
Subject: Yes! Absolutely! I accept!

Dear Mr _____:

I would like to express my appreciation for your letter offering me the position of
_____ in your _____ Department at a starting salary of
£53,000 per year.

I was very impressed with the personnel and facilities at your company in Anytown and am
writing to confirm my acceptance of your offer. If it is acceptable to you I will report to work on
20 November 20–.

Let me once again express my appreciation for your offer and my excitement about joining your
engineering staff. I look forward to my association with ABC and feel my contributions will be in
line with your goals of growth and continued success for the company.

Yours sincerely,

George Keller
12345 678910
gkeller@mindspring.com

Power phrases

Consider using adaptations of these key phrases in your acceptance letters.

I am delighted to accept _____'s generous offer to become their _____. All of the terms in your letter of 13th October are amenable to me.

My resignation was submitted to the appropriate managers at _____ this morning, but we are still working out the terms of my departure.

I am eagerly anticipating starting my new position, particularly at a company with _____'s reputation. During the interim, I will stay in direct contact with _____ to assure a smooth initiation at _____. Thank you again for this opportunity.

We are still working out the terms of my departure from _____, but it is safe to say that I will report to _____ no later than 9th November. It should be possible to confirm a starting date early tomorrow morning. I will telephone you directly when my manager and I have a departure timetable completed.

_____ has arranged my pre-employment physical for _____, and I do not expect any problems to arise. I have found several possible housing alternatives that I will be investigating and I do not expect any problems here, either.

I appreciate the confidence you demonstrated by selecting me to be _____.

I am confident that you made an excellent choice.

I feel that I can achieve excellent results for your company, and I am looking forward to working with you. I am also anxious to get to know you and your organization better.

This letter will serve as my formal acceptance of your offer to join _____. I understand and accept the conditions of employment that you explained in your recent letter.

I will contact your personnel department this week to request any paperwork I might complete for their records prior to my starting date. Also, I will arrange a physical examination for insurance purposes. I would appreciate you forwarding any reading material you feel might hasten my initiation into the affairs of _____.

Yesterday I tendered my resignation at _____ and worked out a mutually acceptable notice time of four weeks, which should allow me ample time to finalize my business and personal affairs here, relocate my family, and be ready for work at _____ on schedule.

You, your board and your staff have been most professional and helpful throughout this process. I eagerly anticipate joining the _____ team and look forward to many new challenges. Thank you for your confidence and support.

I look forward to making a contribution as part of your team.

I look forward to the challenges and responsibility of working in this position.

Negotiation letter (general)

Betsy Kimble

1 Any Street   12345 678910
Anytown AA1 1AA   bkimble@aox.com

(date)

Mr Philip _____
(Title)
ABC Ltd
1 Industry Place
Anytown AA1 1AA

Dear Philip,

I want to thank you for your invitation to join ABC. I have reviewed the offer of the position and salary, as presented in your letter dated _____. I would like to ask for clarification on a few items prior to providing you with a 'formal acceptance'. While none of these items are necessarily 'deal breakers', I believe they will enable both parties to begin the partnership more informed about mutual goals and expectations.

As per the breakdown provided:

- I accept the bonus scheme as proposed.
- I accept the paid holiday and personal days plan as proposed.
- I accept the educational reimbursement plan as proposed.
- I accept the Direct Payroll Deposit plan as proposed (if elected).
- I accept the Medical, Dental, Pension and Life Insurance benefits as proposed, contingent on factors clarified below.

Points of Clarification:

- What is available in regard to 'Share Options'?
- What are the 'standard hours of operation' for ABC employees?
- Would it be possible to have a 'Performance Evaluation' at the end of six months?
- I would like to structure the holiday entitlement as follows: Three days in remainder of year 20–, One week during calendar year 20–, Two weeks during calendar years 20– to 20–, Three weeks beginning January 20–.
- In light of the 'out-of-pocket expenses' anticipated, how might we agree to get the annual base salary to £35,000? I am open to a number of different options to achieve this goal, including profit sharing, commission or 5 per cent annual bonus arrangement.

Page 1 of 2

Betsy Kimble
Page 2 of 2

I am excited about the long-term possibilities that exist at ABC. As you can see by my level of interest, I intend to be with you for a long tenure of success. I believe my skills will be an enhancement to the existing leadership. My presence will enable you and others to focus on new aspects of business development and achieve corporate goals and objectives that will be beneficial to us all. Again, I want to thank you for the gracious offer. I look forward to finalizing these minor details very soon.

Yours sincerely,

Betsy Kimble

Betsy Kimble

Negotiation letter (sales)

Eden Miller

1 Any Street • Anytown AA1 1AA • 12345 678910 • e-mail: salespro@anyserver.co.uk

---

(Date)

Dear Mr _____:

I have reviewed your letter and the specific breakdown regarding compensation. I believe there to be a few items to clarify, prior to providing you with a formal acceptance. I do not consider any of the items to be 'deal breakers' in any way. I also do not perceive them to be issues that cannot be discussed, as we are in fact, moving ahead.

The primary concern has to do with the commission structure, as opposed to salary plus commission, to which I have grown accustomed. I am therefore asking for a one-time initial payment to me in the amount of £5,000. I am trying to diminish some of the 'exposure' that I may experience in the transition from one office to another. I also believe exposure will be felt as a shift occurs from receipt of compensation on a monthly basis, when I am currently accustomed to a biweekly format. Lastly, I am hoping to afford your company the opportunity to share some of the 'risk' in this process and show some 'short-term good faith' toward what I hope will be a long-term relationship of success, productivity and increased profitability.

The second clarification revolves around the bonus scheme: the percentages, timeframes and terms. This is something we can discuss over the course of the next two weeks. You may even be able to pass something specific on to me in writing.

With these two concerns articulated, I want you to know that I will be meeting the owner of our company tomorrow morning, to discuss my plans for departure. In fairness to him and to my current client load, I could not start full-time with you for 21 days.

I would like to set a time for us to have dinner one evening next week, so you can meet my wife and we can talk a bit less formally.

Looking forward to what lies ahead,

Eden Miller

Eden Miller

Negotiation letter (senior lab specialist)

MITCHELL T NORDSTROM

1 Any Street • Anytown AA1 1AA

12345 678910 (days) / 01987 654321 (evenings) • labspecialist@cs.com

(date)

Philip _____
ABC
1 Industry Plaza
Anytown AA1 1AA

Dear Philip:

I want to thank you for the time that we were able to spend together last week. I was encouraged by the invitation to join ABC as Senior Lab Specialist. The position, responsibility and geography are consistent with my career goals and objectives. Based on the information that you gave to me, there are a number of items for clarification, prior to providing you with a formal acceptance. None of the items listed are necessarily 'deal breakers', but they are essential to us beginning this tenure with full disclosure of mutual expectations and responsibilities. Items for clarification are as follows:

- Detailed description of insurance benefits.
- Realistic analysis of the company share and bonus scheme.
- Written explanation of educational reimbursement allowance.
- The mobility plan seems very reasonable, but would like specifics on the Permanent Work Relocation. (Is it an allowance or reimbursement of actual expenses incurred in the move?)
- Detailed explanation of the Variable Pay Plan.

This final item is significant, as it will have an impact on the full compensation potential and modify the suggested salary. In our conversations, I communicated to you that I was making £32K while working part-time and going to college. The salary offer is substantially lower and represents a pay cut. My goal is to discern how feasible it will be for me to meet my financial obligations.

I am interested in your company and this position, but am finding it difficult to give serious consideration to anything less than £40K salary plus benefits. I am hoping to discover a variety of vehicles that will enable you to help me achieve that goal, so that I can help you accomplish your growth and profit targets.

I look forward to discussing these issues with you in the very near future and trust that we will soon be working together in the best interest of Philip _____, Mitchell Nordstrom, and ABC Ltd.

Yours sincerely,

Mitchell Nordstrom

Mitchell Nordstrom

Negotiation letter (product specialist)

MARY A MARTIN

0198765 4321 (Mobile) • 12345 678910 (Home)
productspecialist@email.com
1 Any Street • Anytown AA1 1AA

(Date)

Philip _____
(Title)
ABC Ltd
1 Industry Plaza
Anytown AA1 1AA

RE: Product Specialist/ABC Team

Dear Philip:

Thank you for your offer of employment with ABC Ltd. Your state-of-the-art company would afford me the opportunity to make a contribution while continuing to grow professionally in an ever-evolving industry. I am confident that my strong work ethic would enhance the ABC Team.

As you know from our previous conversations, I have outstanding skills and abilities that I can bring to ABC. First and foremost is my hands-on experience in the medical field. I have a proven track record of relating well to other medical professionals and accommodating their needs. It is my understanding that as Product Specialist, my expert communication skills will be essential to performance success. With my experience in troubleshooting technical problems, I know that technology can be learned but becomes useful only when it can be translated into user effectiveness. My expertise integrates both of these critical components that are key to the Product Specialist role.

The Product Specialist position promises challenge and a high level of professional commitment that I am prepared to embrace. However, based upon the value I can bring ABC, plus the knowledge that the annual salary range for this type of position in our industry normally falls between £34,000 and £46,000, I must request that you reconsider your starting offer of £35,000. I am more than happy to assume all the responsibilities necessary to meet the expectations of the Product Specialist position at a starting salary of £40,000. Of course, I appreciate the generous benefits package that you provide.

I look forward to your response, and hope that we can reach an agreement that will enable me to begin my career with ABC on 4 June.

Yours sincerely,

Mary Martin

Mary Martin

Resignation letter (ITU nurse)

This situation was sensitive. A lot of names and dates were needed to explain the events leading to the decision to resign. Notice how Elizabeth apologizes so she doesn't burn her bridges.

Elizabeth Dixon, RN
1 Any Street ▪ Anytown AA1 1AA ▪ 12345 678910 ▪ criticalcare@med.net

26 April 20–

Ms Dorothy Powell
Director of Special Care
ABC Hospital
111 Any Avenue
Anytown AA1 1AA

Dear Ms Powell:

As requested by Joan Larson, Nursing Manager, I am submitting this letter as written confirmation of my resignation as a per-diem on-call ITU nurse with ABC Hospital.

My employment with ABC was scheduled to begin on 7th April as a permanent part-time ITU nurse; however, in the interim, I accepted a permanent full-time position with XYZ Hospital to begin on 1st May. On 3rd April I met with Gretchen Miller, Human Resources Administrator, to inform her of my decision. I expressed a desire to honour my commitment with the understanding that the need for flexibility in my schedule would be taken into consideration. Ms Miller contacted Joan Larson to discuss an alternative employment arrangement. Subsequently, my status of permanent part-time was changed to per-diem on-call.

Immediately upon completion of the mandatory two-week orientation period, I was faced with a schedule conflict. As a result of an apparent miscommunication, I was scheduled to do my floor orientation from 21st April to the 25th. I approached Diane Willis, Nursing Manager, to resolve the conflict and learned that she was completely unaware of both my situation and agreement between Joan Larson, Human Resources, and myself. As a result, my resignation seemed to be the logical solution.

Ms Powell, it was never my intention to cause you administrative problems; therefore, please accept my apology for any inconvenience experienced. Thank you for the opportunity to be a part of your staff.

Yours sincerely,

Elizabeth Dixon

Elizabeth Dixon

Resignation letter (care coordinator)

Marilyn was offered a new position with another organization, and this letter helped her make a positive exit from her current employer.

Marilyn Cummings

1 Any Street
Anytown AA1 1AA
12345 678910

9 April 20–

Ms Karen Lawrence, RN
Patient Care Manager
Community Care Centre
111 Any Avenue
Anytown AA1 1AA

Dear Karen:

This letter will confirm my resignation from the position of Care Coordinator. I have accepted a new position as Supervisor of Client Services at a growing medical centre in London.

My last day of employment will be on Friday, 9 May 20–, which should provide sufficient time to complete existing projects and assist with the transition to a new coordinator.

The past 10 years at the Centre have been both professionally and personally rewarding. Thank you for your trust and support over the years. I have appreciated the opportunity to expand my skills and work with many talented individuals.

Yours sincerely,

Marilyn Cummings

Marilyn Cummings

Resignation letter (management)

This is a very firm resignation, where a company needs encouragement to live up to obligations.

ROBERT McINTYRE
　　　1 Any Street
　　　Anytown AA1 1AA

home: 12345 678910
mobile: 0198765 4321
robertmcintyre@crpn.com

11 November 20–

Tim Johnson
Title
XTC Ltd
111 Any Avenue
Anytown AA1 1AA

Dear Mr Johnson:

I am writing this letter as a follow-up to the resignation notice I submitted on Wednesday, 5 November 20–. Given the sensitive nature of the events leading to my resignation, I feel it is in everyone's best interest to resolve any issues remaining as quickly as possible.

In this respect, I hope that you will demonstrate swift compliance in delivering to me the management severance package guaranteed as a result of my employment with your firm. I wish to move ahead in my career and put the past few months behind me, as I am sure you can understand; therefore, I am certain you will act upon this request in a professional and forthright manner.

Please be advised that, in the event that there is an attempt to withhold or deny this severance package to me, I will have no other alternative but to seek legal remedy for this situation. **Again, I believe that you will act with integrity concerning this issue**, and I only mention the possibility of legal action in the unlikely event that my request is rejected or delayed.

I can assure you that I, like you, would like for this to be resolved without further complications or additional steps – and as quickly as possible.

Mr Johnson, I thank you in advance for your swift attention and cooperation in this matter.

Yours sincerely,

Robert McIntyre

Robert McIntyre

Resignation letter (sales representative)

.... **Gerard Carlisle**

(Date)

Phillip _____
(Title)
ABC Ltd
1 Industry Plaza
Anytown AA1 1AA

Dear Mr _____:

Please accept my resignation of my position as Sales Representative in the _____ area, effective 25 January 20–. I am offering two weeks' notice so that my territory can be serviced effectively during the transition, with the least amount of inconvenience to our clients.

While I have very much enjoyed working under your direction, I find now that I have an opportunity to develop my career in areas that are more in line with my long-term goals. I thank you for the sales training that I have received under your supervision. It is largely due to the excellent experience I gained working for ABC that I am now able to pursue this growth opportunity.

During the next two weeks, I am willing to help you in any way to make the transition as smooth as possible. This includes assisting in recruiting and training my replacement in the _____ territory. Please let me know if there is anything specific that you would like me to do.

Again, it has been a pleasure working as a part of your group.

Best regards,

Gerard Carlisle

Gerard Carlisle

....
1 Any Street • Anytown AA1 1AA • 12345 678910

Resignation letter (director)

David R Chang

1 Any Street, Anytown AA1 1AA / 12345 678901
chang@earthlink.com

(Date)

Emily _____
(Title)
ABC Ltd
1 Industry Plaza
Anytown AA1 1AA

Dear Ms _____:

As of this date, I am formally extending my resignation as _____. I have accepted a position as Director of _____ at a university medical centre in _____.

My decision to leave ABC was made after long and careful consideration of all factors affecting the company, my family and my career. Although I regret leaving many friends here, I feel that the change will be beneficial to all parties. My subordinate is readily able to handle the company's operations until you find a suitable replacement. I intend to finalize my business and personal affairs here over the next few weeks and will discuss a mutually acceptable leaving date with you in person.

Finally, I can only express my sincere appreciation to you and the entire board for all your support, cooperation, and encouragement over the past years. I will always remember my stay at ABC for the personal growth it afforded and for the numerous friendships engendered.

Yours sincerely,

David Chang

David Chang

Resignation e-mail (general)

From: John Billingsly [systemsoperator@hotmail.com]
To: nbraun@mis.abc.edu
Cc:
Subject: With regrets but many thanks

Dear Mr _____:

This email is to notify you that I am resigning my position with ABC effective Saturday, 26 March 20–.

I have enjoyed my work here very much and want to thank you and the rest of the MIS Department for all the encouragement and support you have always given me. In order to achieve the career goals that I've set for myself, I am accepting a higher level Systems Operator position with another company. This position will give me an opportunity to become more involved in the technical aspects of setting up networking systems.

Please know that I am available to help with any staff training or offer assistance in any way that will make my departure as easy as possible for the department. I want to wish everyone the best of luck for the future.

Yours sincerely,

John Billingsly
12345 678910
systemsoperator@hotmail.com

Power phrases

Consider using adaptations of these key phrases in your resignation letters.

I am offering two weeks' notice so that my territory can be serviced effectively during the transition, with the least amount of inconvenience to our clients.

While I have very much enjoyed working under your direction, I now find that I have an opportunity to develop my career in areas that are more in line with my long-term goals. I thank you for the sales training that I have received under your supervision. It is largely due to the excellent experience I gained working for ABC that I am now able to pursue this growth opportunity.

During the next two weeks, I am willing to help you in any way to make the transition as smooth as possible. This includes assisting in recruiting and training my replacement in the _____ territory. Please let me know if there is anything specific that you would like me to do.

Again, it has been a pleasure working as a part of your sales force.

I have thoroughly enjoyed the work environment and professional atmosphere at _____. Your guidance and counsel have been the source of great personal and career satisfaction, and I am grateful.

These _____ years have made a considerable contribution to my career and professional development and I hope that I have likewise contributed during this time to the growth and development of ABC. I am grateful for the kind of associates I have had the opportunity to work with and the substantial support I have consistently received from management.

Thank-you letter (after success) (general)

Matilda Vixard
1 Any Street ▪ Anytown AA1 1AA ▪ 12345 678910

(Date)

Phillip _____
(Title)
ABC Ltd
1 Industry Plaza
Anytown AA1 1AA

Dear Mr _____:

I want you to be among the first to know that my job search has come to a very successful conclusion. I have accepted the position of _____ Director at _____ Ltd, located in _____.

I appreciate all the help and support you have provided over the last few months. It has made the job search process much easier. I look forward to staying in contact with you. Please let me know if I can be of any assistance to you in the future. Thank you.

Yours sincerely,

Matilda Vixard

Matilda Vixard

Thank-you e-mail (software manager)

From: Shane Franklin [softwarespecialist@yahoo.com]
To: hr@abc.com
Cc:
Subject: Great News! Thanks for the help ;-)

Dear Ms _____:

I am happy to inform you that I received and accepted an offer of employment just after Christmas. I am now employed by _____ Ltd.

I would also like to thank you for all your help the past few months not only in my search for employment but also for your understanding and friendly words of encouragement.

My duties include responsibility for all accounting software (General Ledger, Accounts Payable, Accounts Receivable and Fixed Assets) for _____ worldwide plus the first-year training of several entry-level employees.

I am enjoying my new responsibility and being fully employed again, although at times I feel overwhelmed with all I have to learn.

If there is ever anything I can do for you, please call me. I hope you and your family had a wonderful Christmas and I wish you much luck and happiness in the new year.

Yours sincerely,

Shane Franklin
12345 678910
softwarespecialist@yahoo.com

Power phrases

Consider using adaptations of these key phrases in your thank-you letters.

I am writing to share this good news with you and to thank you for your efforts on my behalf. If there is ever anything that I can do for you, please do not hesitate to call me.

Thank you for all your help. I have accepted a position as a _____ for _____ .

I want you to be among the first to know that my job search has come to a very successful conclusion.

I appreciate all the help and support you have provided over the last few months. It has made the job search process much easier. I look forward to staying in contact with you. Please let me know if I can be of any assistance to you in the future.

I would like to extend my sincere thanks to you for your kind help and encouragement during my job search. If I can be of any assistance to you in the future, please do not hesitate to contact me. I was often reminded during the past few months that we too easily lose contact with old friends. Let's try to stay in touch.

If you ever get a chance to visit _____ , on business or pleasure, please be sure to let me know.

If there is ever anything I can do for you, please call me. I hope you and your family have a wonderful Christmas and much luck and happiness in the new year.

Just a quick note to bring you up to date with what I am doing.

INDEX